Perspectives on Terrorism

Contemporary Issues in Crime and Justice Series
Roy Roberg, San Jose State University: Series Editor

Crime and Justice: Issues and Ideas (1984)
Philip Jenkins, Pennsylvania State University

Hard Time: Understanding and Reforming the Prison (1987)
Robert Johnson, The American University

The Myth of a Racist Criminal Justice System (1987)
William Wilbanks, Florida International University

Gambling without Guilt: The Legitimation of an American Pastime (1988)
John Rosecrance

Ethics in Crime and Justice: Dilemmas and Decisions (1989)
Joycelyn M. Pollock-Byrne, University of Houston, Downtown

Sense and Nonsense about Crime: A Policy Guide, Second Edition (1989)
Samuel Walker, University of Nebraska at Omaha

Crime Victims: An Introduction to Victimology, Second Edition (1990)
Andrew Karmen, John Jay College of Criminal Justice, New York

Death Work: A Study of the Modern Execution Process (1990)
Robert Johnson, The American University, Washington D.C.

Women in Prison (1990)
Joycelyn M. Pollock-Byrne, University of Houston, Downtown

Lawlessness and Reform: The FBI in Transition (1990)
Tony G. Poveda, State University of New York, Plattsburgh

Perspectives on Terrorism (1991)
Harold J. Vetter, Portland State University
Gary R. Perlstein, Portland State University

Perspectives on Terrorism

Harold J. Vetter
Gary R. Perlstein
Administration of Justice Department
Portland State University

Brooks/Cole Publishing Company
Pacific Grove, California

Consulting Editor: *Roy R. Roberg*

Brooks/Cole Publishing Company
A Division of Wadsworth, Inc.

Printed in the United States of America

10 9 8 7 6 5 4 3 2 1

Library of Congress Cataloging in Publication Data

Vetter, Harold J., [date]
    Perspectives on terorism / by Harold J. Vetter, Gary R. Perlstein.
        p.   cm.
    Includes bibliographical references and index.
    ISBN 0-534-14874-3
    1. Terrorism. I. Perlstein, Gary R. II. Title.
  HV6431.V48   1990
303.6′25—dc20

Sponsoring Editor: *Cynthia C. Stormer*
Editorial Assistant: *Cathleen S. Collins*
Production Editor: *Linda Loba*
Manuscript Editor: *Molly Kyle*
Permissions Editor: *Carline Haga*
Interior and Cover Design: *Vernon T. Boes*
Art Coordinator: *Cloyce Wall*
Printing and Binding: *Arcata Graphics-Martinsburg*

To Frances Hartl
    beloved companion

and Carol Perlstein
    with love and devotion

About the Authors

HAROLD J. VETTER, formerly Professor and Chairman of the Department of Criminology, University of South Florida, is now a member of the faculty of the Administration of Justice Department, Portland State University. He is the author of numerous books and articles, including *Theoretical Approaches to Personality* (1982), *Crime and Justice in America* (1984), and *Criminology and Crime* (1986).

GARY R. PERLSTEIN is Professor of Administration of Justice at Portland State University. His published works include "The Mercenary as Social Bandit," in *International Journal of Offender Therapy and Comparative Criminology* (1988) and "Defining Terrorism," in *Jane's Defence Weekly* (1989).

Foreword

Vetter and Perlstein take a multidisciplinary approach to the study of terrorism, and thus provide us with the most comprehensive coverage on the topic to date. The text appropriately begins with a discussion of the difficulty in attempting to adequately define terrorism, concluding that, often, "One man's terrorist is another man's freedom fighter." Of course, such a dilemma creates problems not only in studying, but also in developing policies to respond to, "terrorist" activities. The authors carefully address this situation, incorporating the violent, political, moral and ideological issues, including typologies, into the definition of terrorism.

To appreciate the extent and nature of terrorism today, one must have a solid foundation in its origins and historical development. The authors describe key individuals and groups historically involved in terrorist activities, from the French Revolution to present day acts of vigilante terrorism in the United States. This sets the stage for a discussion of relevant terrorist activities in the United States, including racially motivated letter bombings in the South. The authors thus emphasize the importance of understanding the "domestic side" of terrorism, since many naively believe that terrorism is an international problem only.

Important breakthroughs in coverage on terrorism include chapters on women's involvement; narcoterrorism, or the possible link between drug traffickers and terrorists; terrorism and the law (there is no internationally agreed on definition of terrorism that classifies it as a crime); and United States policies on terrorism. Taking us through the Nixon, Carter, Reagan, and Bush administrations, the authors conclude that we presently have no national policy on terrorism and suggest criteria that such a policy must meet to provide an adequate defensive strategy against terrorist acts.

The authors make a strong argument that international terrorism is a present danger to the United States and other democracies, and must be viewed as a novel kind of warfare. They further suggest that we need to develop policies that allow us to move beyond a merely reactive posture in dealing with terrorists. Hence, the authors take a firm and unwavering stance regarding the need for "active measures" in dealing with terrorism. The implications for such conclusions are far-reaching; policy analysts, as well as students of terrorism, should profit from the debate surrounding this, and other critical issues raised throughout the text.

Roy Roberg

Preface

This book is an introduction to the systematic study of terrorism. It seeks to acquaint the student and general reader with the subject matter, terminology, and basic concepts of both the popular and professional literature on terrorism.

A recent book on terrorism (Poland, 1988) enjoins us to place terrorism in its proper perspective by contrasting the small number of victims slain by acts of *domestic* terrorism between 1979 and 1986 with the large number of Americans murdered in nonterrorist acts of criminal violence during the same period. Our response to this injunction is to point out that such comparisons are misleading because they ignore the threats posed by *international* terrorism to the lives of U.S. citizens abroad. The 241 young men who lost their lives on October 23, 1983, in the devastated headquarters of the Marine Battalion Landing Team at Beirut airport were American victims of terrorism, too.

Until recently, the loss of life and property damage terrorists could inflict on their targets had not changed appreciably since the anarchist bombings and assassinations of the last century. Technological progress, however, has given terrorists, of any persuasion, a degree of mobility and a field of operations that elevate terrorism from the tactical to the strategic level. What Sloan* has called *nonterritorial terrorism*—a form of terrorism not confined to a specific geographic area—must be viewed as a new and dangerous technique for carrying out foreign policy; Iran, Syria, Libya, and a number of other nations have used this technique. Terrorism expert Brian Jenkins goes even further in characterizing terrorism as a manifestation of the changing nature of war:

> The conflict in Lebanon is likely to be representative of armed conflict world-wide in the last quarter of the twentieth century: a mixture of conventional warfare, classic guerrilla warfare, and campaigns of terrorism, openly fought and secretly waged, often without regard to national frontiers, by armies, as well as irregular forces, directly or indirectly.**

Whether or not one agrees with assessments of this kind—and many critics question their accuracy and validity—it is necessary for a textbook that attempts even-handed coverage of terrorism to discuss the growing importance accorded to *low-intensity conflict* in official quarters.

The momentous events that occurred recently in Eastern Europe and Latin America appear to have engendered a euphoric mood in Washington and other democratic capitals throughout the world of a kind not experienced since the VE-Day and VJ-Day celebrations at the end of World War II. These events are obviously fraught with significance for the nature and direction of future terrorist activities, but it is much too early to gauge their impact on terrorism. Internal social, economic, and political disturbances in the USSR and former Soviet-bloc nations may have already significantly altered both the inclination and capacity of these countries to continue supporting terrorism as an acceptable form of sub-rosa diplomacy. On the other hand, killing or imprisoning narcoterrorist figures such as Gacha and Noriega is not likely to have much effect on drug-related terrorism other than to change the cast of top players. In addition, the Middle East and Africa remain politically volatile areas. The *intefadeh* continues to claim victims; Lebanon seems no closer than ever to resolving its internal problems; and civil wars in the Sudan, Ethiopia, and Zambia provide the kind of political instability in which terrorism can flourish and proliferate. At this time in world affairs, it is more important than ever to devote serious study to terrorism.

The presentation in this book is multidisciplinary and extremely broad in focus. Specialists in a variety of fields have already made, and continue to make, substantial and important contributions to understanding contemporary terrorism. Historians have traced the development of terrorist strategy and tactics to origins in the activities of the Sicarii and Zealots in Biblical times. Psychologists and psychiatrists have explored the motivations, group affiliations, psychological dynamics, and defensive rationalizations of terrorist groups, organizations, movements, and individuals. Biographers have probed the forces and factors that shaped the lives of some of history's most prominent—or notorious—terrorists. Legal scholars have examined terrorism and terrorist acts within the context of domestic and international law. Military experts have searched for fundamental linkages between low-intensity conflict and terrorism. Weapons experts have assessed the effects of incredibly rapid development of technology on both terrorism and counterterrorism. Political scientists have addressed the policy issues raised by terrorism for democratic nations such as the United States, Britain, France, West Germany, and Italy during a period when international relations, especially those involving the superpowers, appear to be undergoing significant changes.

For a course dealing with terrorism, all these viewpoints and disciplinary perspectives are valid and relevant—and this list is merely suggestive, not exhaustive.

Part One: Systematic and Historical Perspectives begins with a review of concepts and typologies of terrorism, so that we can identify, analyze, and understand the major types of terrorism that confront us. Chapter 2 examines the historical antecedents of terrorism, in some instances extending back as far as antiquity. The third chapter looks closely at terrorist groups and organizations in the U. S. that, for the most part, are rooted in the ideological extremes of the Right and the Left. Chapter 4 addresses a topic often overlooked or neglected in accounts of terrorism: the victims. The fifth chapter explores the relationship between terrorism and the mass media on which the success of terrorist activity so closely depends. Chapter 6 deals with another neglected but important theme: the increasingly significant role of women in terrorism.

Part Two: Operational Perspectives is devoted to detailed accounts of terrorist tactics and strategy. Chapter 7 analyzes terrorist kidnapping and the various techniques devised for negotiating the release of hostages. In Chapter 8, the "unholy alliance," as it is referred to in Drug Enforcement Administration jargon, between drug traffickers and terrorism is discussed in detail; particularly, we try to distinguish between factual knowledge and official propaganda on narcoterrorism. Chapter 9 is devoted to the ominous prospects created for the terrorist arsenal by developments in chemical, biological, and nuclear weaponry.

The concluding section, *Part Three: Transnational Perspectives*, focuses on legal and policy issues affecting the containment of terrorist threats. Terrorism as a series of problems for the U.S. criminal justice system and for international law is discussed in Chapter 10. Chapter 11 seeks an answer to the question: Does the U.S. have a cohesive national policy on terrorism? The final chapter addresses the development of operational doctrine leading to preemption and other counterterrorism initiatives.

The authors would like to thank the following reviewers for their helpful suggestions in the preparation of this book: Dr. Harold Becker, California State University-Long Beach; Dr. Dilip Das, Western Illinois University; Dr. Daniel Georges-Abeyie, Florida State University; Dr. Richard Holden, Central Missouri State; Dr. Philip Jenkins, Pennsylvania State University; Dr. Paul Lawson, Montana State University; Dr. Thomas Phelps, California State University-Sacramento; and Dr. Roy Roberg, San Jose State University.

Harold J. Vetter
Gary Perlstein

*Sloan, S. Beating International Terrorism: An Action Strategy for Preemption and Punishment. Maxwell Air Force Base, AL: Air University Press, 1987.
**Jenkins, M.M. Talking to Terrorists. Santa Monica, CA: The Rand Corporation, 1983.

Contents

Part One

Systematic and

Historical Perspectives

1

Patterns of Terrorism

It has almost become pro forma for writers on terrorism to begin by pointing out how hard it is to define the term *terrorism*. One author (Schmid, 1983) collected more than one hundred definitions of terrorism provided by writers between 1936 and 1983, and there is every reason to believe the number has increased since the year of Schmid's publication. Why should it be so extraordinarily difficult to formulate a clear, concise, and generally acceptable definition of terrorism?

Before trying to deal with the problems of clarity and conciseness, let us begin with the issue of general acceptability. According to Wardlaw (1989), a major obstacle to a definition that commands broad acceptability is that, in many instances and contexts, terrorism involves an issue of *morality*. That is, the term *terrorist* has often been applied to individuals, groups, organizations, nations, and events in a way that involves making a moral judgment, based on the assumption that some categories of violence are justifiable, whereas others are not. Wardlaw uses as an example the Palestine Liberation Organization (PLO), which officials of some nations see as a terrorist group that lacks political legitimacy and uses morally unjustifiable methods of violence to achieve unacceptable ends, whereas other nations view the PLO as legitimate representatives of an oppressed people using necessary and justifiable violence—not terrorism—to achieve just and inevitable ends. A shorthand expression of this distinction is contained in the dictum: "One man's terrorist is another man's freedom fighter."

Wardlaw goes on to suggest, however, that the issue of morality relates primarily to the written or spoken utterances of politicians, law enforcement authorities, and other kinds of government officials, whereas many academicians appear capable of identifying events as "terrorist" without making moral judgments about those acts. According to Wardlaw (1989, 4), for a definition of terrorism to be universally accepted, it must go beyond behavioral descriptions to include individual motivation, social milieu, and political purpose. This ensures that the same behavior will or will not be viewed as terrorism by any particular observer according to differences in these other factors. To meet these criteria, he offers the following working definition:

> Political terrorism is the use, or threat of use, of violence, by an individual or a group, whether acting for or in opposition to established authority, when such action is designed to create extreme anxiety and/or fear-inducing effects in a target

3

group larger than the immediate victims with the purpose of coercing that group into acceding to the political demands of the perpetrators. (1989, 16)

The most noteworthy feature of Wardlaw's definition, which is also clear and concise, is that it restricts terrorism to *political terrorism*. As we shall see, another source of variability in definitions of terrorism has been the inclusion of violence perpetrated by individuals of unsound mind or individuals and groups motivated by criminal intent. Although it is important to be aware of these considerations and to look at some examples of violence instigated by psychiatric or criminal motives, the focus of this book is on politically motivated terrorism.

The definition also recognizes that terrorism is not only a tactic that insurgents or revolutionaries can employ; it is also a strategy that can be employed by the state. Repressive regimes in countries with widely differing cultures, economies, and political systems have used—and continue to use—violence to maintain political power. To the extent that state terrorism, however, is much less newsworthy than the dramatic incidents likely to characterize the activities of the insurgent or revolutionary terrorist, it is much more difficult to document state terrorism because official actions are usually covered by the concealing mantle of "state security." The disparity in media coverage of the two categories of politically motivated violence has produced a popular and professional literature on terrorism that is top-heavy with material on what one author designated *agitational terrorism*, at the expense of detailed descriptions of *enforcement terrorism* (Thornton, 1964).

As Wardlaw's analysis suggests, most authors appear to agree that terrorism involves the use or threat of violence as a method or strategy to achieve certain goals, and that, as a major part of this coercive process, it seeks to induce fear in its victims. Beyond this point, definitions of terrorism are likely to diverge because analysts differ in their focus on various aspects or dimensions of terrorist events and the individuals, groups, or organizations involved in their perpetration.

Typologies of Terrorism

Classifications and typologies are an attempt to understand one another and the world about us. Finding similarities and differences among objects and events is the first step toward determining their composition, functions, and causes. The notion of *type* implies that phenomena possess some relatively enduring properties or characteristics that allow them to be grouped together as part of a category; that is, membership in a group is based on sharing certain common features that distinguish an identifiable type or class. Classifying terrorists according to aims, motives, and ideologies is one way to try to understand the dynamics and consequences of terrorist acts.

The methodological and theoretical issues raised by Flemming, Stohl, and Schmid (1988) in their detailed review of terrorist typologies are outside the concerns of the present volume. For our purposes, it is sufficient to recognize that none of the various classifications of terrorism thus far proposed, from the simplest to the most complex, provide more than a rough sorting of terrorists, terrorist groups, or terrorist organizations according to one or more variables: motives, organizational composition, tactics and targets, and origins.

One of the more useful typologies was developed by a psychiatrist, Frederick Hacker, who distinguishes three kinds of terrorists: *crusaders, criminals,* and *crazies* (1977). The crusader is one who seeks prestige and power in the service of a "higher cause" and acts to attain a collective goal. Criminals may commit acts of terrorism as individuals, such as the bank robber who tries to secure his getaway by seizing bank personnel or customers and holding them hostage, or as part of the pattern of intimidation and coercion practiced by syndicated (organized) crime. As noted by the members of the National Advisory Committee on Criminal Justice Standards and Goals in their *Report of the Task Force on Disorders and Terrorism,*

> There is a vast area of true terroristic activity that clearly cannot be termed political, notably that ascribed to the present-day operations of organized crime. This is true terrorism, exhibiting conscious design to create and maintain a high degree of fear for coercive purposes, but the end is individual or collective gain rather than the achievement of a political objective. (1976, 4)

Acts of terrorism—bombings or bomb threats, capture of hostages, killing of innocent persons—can be carried out by *crazies,* individuals who are mentally and emotionally disturbed. In these cases, the target of the terrorist attack is likely to be significantly related to the disturbed individual's psychopathology. On February 22, 1974, for example, an unemployed salesman, who had previously been admitted to a Philadelphia hospital for mental observation and twice had been arrested for picketing the White House, killed a guard and a pilot in a bungled attempt to seize an airliner at the Baltimore airport and crash it into the White House.

Hacker cautions that the pure, ideal type of terrorist is rarely, if ever, encountered. Crusading terrorists may suffer from severe psychological problems, and individuals with criminal backgrounds can be found among the ranks of crusaders—a discovery that British police authorities made quite early in their confrontation with the Irish Republican Army. It was not Hacker's intention to suggest that these were mutually exclusive categories; in fact, Hacker contends that there is considerable overlap among the three types.

Although terrorism perpetrated by criminals and crazies is of interest and concern to the student of terrorism, by far the most numerous and significant terrorist actions are those committed by persons belonging to Hacker's category of crusaders. Their terrorism involves acts of *political violence.* According to Newman,

Political violence is instrumental violence. It is violence used to achieve a political end—whether a radical change in the authority structure or a reaffirmation of authority. It may be a means to power, but it may also be a way of exercising power. The concepts of power and authority are essential to an understanding of political violence. (1979, 11)

Violence or terrorism, in brief, can be used both by those who seek to change or destroy the existing government or social order and those who seek to maintain the status quo. This distinction provides the basis for Thornton's (1964) typology, which, as noted earlier, includes the categories of *agitational* terror (violence perpetrated by an organized group seeking to disrupt an existing political establishment and seize control), and *enforcement* terror (violence employed by governments to extinguish threats to their power and authority).

A Matter of Ideology

Ideology is a central element in the complex patterns of political change and stability. The term *ideology* has many meanings, but we use it here merely to refer to a set of general and abstract beliefs or assumptions about the proper state of things, particularly with regard to moral order and political arrangements, that shape one's positions on specific issues (Miller, 1974). As used in this sense, we need to note several aspects of ideology.

First, ideological assumptions are generally preconscious rather than explicit. They serve, under most circumstances, as unexamined presumptions that underlie positions that are taken openly. Second, ideological assumptions bear a strong emotional charge. This charge is not always evident, but it can readily be activated by appropriate cues, especially by a direct challenge. During their formation, ideological premises for particular individuals are influenced by information from a variety of sources, but once established, they become extremely resistant to change, because they receive or reject new evidence in terms of a self-contained and self-reinforcing system.

Ideological positions are conventionally represented by a one-dimensional scale that runs from left to right, as shown in Figure 1–1. The various terms used to identify scale positions, especially those on the extremes, cannot be defined with anything approaching precision; however, the scale provides a simple device for depicting ideologically divergent positions on any number of significant issues.

Categories such as "left-wing" and "right-wing" are admittedly crude and, inevitably, subtle distinctions are blurred. Even more controversial are labels such as "radical" and "reactionary," which refer to positions on the extremities of the ideological continuum. Despite their limitations, this classification scheme helps us think systematically about the various groups or organizations associated with the ideological scale positions by directing our attention to the assumptions that underlie them. According to Smith,

For the right, the paramount value is order—an ordered society based on a pervasive and binding morality—and the paramount danger is disorder—social, moral, and political. For the left, the paramount value is justice—a just society based on a fair and equitable distribution of power, wealth, prestige and privilege—and the paramount evil is injustice. (1982, 137)

RADICAL	LIBERAL	MODERATE		REACTIONARY
•Far Left	•Left	•Middle	•Right	•Far Right

The distance between scale values is entirely arbitrary and is not meant to imply differences in strength of conviction.

Figure 1-1
The Ideological Continuum

Left-wing groups oppose the existing government or social order and seek change; they deny the government's legitimacy and authority. Those on the right want to maintain the status quo and oppose those who seek change; they deny the legitimacy of the opposition. These distinctions become clearer when we look at the dimensions—power and authority—that underlie various forms of political violence.

Violence, Power, and Authority

Van den Haag (1972, 53–54) outlined the distinctions between power, authority, and influence within the context of political violence:

1. Authority (the legal aspect): the right of officeholders to order, and the duty of those subject to their authority to comply.
2. Authority (the consensual aspect): the effective exercise of authority by the officials vested with it, and acceptance by those subject to it.
3. Power: the ability to compel others to comply with one's wishes, regardless of authority.
4. Influence: the ability to make others acquiesce (by persuasion, prestige, or loyalty) without relying altogether on authority or on actual power.
5. Violence: "physical force used by a person, directly or through a weapon, to hurt, destroy, or control another or to damage, destroy, or control an object (e.g., territory or property). Violence can be used for the acquisition and exercise of power and to challenge authority or to enforce it."

From this schema, Van den Haag derives four political uses of violence: (1) to acquire power; (2) to exercise power; (3) to challenge authority; and (4) to enforce authority. The distinction between the legal and consensual meaning of authority, as Newman observes, is crucial with respect to political violence.

Terrorism from Above

Hacker (1977) uses the terms "above" and "below" to refer to whether terrorism is employed in the acquisition or exercise of power and in the challenge to, or enforcement of, authority. What Hacker calls "violence from above" is consistent with Van den Haag's characterization of two of the four political uses of power: to exercise power and to enforce authority. According to our ideological scale, one would identify these uses of power as a conservative or "right-wing" position. If one accepts the basic Hobbesian premise that all social order rests ultimately on the use of power (i.e., violence) as the source of authority, then violence used to enforce authority can take two different forms: *legitimate* and *illegitimate*.[1]

Legitimate use of violence is implicit in the authority of the police officer to take a suspect into custody—that is, the power of arrest. The police are, in Egon Bittner's expressive phrase, "a mechanism for the distribution of situationally justified force in society" (1970, 38). Within the boundaries of situations that, in the judgment of the officer, are "nonnegotiably coercible," the amount of power available to the discretion of the officer, acting as a representative of society, extends to the utmost extremity—the use of deadly force.

To the extent that legal authority makes the use of violence legally permissible to maintain order, there is likely to be a close correspondence between legal and consensual authority. In democratic societies such as the United States, Britain, France, West Germany, and Italy, there is room for a certain amount of disagreement with the moral or political base on which the social order rests. When dissent exceeds the legally permissible limits of disagreement, however, individuals may find themselves compelled to pursue the path of *principled deviance* and engage in acts of civil disobedience, one of whose aim is to underscore the alleged immorality of the law or laws that are broken (Clinard & Quinney, 1973). Nelson Mandela, a black South African leader, was recently released from 27 years of captivity for the political crime of belonging to the African National Congress (ANC), an organization seeking an end to apartheid and the disenfranchisement of black people within their own country.

Illegitimate use of violence from above represents the intentional choice of a policy, strategy, or technique of domination that claims the right to deny rights to everyone else, especially those identified as "enemies of the people." Terrorism from above rests on the claim that its practitioners are compelled to use violent methods to protect, unite, educate, and lead the people—the objects of terror—against disturbances of law and order. Terror from above is totalitarian and total:

> It respects neither privacy nor any sphere of intimacy. The inner circle discloses nothing, but it has the right and duty to disclose everything about everybody at its discretion. The ruling clique is not accountable to anybody except the leader, who is responsible only to his conscience, to history or to the will of the people, which he represents; but everyone else is held strictly accountable for every thought or action. There is no such thing as illegal search or seizure or any other

constitutional guarantee; everything that the masters deem necessary is by definition legal, legitimate, and in the interest of the sacred cause. (Hacker, 1977, 276)

Terror provides its own justifications. Terror regimes are often launched
and maintained on the premise that they alone can effectively provide a
defense against terrorism from below. From Hitler and the Nazis to Nixon and
Watergate, from Lenin and the Bolsheviks to Pol Pot and the Khmer Rouge,
supreme rights and the highest principles—national survival, the will of God,
or the general welfare—are always invoked to justify brutality and acts of
violence.

Government or state terrorism within the domestic political process in
some countries has grown to staggering proportions. The numbers are simply
overwhelming. In Latin America, the high level of insurgent or agitational
terrorism, which has concentrated mainly on bombings, kidnappings, and
assassinations, has been far exceeded by the level of enforcement terrorism
performed by, and on behalf of, ruling governments. Between 1970 and 1980,
more than 30,000 people are reported to have been abducted or assassinated
by agents of the state for political reasons (*Matchbox*, Spring 1980). They have
given rise to a new noun: *los desaparecidos* ("the disappeared"). Timmerman
(1981), in his memoirs of imprisonment (*Prisoner Without a Name, Cell Without
a Number*) refers to the disappearance of 15,000 Argentinians in a five-year
period. In August 1980, in the Bolivian town of Caracoles following atrocities
by government troops, some 900 people disappeared (*Amnesty Action*, September 1980).

Duvall and Stohl suggest that this strategy of political abduction—creating the "disappeared"—seems to have two objectives: to directly eliminate an
important person opposed to the government, and indirectly to communicate
to the *potential* opposition more generally—especially the political left—that
opposition is dangerous.

> To the extent that the first of these objectives is paramount, the strategy is not
> appropriately regarded as terrorism; it is a form of political assassination or
> murder. But the second objective *is* the objective of terrorism. (1983, 245)

The "disappearances" appear to be created by vigilantes—groups that are
widely recognized within society as agents of the state but who are not subject
to legal constraints. In Brazil, the *Esquadrao de Morte* (Death Squad), consisting
mostly of off-duty policemen, is accused of having executed more than 1,000
persons because of the—in their words—"inefficiency" of the Brazilian judicial process (Rosenbaum & Sederberg, 1976).

Newman claims that radical opponents of existing social orders typically
overstate the prevalence of the illegitimate use of force, at least in the Western
democracies.

> Most modern established states have a legal system which clearly forbids the
> unbridled use of violence by those in authority, and this includes the South
> American states where there is said to be widespread torture of suspects. The use
> of violence by such torturers must be seen as illegitimate violence since it is

violence that exceeds the limitations imposed on it by the legal codes. Therefore, because in some states, those in legal authority exceed the limitations on the use of violence placed on them by the law, we should not leap to the conclusion that therefore all states can survive over time only because they have an unbridled or unconstrained access to violence. (1979, 13–14)

Most states, Newman claims, are severely constrained in their employment of violence and are only able to break those constraints at times of severe crisis. This may be true for liberal democracies: witness the internal political problems created for the Israelis by the "iron fist" policies of suppression directed against the Palestinian *intefadeh* rioters on the West Bank and in the Gaza Strip. It is much more difficult to support this claim with regard to states that are controlled by totalitarian or dictatorial regimes, such as the one that ruled Romania under Nikolai Ceaucescu until his fall from power and execution.

Terrorism from Below

Remediable injustice, according to Hacker, is the basic motivation for terrorism from below. It is not deprivation or oppression as such, but the perception and experience of injustice—and the belief that such injustice is not natural or inevitable but is arbitrary, unnecessary, and remediable—that are the fundamental causes of terrorism from below. Poverty, oppression, and economic exploitation are no longer accepted as part of the inevitable scheme of things or the product of natural catastrophes: they are attributed to societal and political arrangements that can be altered by appropriate measures.

The mass media show examples of widespread hunger, torture, and oppression all over the world. They also show occasional instances of successful uprisings and revolutionary changes brought about by violent means. Even though these reports are purely factual, they cannot help but be inflammatory. When the media tantalizingly dangle the availability of goods and services before everybody's eyes, those who cannot afford to buy the products of abundance experience their limitations not just as scarcity but as deprivation and injustice.

Crusaders: Nationalistic Groups

Under Hacker's heading of crusaders, we can distinguish a category of *nationalistic groups*. Groups that belong to this category are united in the goal of political self-determination and include terrorist groups, which may cross national frontiers to carry out their attacks or may operate within their own countries. Members of these groups usually see themselves as soldiers or guerrilla fighters and reject the terrorist label. Menachem Begin, former prime minister of Israel, was a member of the Irgun Zvai Leumi, an underground organization that carried out unlimited war and committed many acts of terror against Arabs and British alike during the 1940s, before Israel achieved its independence. In his biography, Begin (1951) had this to say about being identified as a terrorist:

> Our enemies called us terrorists. People who were neither friends nor ene-mies, like the correspondents of the New York Herald-Tribune, also used this Latin name, either under the influence of British propaganda or out of habit. Our friends, like the Irishman O'Reilly, preferred, as he wrote in his letter, to "get ahead of history" and called us by a simpler, though also a Latin name: patriots.

Despite Begin's disclaimer, the historical record indicates that at least some of the actions of the Irgun toward noncombatants violated the rules of war—which is the reason the organization was stigmatized as a terrorist group.

The category of nationalistic terrorists includes some of the best-known terrorist groups, such as the Irish Republican Army (IRA); the Palestine Liberation Organization (PLO); various splinter factions of the PLO, including the Popular Front for the Liberation of Palestine (PFLP) and the "Abu Nidal" movement; the Front de Liberation Nationale (FLN); and groups that are less well-known, such as the FALN (Puerto Rico); FLNC (Corsica); ASALA and JCAG (Armenia); "Croatian Liberation Movement" and the "Croatian Free-dom Forces" (Yugoslavia); and the ETA (Basques in Spain).

In chapter 2 we will try to do justice to the centuries-long Irish struggle for independence and the emergence of the Irish Republican Army; for now we focus on the IRA and its activities as a contemporary terrorist group.

The Irish Republican Army (IRA)

The people of Ireland have been in rebellion against British occupation every generation for hundreds of years. The first organized opposition to the English invasion of Ireland was in 1791, when Wolfe Tone founded the Society of United Irishmen. Under Tone's leadership, Catholics and Protestants joined in the rebellion. The rebellion failed, but this uprising set the stage for the formation of the Irish Republican Brotherhood, also known by the Gaelic name *Fenians*, in 1858 (Coogan, 1970, 13). The Brotherhood, committed to a violent overthrow of British rule, engaged in various acts of violence and terrorism. During the 1890s better political relations developed between Brit-ain and Ireland; restrictions against Catholics were removed and inequities in the land system were changed. The Liberal party of Britain was bringing about changes that removed many of the conditions favorable to terrorism (Bell, 1974). By 1912 Britain appeared to be ready to grant Ireland autonomy, but the Protestants in Ulster fiercely resisted this plan. Ulster threatened to use force to halt the home rule movement, and the southern part of Ireland retaliated by organizing the Volunteers. Before violence could break out, World War I began, and many members of the Volunteers obeyed the com-mand of constitutionalist John Redmond and enlisted in the British army. A minority of the Volunteers refused to join the army, however, and members of this group organized the famous Easter Rising of 1916. The majority of the Irish people viewed the rebellion as madness, but when the British executed the leaders of the rebellion for treason instead of treating them as prisoners of war, the sympathies of the Irish people began to change.

The elections of 1918 brought victory to the Sinn Fein, who proclaimed Ireland a republic and formed the Dail Eireann (National Assembly of Ireland). A new group of Volunteers was created, which was called the Irish Republican Army. From 1919 to 1921, the IRA fought the British using a combination of guerrilla warfare and terrorism. The British were unable to defeat their elusive enemy and responded by levying new troops composed of men from disciplinary battalions and civil-law prisoners who, because of their uniform, were nicknamed the Black and Tans. The Black and Tans engaged in their own forms of indiscriminate brutality and terrorism that included acts of murder and torture (Breen, 1974; Cronin, 1971). The IRA retaliated with attacks on English soil and on the Irish who remained loyal to Britain. In 1932, the IRA began to ask for funds from Irishmen who had emigrated to the U.S. These transplanted Irishmen responded with funds, and the British, concerned by the American response and by the Irish problem's increasing unpopularity in Britain, proposed a truce (see Monsergh, 1976). The truce produced a treaty that granted dominion status to Ireland, but continued partition of Ireland with British forces remaining in Northern Ireland. The IRA continued to repudiate the treaty, and a civil war broke out that saw terrorism and assassination countered by repression and executions (Younger, 1969). The civil war ended by 1923, but the IRA was not destroyed—it only went underground, and, as Hachey (1982) points out, some of its members began to espouse a social radicalism that moved them toward the ideological left. In 1949 the Republic of Ireland was formed, but it did not include the six northern counties. The desire to include the six counties in the Republic set the stage for the terrorism in Ireland today.

In 1956, the IRA began a terrorist campaign in the North, and were using the South as a sanctuary. The government of the Republic of Ireland responded by arresting and imprisoning members of the IRA. Internment of IRA members by both the North and the South was a major cause for the failure of this campaign, and for the relative calm until the end of the 1960s (O'Brien, 1972). During this period, a split had developed among the IRA. On one hand was the so-called official IRA, which advocated a political solution to the problem by creating a socialist republic of thirty-two counties, and on the other hand, the provisional IRA, which wanted a united Ireland of thirty-two counties and expulsion of all British troops. The situation today is not too different from what it was in the 1970s. The Provisional IRA currently uses terrorist tactics against the British and Protestant Paramilitaries, and the Protestant Paramilitaries murder Catholics in the North and, on occasion, plant bombs in the South (Bell, 1985).

The Provisional IRA remains the oldest operating revolutionary group in the world and still commits acts of terrorism for a nationalistic cause that many regard as unattainable.

Front de Liberation Nationale (FLN)

The FLN (Front de Liberation Nationale) no longer exists because, unlike the IRA, it achieved its goal of ending the occupation of its homeland by a foreign power. The FLN demonstrated how a small insurgent group can use the strength of the occupying power against itself. It also showed, in the words of Abane Ramdane, that its leaders realized the importance of the media for terrorist activity:

> Our brothers know that we are outnumbered and outgunned by the colonialist army and hence, cannot achieve great, decisive military victories. Which is better for our cause? To kill ten enemies in some gulch in Telergma—which will go unnoticed—or one in Algiers—which will be written up in the American press the next day? If we are going to risk our lives, we must make our struggle known. We could kill hundreds of colonialist soldiers without ever making news. Let us reflect on the consequences of our acts and be sure that they will be profitable, that they will unfailingly draw attention to the noble struggle of our people and its army. (Gaucher, 1968, 230)

The war for Algeria and France's battle with the FLN began on October 31, 1954, when small bands of Algerian nationalists simultaneously attacked several French interests across the country. The FLN wanted national liberation for Algeria, but this was confusing to the French. Tunisia and Morocco were protectorates, but Algeria was considered part of the French Republic (Clark, 1960, 118). The French saw the revolt as seditious acts by a few extremists. The FLN continued its offensive with guerrilla tactics and terrorism; it recruited bandits who were already fighting the existing government (Gaucher, 1968, 226–227). The FLN could not defeat the French Forces, but used terrorism to intimidate the Moslem, pro-French elements. By 1956 the FLN offensive had moved from the countryside to Algiers, and the European community became the target of terrorism. The FLN placed bombs in cafes, stadiums, and bus stops (Clark, 1960, 326). These actions caused retaliations by European activist groups, such as the ORAF (Organisation de Resistance de l'Algerie Francaise), which would go on "Arab Hunts" (Gaucher, 1968, 230). The retaliations caused the beginning of a separation between the French born in Algeria and the Moslems, and created an environment from which the FLN could gain more recruits.

Terrorism also caused authorities to use the army instead of the police to keep public order. On January 7, 1957, General Jacques Massu, commander of the Tenth Parachute Division, became the security chief for Algiers. The "Battle for Algiers" had begun, and, by October, the leaders of the FLN had either been killed, captured, or had escaped to Tunisia (Clark, 1960, 328; Gaucher, 1968, 236–237).

After its defeat in Algiers, the FLN began a campaign of terror in metropolitan France. The FLN wanted to duplicate the "Battle of Algiers" in Paris, but the plans were never carried out (Duchemin, 1962); however, terrorist attacks were made on various French authorities and Moslems living in France who were not loyal to the FLN (Gaucher, 1968, 238). Even with the acts of terrorism on French soil, the FLN realized it could never achieve a military victory, but the struggle was receiving international attention. World opinion turned away from France, and the FLN was seen as representative of a people fighting for freedom. France was pressured into allowing Algeria to vote on self-determination, although Europeans who lived in Algeria and some segments of the army were not in agreement.

In 1961 several officers and the 1st Regiment of the Foreign Legion's parachutists attempted a putsch. The putsch failed, and Algeria received its independence on July 5, 1962. The FLN's terrorism could not defeat the French army, but the army's use of torture and brutality caused world opinion to give the FLN its victory.

Crusaders: Ideologues

The second category of crusader-terrorists can be identified as *ideologues*. Groups in this category have the avowed purpose to change social, economic, and political systems. Some groups, however, may not embrace a specific ideological doctrine or objective and may resemble, in some ways, the anarchists of the last century, whose aim was the total abolition of all government. (We will trace the origins and historical impact of the anarchists in chapter 2.)

Over the past quarter-century, the most notorious of the European terrorist groups were the "Baader-Meinhof Gang" of West Germany and the Red Brigades of Italy. The Baader-Meinhof Gang is referred to in official documents as the Red Army Faction. Originating in student disorders of the 1960s, it declared as its goal the complete overthrow and destruction of the bourgeois establishment and introduction of the rule of the freed masses (Parry, 1976, 395).

The group's first important terrorist act occurred in 1968, when Andreas Baader—a former student radical of the New Left—set fire to a Frankfurt department store. Baader was imprisoned, and in 1970 was broken out of prison by Ulrike Meinhof, a radical journalist, along with several gunmen. After the breakout, Baader and Meinhof went underground and began a campaign of terror. Terrorist attacks under their leadership continued until 1972, when both were arrested. The Red Army Faction continued terrorist activities after the arrest of its leaders. Ulrike Meinhof was found hanged in her cell in 1976, and Andreas Baader apparently also committed suicide in 1977. Since the deaths of the two leaders, the Red Army Faction has not only continued terrorist attacks in the Federal Republic, but has been involved in terrorist incidents outside West Germany. Its members have been arrested in the Netherlands, France, the United Kingdom, the United States, and Australia (Pluchinsky, 1982, 52). The Red Army Faction continues to commit acts of terrorism with linkages to groups in other countries. As recently as December 1989, the Red Army Faction claimed responsibility for the car-bombing death of Alfred Herrhausen, head of the huge and powerful Deutsche Bank (*Newsweek*, December 14, 1989).

The Italian Red Brigades have been an active terrorist group since 1970. They declared that they were "against the institutions that administer our exploitation, against the laws and the justice of the bosses, the most decisive and conscious part of the proletariat in struggle has already begun to fight for the construction of a new legality, a new power" (Drake, 1982, 105). Activities include kidnapping prominent people for either money or the release of political prisoners and murder. In 1982 the Red Brigades suffered a setback when Brigadier General James Dozier was rescued after being kidnapped; however, the Red Brigades are still the most prominent ideological terrorist group in Italy.

Asia has also been the scene of an ideological terrorist group. The Red Army (Sekigen) of Japan first gained prominence in 1970 by hijacking an airline to North Korea and by committing robberies and kidnappings in Japan. Its ideology has been described as revolutionary Socialist-Communist, with nihilist tendencies (Parry, 1976, 434). The Japanese Red Army has strong ties with Palestinian terrorist organizations (Gad, 1985; Laqueur, 1977, 207–208; Parry, 1976, 435). Their most famous terrorist attack occurred in May 1972 at the Lydda (Lod) airport in Israel, when three members of the Red Army opened fire with automatic rifles and killed twenty-eight people. The attack was organized and planned with the PFLP, a Palestinian organization. The Japanese Red Army continues to be the ideological terrorist group most involved in transnational terrorism.

Criminals and Crazies

The remaining two categories in Hacker's threefold classification are *criminals* and *crazies*. In contrast with idealistically inspired crusaders, criminal terrorists are those who use illegitimate means to achieve personal gains. Crazies, on the other hand, include people who are emotionally disturbed and driven by reasons that often do not make sense to anyone else. Hacker reluctantly uses the colloquial "crazy" because of its judgmental connotations.

Criminal Terrorists

Criminal terrorists can be further subdivided into those who employ terrorism from above or below. We can identify criminal terrorists from above as individuals who, because of their consistent selfishness and their long criminal careers before advancing to terrorism, can safely be called criminals (Hacker, 1977, 23).

Criminal Terrorists from Above: Trujillo and Noriega

General Rafael Trujillo was dictator of the Dominican Republic for thirty-one years. Before becoming "the benefactor of the people, genius of peace, savior of the country, protector of workers, and father of all Dominicans," as his people were required to call him, Trujillo had been a thief, pimp, informer, and convicted forger. He owned private monopolies in such staples as milk, salt, tobacco, meat, cocoa, and matches; and he had total control over the iron and cement industries, shipping, air travel, insurance, drugs, and the mass media. His career came to a violent end in the trunk of an abandoned car near the Dominican capital, his mutilated body a testament to three decades of dictatorial rule (Hacker, 1977, 24).

The later career of General Manuel Noriega of Panama parallels that of Trujillo in a number of ways. Noriega had been preceded by Brigadier General Omar Torrijos, who died in August 1981 in the crash of a Panamanian Air Force plane. As chief of the Panamanian Defense Forces, Noriega was the real power in Panama; Eric Arturo Delvalle, who was elected President of Panama in 1985, was viewed as a puppet of the corrupt military regime. When Delvalle resigned his office in 1988, however, he became something of a folk hero to the Panamanian people.

From the beginning of his dictatorial rule, Noriega displayed most of the features that characterized the Trujillo regime. He has been charged with political murder, election fraud, money laundering, gunrunning, drug trafficking, and selling U.S. military secrets and technology to Cuba's Fidel Castro and Libya's Moammar Gadaffi. Noriega managed to amass an estimated fortune of more than $500 million, while drawing an official salary of less than $50,000 annually.

The duel between Noriega and the U.S. holds a certain ironic interest for the student of terrorism. In April 1988, after a month of American economic pressure, Panamanians who feared and despised Noriega were saying that U.S. policy was destroying Panama in order to save it. To many Panamanians, it appeared that both Noriega and the nation of Panama were being held for ransom, just like hostages in a skyjacking.

The standoff ended when Noriega, who had seized power illegally from the duly elected representatives of the Panamanian people, became the target of a flagrant act of military aggression by the armed forces of the United States. But the duel between Noriega and the United States is not over. The case of *U.S. v. Manuel Noriega* illustrates some of the complexities posed by the trial of a foreign national on criminal charges in a U.S. court. A substantial body of legal opinion, in the United States and abroad, has argued that both Noriega's rights as a Panamanian citizen and the national sovereignty of Panama were violated by the American armed incursion that led to Noriega's capture.

Criminal Terrorists from Below: The Autobahn Bandits

In August 1988, in the West German city of Gladbeck, two ex-convicts named Hans-Jurgen Rosner and Dieter Degowski tried to hold up a bank. When police arrived on the scene in strength, the two robbers grabbed a pair of hostages; after ten hours of talks, they made off in a getaway car with their captives and $220,000. They drove all night, and picked up Rosner's girlfriend, Marion Loblich, in Bremen. Unable to shake off the pursuing police, they boarded a city bus and took thirty people hostage. Reporters and television crews moved in to record Rosner's declaration: "If our demands are not met, we will shoot."

He meant it. As the desperadoes headed for the Dutch border, Degowski killed one hostage, a fifteen-year-old Italian boy who was trying to protect his younger sister. A police officer named Ingo Hagen was killed when his motorcycle was rammed by a police vehicle during the high-speed pursuit. Three miles into Holland, the criminals exchanged the bus for a gray BMW and released all the hostages except two eighteen-year-old girls, Silke Bischoff and Ines Voitle. Then they drove to Cologne. There, as cameras whirred, Rosner aimed a gun at Silke Bischoff and explained his motivation. "If I have money," he said, just before the BMW took off down the Autobahn, "I'm a king."

Determined to end the two-day ordeal, police rammed the car. One of the fugitives killed Silke Bischoff. The other hostage, Ines Voitle, was wounded in the shoot-out, and the gunmen were captured. The bloody saga was over, but not the controversy; many Germans blamed both the police and the media for prolonging the ordeal.

We will discuss this episode further in terms of terrorism and the media in chapter 5; it is mentioned here as a prototypical example of Hacker's criminal terrorist from below.

Crazy Terrorists

Crazy Terrorist from Above: Idi Amin

The former dictator of Uganda, Idi Amin, is an archetypical example of what Hacker calls a crazy terrorist from above. Crazy, as Hacker uses the term, describes unusual, unforeseen, and incomprehensible conduct. In Amin's case, "His grotesquely irrational, bizarre actions seem to be the result of thought processes so disturbed that, in contrast with other terrorist dictators such as Hitler or Stalin, he would be considered deranged in any conceivable setting" (Hacker, 1977, 11).

Amin was the heavyweight boxing champion of Uganda for a number of years, and it has been suggested that his career in the ring may have left him with brain damage. Whatever the source of his psychopathology, he established and maintained a barbarous, bloody, and oppressive regime. His personal goon squad—the Public Safety Unit—was called the worst-trained and best-paid security force in the world. At Idi Amin's direction, torture, mutilation, and murder were commonplace in Uganda.

Hacker makes the point that to achieve the pinnacle of political power requires a certain degree of consistency, self-control, and personal strength that is lacking in most persons who are seriously disturbed. For obvious reasons, psychotic individuals do not succeed in realizing their fantasies of becoming emperors or presidents. As a rule, psychotics can neither reach nor maintain themselves in top positions. Until his overthrow, Idi Amin may have been the exception.

Crazy Terrorist from Below: The Mad Bomber

It does not require a professional background in clinical psychology or psychiatry to recognize that the type of mental disturbance most likely to produce terrorist actions is some form of paranoid disorder. The individual afflicted with a paranoid disorder is likely to suffer from persecutory delusions in which he perceives himself as the target of harassment by enemies. The individual vigorously defends these delusional or false beliefs despite logical absurdity or proof to the contrary and despite their serious interference with his social adjustment.

This profile fits the celebrated case of New York City's "Mad Bomber," a paranoid individual named George Metesky. Over a period of seventeen years, Metesky planted more than thirty homemade bombs in public places around the city. Occasionally he wrote letters to the police and the newspapers. Wrapped around his first bomb was a note: "Con Edison crooks, this is for you." In subsequent letters, it was apparent that he bore a murderous grudge against the New York supplier of electrical power, Consolidated Edison.

The Metesky case is described in detail by Dr. James Brussel in *Casebook of a Crime Psychiatrist* (1968). The significance of the case from our perspective is the amount of public fear that a single individual was able to generate by his actions—and the length of time he was able to escape detection. Metesky may have been a seriously disturbed person, but his psychotic condition did not prevent him from carrying out his terrorist plans with intelligence, foresight, and consummate craftiness.

State-Sponsored Terrorism

In many cases terrorism can be viewed as nothing more than the addition of ideology to crimes such as murder, kidnapping, and extortion. International terrorism, however, where groups or individuals are controlled or under the direction of a sovereign state, can be considered an act of war (Farrell, 1982, 6–18). The main distinction between international and transnational terrorism is determined by who is giving the orders or suggesting the target to the terrorist group. International terrorism is a *method of warfare in which a sovereign state uses surrogates to disrupt and create political and economic instability in another country.* Countries that have been reported to engage in this method of warfare include Libya, the Soviet Union, and Syria (Kupperman, 1986a, 37).

The use of surrogates to fight a war is not a new phenomenon. Throughout history, countries with imperial responsibilities have employed mercenaries to fight their wars. The British hired Native Americans and Hessian troops[2] to fight the colonists during the American Revolution, and more recently, the British used Gurkhas in the Falklands; the French are using their Foreign Legion[3] in Chad (Mockler, 1986, 15–36). Perhaps the main difference between the use of mercenaries and the use of terrorists is that by using terrorists, the sovereign state can manipulate international events and continue to remain anonymous.

Why Surrogate War?

When one thinks of war, one usually imagines two great armies clashing on a battlefield; however, as Halle points out: "the day of general wars, directly involving great powers on both sides, may also be past" (1973, 33). He did not predict an end to conflict, but instead foresaw widespread and continual disorder in the form of guerrilla warfare or terrorism.

There are several reasons for this shift to low-intensity warfare. The nuclear weapons available to the superpowers make conventional warfare too destructive. Gaucher comments on this reason for the change from individual acts of terrorism to terrorism as a surrogate for conventional warfare: "In our time, when it is difficult to mobilize large masses of men without provoking a world war and all its inevitable consequences, the selective brutality of terrorism is tending to replace the impartial horror of war" (1968, 310). Looking at the future of warfare, Jenkins concurs:

> The alternative to modern conventional war is low-level protracted war, debilitating military contests, in which staying power is more important than fire power, and military victory loses its traditional meaning. . . . Terrorism, though now rejected as a legitimate mode of warfare by most conventional military establishments, could become an accepted form of warfare in the future. Terrorists could be employed to provoke international incidents, create alarm in an adversary's country, compel it to divert valuable resources to protect itself, destroy its morale, and carry out specific acts of sabotage. Governments could employ existing terrorist groups to attack their opponents, or they could create their own terrorists. (1978, 243–244)

Paul Wilkinson believes that Jenkins's future may be happening now.

> I conclude that the most probable development in the 1980s will be an escalation of proxy unconventional war in third-party states. It is highly improbable that major powers would unleash covert attacks against each other's own territories. The fear of provoking a retaliatory war or punitive attack by a powerfully armed adversary is an effective deterrent against such adventures. The covert war in third party states is likely to be in many modes and combinations, with the use of terrorism figuring as an effective auxiliary in certain circumstances. (1986, 216–217).

Loren B. Thompson (1989) shares this belief.

Another reason for the rise of state-sponsored terrorism is that it is cost-effective—compared to conventional warfare, terrorism is extremely cheap. A third advantage of state-sponsored terrorism is that the sponsoring state can remain anonymous. Evidence of state-sponsored terrorism is usually only circumstantial and, therefore, can easily be hidden or denied by the sponsoring state.

Who Sponsors Terrorism?

The anonymous nature of state-sponsored terrorism makes it difficult to determine the identity of sponsors. Many researchers in the field of terrorism believe, however, that the Soviet Union has a lengthy history of sponsoring terrorist acts. Claire Sterling's book (1980), which became a best-seller, charged the Soviet Union with the strategic use of terrorism to undermine Western democracies. Her work and the Soviet-conspiracy thesis have been criticized by some researchers (Schmid, 1983, 210–218; Green, 1985, 42–43). But even though the Soviet Union may not have been responsible for every terrorist incident that has occurred in recent years, they have been implicated in many terrorist activities.

> They have been involved in training; in providing logistics and weaponry; in operating schools (including graduate-level education at Patrice Lumumba University in Moscow); in what to do to disrupt nations; in penetrating satellite countries, where in one case they apparently engineered the near assassination of the Pope; in running proxy operations everywhere in the world, from North Korea to Central and South America; in providing aid and comfort to proxy nations that affect client states, such as Syria; and in providing aid—indirectly and covertly—to people they are trying to bring under their umbrella, namely, Iran. (Kupperman, 1986b, 256)

The debate on how much influence the Soviet Union has had—and continues to have—on terrorist activities goes on. Edward S. Herman (1982) believes that the so-called Soviet terror network is nothing but a new form of Red Scare. On the other hand, researchers such as Alexander (1985, 101–118), Cline & Alexander (1985), and Francis (1985) believe there is adequate evidence to show that the Soviet Union and its satellites have used terrorism as a form of surrogate warfare.

The researchers' evidence indicates that the Soviets have primarily supported terrorist movements by providing training and equipment; there is only circumstantial evidence that they have had direct control over policy or actions of terrorist groups.

Another country reported to control some activities of terrorists is Libya. The most blatant example of Libyan "state-directed" terrorism has been the assassinations of dissident Libyan exiles. Assassinations of Libyan exiles by agents of the Libyan government have taken place in London, Rome, Bonn, Athens, and Milan (Pluchinsky, 1982, 62). Colonel Gaddafi has strongly supported the Arab National Youth Organization, which was responsible for skyjacking a Lufthansa plane over Turkey and forced the Bonn government to free the surviving members of Black September, who killed the Israeli Olympic athletes (Parry, 1976, 463). After the murder of British policewoman Yvonne Fletcher outside the Libyan People's Bureau in London in 1984, large quantities of weapons were found inside the building. It is suspected that the Bureau was being used as a base for operations against Libyan dissidents living in Europe. Libya is also thought to have been responsible for the attempted assassination of the head of

Chad's government in 1983, a bombing in the Kinshasa airport in Zaire, and in plots to attack the French and American embassies in Chad (Livingstone & Arnold, 1986, 17–18).

On November 4, 1979, the world learned of Iran's involvement in terrorist activities. Iranian students attacked the U.S. embassy in Tehran and seized the diplomatic personnel. The Islamic government, under the Ayatollah Khomeini, not only did nothing to protect the U.S. diplomatic mission, but used the hostage crisis to embarrass and humiliate the United States. Wilkinson (1986, 266–267) points out that this is the first time in recent history that a government has sanctioned the kidnapping of an entire embassy. When vehicle bombs destroyed the U.S. Marine barracks and the headquarters of the French Multinational Force on October 23, 1983, credit for the attacks was claimed by the Islamic Jihad, which receives direct support from the Iranian government (Livingstone & Arnold, 1986, 15). The government of Iran also sponsors other Islamic fundamentalist groups, such as the Islamic Amal and Hezbollah, which engage in terrorist activities such as car-bombing the U.S. Embassy annex in Beirut (Motley, 1986, 74).

Iran's sponsorship of terrorists can also be inferred from several kidnappings in Beirut. Victims include Jeremy Levin (Cable News Network Bureau Chief), University of Beirut Professor Frank Regier, and Minister Benjamin Weir. (Reverend Weir was kidnapped again while trying to negotiate with the kidnappers.) The Islamic Jihad claimed responsibility for the kidnappings (Livingstone & Arnold, 1986, 17).

The Iranian involvement in terrorism was part of the Khomeini regime's strategy to internationalize their religious revolution. Iranians have also used terrorism against France and Italy in an attempt to intimidate business from providing assistance to Iraq during its long war with Iran (Pluchinsky, 1982, 65). If political rhetoric is any indication, the Rafsanjani administration, which succeeded the Khomeini regime following the death of the Ayatollah, seems more concerned with rebuilding the war-ravaged Iranian economy than furthering the cause of Islamic fundamentalism.

Syria is another Middle Eastern country that includes terrorism in its strategic arsenal. The Syrian use of the Saiqa Faction of the Palestinian Liberation Organization (PLO) is an example. The Saiqa have been employed against other Palestinian factions to make sure that PLO policies do not deviate from the objectives of the Syrian government. It is also believed that the Saiqa have used the cover name "Eagles of the Palestinian Revolution" (Asa, 1985, 124–125).

Syria has also formed some kind of link with Abu Nidal and his organization, Black June. The agreement appears to call for the assassinations of moderate Arab and Palestinian leaders (Livingstone & Arnold, 1986, 19). Abu Nidal formerly operated from Iraq, but he now considers himself a Syrian citizen and has established headquarters in Damascus (Nidal, 1986, 116).

The United States has not escaped the charge of using terrorism as a form of surrogate warfare (Herman, 1982; Chamorro, 1986). In 1975, when the first Cuban troops arrived in Angola, the U.S. government—realizing that, after

Vietnam, public opinion would not allow the use of American troops in Angola—had the CIA set up an Angolan Task Force under the control of CIA operative John Stockwell (Stockwell, 1978). Apparently, the CIA, working with Robert Denard[4], hired twenty French mercenaries as instructors to UNITA (a pro-Western Angolan independence movement). According to one authority, the CIA was not involved with the English-speaking mercenaries who were working for the FNLA (another pro-Western Angolan group) and never recruited them (Mockler, 1986, 242). The CIA's use of mercenaries and the terrorist activities of which they were accused, however, certainly fit the conventional pattern of surrogate warfare.[5]

A more familiar instance of U.S. involvement in surrogate warfare is American support for the Contras, who waged war for a decade against the Sandinistan government of Nicaragua, until it was defeated by the UNO coalition in the February 1990 general election.

Other governments, such as Yugoslavia, Bulgaria, and Israel, have been accused of using terrorist techniques of assassinations and bombings. The available evidence indicates, however, that Yugoslavia and Bulgaria conducted state terrorist actions against internal dissension within their own nations, not surrogate warfare against other countries (Pluchinsky, 1982, 63–64). Israel, on the other hand, has used terrorist tactics for retaliatory purposes, such as the assassinations of the terrorists involved in the Munich massacre (Dobson, 1974, 89–133; Bar-Zohar & Haber, 1983; Jonas, 1984). It has also been speculated that Israel has used terrorist tactics against France in an attempt to stop that government from helping Iraq develop a nuclear capability (Pluchinsky, 1982, 65–66).

Summary

It is nearly impossible to find a single definition that reflects all, or even most, of the meanings ascribed to the term *terrorism*. An effort toward simplification, however, can be seen in the development of terrorist *typologies*. These schemas or devices try to classify terrorists according to such underlying factors as motives, tactics, targets, origins, or group composition.

One of the simpler and more useful of the typologies divides terrorists into *crusaders*, *criminals*, and *crazies*. Crusading terrorists seek to achieve political goals through violent means: they can be conveniently grouped according to where they fall on a continuum of *ideology*, from extreme left to extreme right. Leftists generally seek revolutionary changes in political or social arrangements; rightists tend to assert the maintenance of the status quo or "things as they are." Crusaders also include those, such as members of the Irish Republican Army (IRA), whose objectives are nationalistic.

Criminal terrorism can be exhibited by individual acts of violence and coercion or in the systematic arrangements for intimidation and corruption practiced by organized (syndicated) crime. Crazies are persons who carry out violent actions for reasons that are usually associated with the major factors involved in their mental or emotional disturbance.

A significant and growing terrorist threat to the free world is *state-sponsored terrorism*. Although the use of surrogates to fight wars is anything but new, technological innovations have made it increasingly cost-effective for nations to carry on a kind of *low-intensity warfare* against states that cannot be directly affected by economic, political, or military aggression. This form of terrorism far outweighs in potential seriousness the kind of threat posed by small groups of insurgents.

Key Terms

Idi Amin	Andreas Baader
crazies	criminals
crusaders	FLN
Frederick Hacker	ideology continuum
ideologues	illegitimate violence
IRA	"left-wing" and "right-wing"
legitimate violence	the "Mad Bomber"
Ulrike Meinhof	Manuel Noriega
principled deviance	state-sponsored terrorism
terrorism from above	terrorism from below
typologies of terrorism	

Questions for Discussion and Review

1. What is a terrorist typology? How can typologies help us understand terrorism and terrorists?
2. Briefly define *ideology* and identify some of the more important dimensions that underlie the ideological continuum depicted in this chapter.
3. Is there any real distinction between authorized and unauthorized forms of coercion?
4. What is the major difference between "terrorism from above" and "terrorism from below"?
5. What are the goals sought by the Irish Republican Army? Is there any likelihood that these goals will be achieved in the foreseeable future?
6. Identify the following individuals: Manuel Noriega, Idi Amin, George Metesky.
7. Define state-sponsored terrorism and identify some of the nations that provide direction or active support for terrorism and terrorists.

Notes

1. Wilkinson (1986, 23–24) has argued for retaining a "traditional distinction" between force and violence as *authorized* and *unauthorized* forms of coercion. He restricts the definition of violence to "the illegitimate use or threatened use of

coercion resulting, or intended to result, in the death, injury, restraint or intimidation of persons or the destruction or seizure of property." In our judgment, this
distinction fails to allow for the many instances in which the legitimate use of
coercion by duly authorized representatives of the state (police or the military)
results in "death, injury, restraint or intimidation of persons or the destruction or
seizure of property," or the other instances in which unauthorized coercion takes
a nonviolent form of expression. The U.S. National Commission on the Causes and
Prevention of Violence (1970) appears to have agreed with our conclusion that
evidence does not support this kind of distinction, because, as Wilkinson himself
points out, they abandoned it in their terminal report.
2.   Hessian troops were German soldiers under the direct control of His Most Serene
Highness the Landgrave of Hesse Cassel. They were considered the best-disci-
plined troops in Germany.
3.   The French Foreign Legion is probably the most famous mercenary unit in history.
It was officially formed on March 9, 1831, for service outside France. Readers
interested in the Legion should read Wren (1976, 1984) and Murray (1978).
4.   Robert Denard gained his fame when he commanded the mercenary troops for
the last battle against the United Nations in Katanga. He is one of the world's most
respected mercenary leaders (Bradshaw, 1979).
5.   Details on the use of mercenaries during the Angolan conflict can be found in
Burchett and Roebuck (1977) and Dempster and Tomkins (1978).

References

Alexander, Y. "Terrorism and the Soviet Union." In *On Terrorism and Combatting Terrorism*, edited by A. Merari, pp. 101–118. Frederick, MD: University
Publications of America, 1985.

Amnesty Action. New York: Amnesty International, September, 1980.

Amnesty Action. New York: Amnesty International, March, 1981.

Asa, M. "Forms of State Support to Terrorism and the Supporting States." In
On Terrorism and Combatting Terrorism, pp. 119–133. Frederick, MD: University Publications of America, 1985.

Bar-Zohar, M., and Haber, E. *The Quest for the Red Prince.* New York: Morrow,
1983.

Begin, M. *The Revolt: Story of the Irgun.* New York: Schuman, 1951.

Bell, J.B. *The Secret Army: A History of the IRA 1916–1970.* Cambridge, Massachusetts: M.I.T. Press, 1974.

Bell, J.B. "Terrorism and the Eruption of War." In *On Terrorism and Combatting
Terrorism*, edited by A. Merari, pp. 41–51. Frederick, MD: University
Publications of America, 1985.

Bittner, E. *The Functions of the Police in a Modern Society.* Chevy Chase, MD:
National Institute of Mental Health, 1970.

Bradshaw, J. "The Man Who Would be King: Robert Denard." *Esquire* 91
(March 1979): 54–59.

Breen, D. *My Fight for Irish Freedom.* Dublin: Talbot Press, 1984.

Brussel, J. *Casebook of a Crime Psychiatrist.* New York: Grove Press, 1968.

Burchett, W., and Roebuck, D. *The Whores of War.* London: Penguin, 1977.

Chamorro, E. "U.S.-sponsored Contras are Terrorists." In *Terrorism: Opposing Viewpoints*, edited by B. Szumski, pp. 137–141. St. Paul, MN: Greenhaven Press, 1986.

Clark, M.K. *Algeria in Turmoil*. New York: Praeger, 1960.

Clinard, M.B., and Quinney, R. *Criminal Behavior Systems: A Typology*. New York: Holt, Rinehart & Winston, 1973.

Cline, R.S., and Alexander, Y. *Terrorism: The Soviet Connection*. New York: Crane, Russak & Company, 1985.

Cline, R.S., and Alexander, Y. *Terrorism as State-Sponsored Covert Warfare*. Fairfax, VA: Hero Books, 1986.

Clutterbuck, R. *Living With Terrorism*. New Rochelle, NY: Arlington House, 1975.

Coogan, T.P. *The IRA*. New York: Praeger, 1970.

Cronin, S. "Internment in Ireland: Everyone but the Terrorists." *Commonweal* 94, no. 20 (Sept. 17, 1971): 470–471.

Dempster, C., and Tomkins, D. *Firepower*. London: Corgi Books, 1978.

Dobson, C. *Black September: Its Short, Violent History*. New York: Macmillan, 1974.

Drake, R. "The Red Brigades and the Italian Political Tradition." In *Terrorism in Europe*, edited by Y. Alexander and K.A. Myers, pp. 102–140. New York: St. Martin's Press, 1982.

Duchemin, J.C. *Histoire du F.L.N.* Paris: La Table Ronde, 1962.

Duvall, R.D., and Stohl, M. "Governance by Terror." In *The Politics of Terrorism*, edited by M. Stohl, pp. 179–219. New York: Marcel Dekker, 1983.

Farrell, W.R. *The U.S. Government Response to Terrorism*. Boulder, CO: Westview Press, 1982.

Fleming, M. "Propaganda by the Deed: Terrorism and Anarchist Theory in Late-Nineteenth Century Europe." In *Terrorism in Europe*, edited by Y. Alexander and K.A. Myers, pp. 8–28. New York: St. Martin's Press, 1982.

Flemming, P.A., Stohl, M., and Schmid, A.P. "The Theoretical Utility of Typologies of Terrorism: Lessons and Opportunities." In *The Politics of Terrorism*, edited by M. Stohl, pp. 153–195. New York: Marcel Dekker, 1988.

Forsyth, F. *The Biafra Story*. Hammondsworth, England: Penguin, 1969.

Francis, S.T. *The Soviet Strategy of Terror*. Washington, DC: The Heritage Foundation, 1985.

Fromkin, D. "The Strategy of Terrorism." In *Contemporary Terrorism: Selected Readings*, edited by J.D. Elliot and L.K. Gibson, pp. 11–24. Gaithersburg, MD: International Association of Chiefs of Police, 1978.

Gad, Z. "International Cooperation among Terrorist Groups." In *On Terrorism and Combatting Terrorism*, edited by A. Merari, pp. 135–144. Frederick, MD: University Publications of America, 1985.

Gaucher, R. *The Terrorists*. London: Secker & Warburg, 1968.

Green, L.C. "Terrorism and Its Responses." *Terrorism: An International Journal* 8, no. 1 (1985): 33–77.

Hachey, T.E. "A Courtship with Terrorism: The IRA Yesterday, Today, Tomorrow." In *The Rationalization of Terrorism*, edited by D.C. Rapoport, and Y. Alexander, pp. 178–187. Frederick, MD: University Publications of America, 1982.

Hacker, F.J. *Crusaders, Criminals, Crazies*. New York: Norton, 1977.

Halle, L.J. "Does War Have a Future?" *Foreign Affairs*, 52 (1973): 20–39.

Herman, E.S. *The Real Terror Network*. Boston: South End Press, 1982.

Hill, C. "The Political Dilemmas for Western Governments." In *Terrorism and International Order*, pp. 77–100. London: Routledge & Kegan Paul, 1986.

Homer, F.D. "Terror in the United States: Three perspectives." In *The Politics of Terrorism*, edited by M. Stohl, pp. 145–177. New York: Marcel Dekker, 1983.

Ivianski, Z. "The Blow at the Center: The Concept and Its History." In *Terrorism and Combatting Terrorism*, edited by A. Merari, pp. 53–62. Frederick, MD: University Publications of America, 1985.

Jenkins, B. "International Terrorism: A Balance Sheet." In *Contemporary Terrorism: Selected Readings*, edited by J.D. Elliott and L.K. Gibson, pp. 235–245. Gaithersburg, MD: International Association of Chiefs of Police, 1978.

Joll, J. *The Anarchists*. Cambridge, MA: Harvard University Press, 1980.

Jonas, G. *Vengeance: The True Story of an Israeli Counter-Terrorist Mission*. London: Collins, 1984.

Kupperman, R.H. "Terrorism is International Warfare." In *Terrorism: Opposing Viewpoints*, edited by B. Szumski, pp. 33–38. St. Paul, MN: Greenhaven Press, 1986.

Kupperman, R.H. "Terrorism and National Security." *Terrorism: An International Journal* 8, no. 3 (1986b): 255–261.

Laqueur, W. *Terrorism*. Boston: Little, Brown, 1977.

Laqueur, W. *The Age of Terrorism*. Boston: Little, Brown, 1987.

Ledeen, M. "Covert Operations Can Fight Terrorism." In *Terrorism: Opposing Viewpoints*, edited by B. Szumski, pp. 218–222. St. Paul, MN: Greenhaven Press, 1986.

Livingstone, N.C. "Proactive Responses to Terrorism: Reprisals, Preemption and Retribution." In *Fighting Back: Winning the War Against Terrorism*, edited by N.C. Livingstone and T.E. Arnold, pp. 109–131. Lexington, MA: D.C. Heath, 1986.

Livingstone, N.C., and Arnold, T.E. "The Rise of State-Sponsored Terrorism." In *Fighting Back: Winning the War Against Terrorism*, edited by N.C. Livingstone and T.E. Arnold, pp. 11–24. Lexington, MA: D.C. Heath, 1986.

Matchbox. Amnesty International, Spring 1980.

Mickolus, E. "International Terrorism." In *The Politics of Terrorism*, edited by M. Stohl, pp. 221–253. New York: Marcel Dekker, 1983.

Milbank, D.L. "International and Transnational Terrorism: Diagnosis and Prognosis." In *Contemporary Terrorism: Selected Readings*, edited by J.D. Elliot and L.K. Gibson, pp. 51–80. Gaithersburg, MD: International Association of Chiefs of Police, 1978.

Miller, W.B. "Ideology and Criminal Justice Policy." In *Criminology: Crime and Criminals*, edited by C.E. Reasons, pp. 19–50. Pacific Palisades, CA: Goodyear, 1974.

Mockler, A. *The New Mercenaries*. London: Transworld Publishers, 1986.

Monsergh, N. *The Irish Question: 1840–1921*. 3rd ed. Toronto: University of Toronto Press, 1976.

Motley, J. B. "Target America: The Undeclared War." In *Fighting Back: Winning the War Against Terrorism*, edited by N.C. Livingstone and T.E. Arnold, pp. 59–83. Lexington, MA: D.C. Heath, 1986.

Murray, S. *Legionnaire*. London: Sidgwick and Jackson, 1978.

Newman, G. *Understanding Violence*. New York: Harper & Row/Lippincott, 1979.

Newsweek. "The Bloody Return of the Red Army Faction." (December 11, 1989), p. 62.

Nidal, A. "The Palestinian Goal Justifies Terrorism." In *Terrorism: Opposing Viewpoints*, edited by B. Szumski, pp. 113–118. St. Paul, MN: Greenhaven Press, 1986.

O'Brien, C.C. *States of Ireland*. New York: Random House, 1972.

Parry, A. *Terrorism: From Robespierre to Arafat*. New York: Vanguard Press, 1976.

Pluchinsky, D. "Political Terrorism in Western Europe: Some Themes and Variations." In *Terrorism in Europe*, edited by Y. Alexander and K.A. Meyers, pp. 40–78. New York: St. Martin's Press, 1982.

Pyle, C.H. "Defining terrorism." *Foreign Policy* 64 (Fall 1986): 63–78.

Roberts, G.B. "Covert Responses: The Moral Dilemma." In *Fighting Back: Winning the War Against Terrorism*, edited by N.C. Livingstone and T.E. Arnold, pp. 133–144. Lexington, MA: D.C. Heath, 1986.

Rosenbaum, J.H., and Sederberg, P. *Vigilante Politics*. Philadelphia: University of Pennsylvania Press, 1976.

Schmid, A.P. *Political Terrorism: A Research Guide to Concepts, Theories, Data Bases and Literature*. Amsterdam: North Holland Publishing Company, 1983.

Sloan, J.W. "Political Terrorism in Latin America." In *The Politics of Terrorism*, edited by M. Stohl, pp. 1–19. New York: Marcel Dekker, 1983.

Smith, D. "Ideology and the Ethics of Economic Crime Control." In *Ethics, Public Policy, and Criminal Justice*, edited by F. Elliston and N. Bowie, pp. 133–155. Cambridge, MA: Oelgeschlager, Gunn and Hein, 1982.

Sterling, C. *The Terror Network: The Secret War of International Terrorism*. New York: Holt, Rinehart & Winston, 1981.

Stockwell, J. *In Search of Enemies*. New York: Norton, 1978.

Stohl, M. "Myths and realities of political terrorism." In *The Politics of Terrorism*, edited by M. Stohl, pp. 1–19. New York: Marcel Dekker, 1983.

Thompson, L.B. "Who Dares Wins: The Story of the Special Air Service." In *Fighting Elite*, pp. 36–41. Boulder, CO: Omega Group, 1986.

Thompson, L.B. *Low-Intensity Conflict: The Pattern of Warfare in the Modern World*. Lexington, MA: D.C. Heath, 1989.

Thornton, T.P. "Terror as a Weapon of Political Agitation." In *Internal War*, edited by H. Eckstein, pp. 71–99. New York: Free Press, 1964.

Timmerman, J. *Prisoner Without a Name, Cell Without a Number*. New York: Knopf, 1981.

Van den Haag, E. *Political Violence and Civil Disobedience*. New York: Harper & Row, 1972.

Walter, E.V. *Terror and Resistance: A Study of Political Violence*. London: Oxford University Press, 1969.

Wardlaw, G. *Political Terrorism*. New York: Cambridge University Press, 1989.

Wilkinson, P. *Terrorism and the Liberal State*. New York: New York University Press, 1986.

Wilkinson, P. "Trends in international terrorism and the American response." In *Terrorism and the International Order*, pp. 37–55. London: Routledge & Kegan Paul, 1986.

Wren, P.C. *Beau Ideal*. Cutchoghe, NY: Light Year, 1976.

Wren, P.C. *Beau Sabreur*. Cutchoghe, NY: Light Year, 1976.

Wren, P.C. *Beau Geste*. Cutchoghe, NY: Buccaneer Books, 1984.

Younger, C. *Ireland's Civil War*. New York: Taplinger, 1969.

Zenker, E.V. *Anarchism*. London: Methuen, 1898.

2
Terrorism in Historical Perspective

The origins of terrorism are lost in antiquity. As Hacker (1977, ix) points out, terror and terrorism "are as old as the human discovery that people can be influenced by intimidation." The use or threat of violence to achieve political purposes was already familiar to the ancestors of Brutus, Cassius, and the rest of the conspirators who assassinated Julius Caesar. But the terms *terrorism* and *terrorist* are comparatively recent; they can be traced to the period of the French Revolution. More precisely, they are associated with the so-called "Reign of Terror," which some historians date from September 4, 1793—the day that Barere's motion was carried "to place the Terror on the order of the day." Other historians have identified the Terror with all popular violence after the Tennis Court Oath of June 20, 1789. There is general agreement, however, that the Terror ended with the death of Robespierre on the ninth of Thermidor.

Laqueur (1987, 11) claims that, according to a French dictionary published in 1796, the Jacobins had occasionally used "terrorist" to refer to themselves in a positive sense. After the ninth of Thermidor, however, the word acquired the connotations of abuse with criminal implications.

Attila and the Huns, Genghis Khan and the Mongols, Tamerlane and the Seljuk Turks made calculated use of terror in the service of military conquest. As an ancient Chinese proverb puts it, "Kill one person, frighten ten thousand"—manifested in the later German practice of *Schrecklichkeit* ("frightfulness") in attempting to subdue and intimidate captive populations in the two world wars.

An eighteenth-century contribution of colonial America to terrorism and terrorist tactics was the Sons of Liberty, part patriot and part ruffian, who helped fan the fires of resistance to the Crown by such undertakings as the Boston Tea Party and who were thus instrumental in bringing about the coercive countermeasures by George III and Parliament that led to the Revolutionary War.

When a full historical account of terrorism is written, it will abound with examples of parallels between earlier and later uses of violence to achieve political objectives. It is not part of the record that the Sons of Liberty—or their leaders—were keen students of history, but the tactics they employed in eighteenth-century Boston against the British had already reached a respectable level of sophistication in the first century after the birth of Jesus Christ.

Early Antecedents

The Jewish Zealot movement fought against the harsh and oppressive rule of Rome. The *Sicarii*, a religious sect whose members were active within the Zealot struggle in Palestine, employed terrorist tactics that were also directed against Jewish moderates. Between 66 and 70 A.D., the *Sicarii* and Zealots managed to polarize the Jewish population by acts of violence designed to provoke retaliatory violence from the Roman military government: imprisonment of Jewish religious leaders, desecration of religious symbols, use of excessive military force to break up demonstrations, and similar measures. Rapoport and Alexander (1983) have noted that the *Sicarii*—a term derived from *sica*, the short sword that was the favorite weapon of the sect members—chose to intensify the histrionic effects of their violence by making it a point to attack their targets, Roman soldiers or administrators and Jewish moderates, in broad daylight, especially when their victims were surrounded by supporters and friends, to demonstrate that no circumstances could guarantee immunity from assault.

Rapoport (1988) observes that the messianic fervor of the *Sicarii* carried them to the extreme of being willing to violate the most hallowed taboos in the name of their cause. They chose the holiest days to assassinate Jewish priests who, they charged, had succumbed to Hellinistic influences. A drastic example was the description by Flavius Josephus of the dreadful fate suffered by a Roman garrison that surrendered after receiving a safe passage agreement secured by a covenant—the most inviolable pledge that Jews could make.

> When they had laid down their arms, the rebels massacred them; the Romans neither resisting nor suing for mercy but merely appealing to the Covenant! . . . The whole city was a scene of dejection, and among the moderates everyone was racked by the thought that he should personally have to suffer for the rebels' crime. For to add to its heinousness the massacre took place on the sabbath, a day on which from religious scruples Jews abstain from the most innocent acts.

A similar combination of religious zeal and political extremism characterized the Assassins, a sect that emerged during the eleventh century and became familiar to the Crusaders. Led by a founder known only as the "Old Man of the Mountains," the Assassins gained widespread repute in the Middle East as murderers who carried out their lethal missions while under the influence of hashish (hence the name, Assassin, which derives from the Arabic *hashashim* or "eaters of hashish").

It is tempting to draw parallels between the Assassins and contemporary movements such as The Islamic Jihad and Hezbollah in terms of their mutual dedication to violence, hatred of foreigners, and religious fanaticism. But the existence of other religiously motivated extremist groups, such as the Thugs of India, the Boxers of China, and the Fenian Brotherhood in the U.S. and Ireland during the nineteenth century, strongly suggests that political, economic, and religious oppression—real or perceived—in widely differing places and times tend to elicit similar kinds of reactions.

Thuggee was a cult that worshipped the many-armed Kali, goddess of destruction. Its devotees—called Thugs—carried out ritual murder of victims, who were strangled with a silk scarf. For centuries, the Thugs preyed on travelers who used India's meandering, unprotected roads and footpaths. They joined parties of merchants, couriers, porters, and others with property, killed them, robbed them, and buried them in graves dug before the murders.

A British officer, William Sleeman, carried on a campaign over a twenty-year period to suppress the cult of Thuggee, but Sleeman hastened its end by only a short time. The coming of the railroad and telegraph in the middle of the century deprived the Thugs of the isolation they needed for their practices. The Thugs held death in contempt; and their political aims, if they had any, were not easily discernible. As Laqueur (1987) observes, in a survey of political terrorism, this phenomenon rates no more than a footnote.

Also worth a footnote were the militant secret societies or *triads* in China. One of the more famous—or notorious—of these was the Boxers ("Society of Righteous Fists"), which hated foreigners and was opposed to the ruling Manchu dynasty. The Boxers were only one of a number of such groups, but they gave their name to the Boxer Rebellion in 1905 and contributed substantially to the nationalist movement headed by Sun Yat-sen. Politics was only one of their interests, however, and in this respect, as Laqueur points out, they resembled more closely the Mafia than modern political terrorist movements.

The Anarchist Heritage

The modern era of terrorism can be said to have begun with the Anarchist movement in Europe during the nineteenth century. A "daydream of desperate romantics," as it was called by a historian of revolt, Anarchism sought the destruction of all existing governments and the abolition of private property. It called for a "propaganda of the deed," and its symbol was a bomb with a lighted fuse. In pursuit of this impossible dream, six heads of state lost their lives in the two decades that preceded World War I; among them was President McKinley of the United States.

It was in Russia during this period that writers developed doctrines proclaiming the virtue of terror. One writer was Serge Nachaeyev, whose *Revolutionary Catechism* contains the following statements regarding the duties of the revolutionary:

> The revolutionary is a dedicated man. He has no personal inclinations, no business affairs, no emotions, no attachments, no property, and no name. Everything in him is subordinated towards a single exclusive attachment, a single thought, and a single passion—the revolution.
>
> In the very depths of his being, not only in words but also in deeds, he has torn himself away from the bonds which tie him to the social order and to the

cultivated world, with all its laws, moralities, and customs and with all its generally accepted conventions. He is their implacable enemy, and if he continues to live with them, it is only to destroy them more quickly.

The revolutionary despises all dogmas and refuses to accept the mundane sciences, leaving them for future generations. He knows only one science: the science of destruction. For this reason, and only for this reason, he will study mechanics, physics, chemistry, and perhaps medicine. But all day and night he studies the living science of peoples, their characteristics and circumstances, and all the phenomena of the present social order. The object is the same: the prompt destruction of this filthy order.

Fueled by such ideas, the *Narodniki*—members of a nihilist group called *Narodnaya Volya (People's Will)*—assassinated Czar Alexander II of Russia. Narodnaya Volya bears the dubious distinction of having been the first terrorist organization to use dynamite on a wide scale. Indeed, it was a crude bomb containing dynamite that ended Czar Alexander's life.

The assassination of the czar set the stage for a meeting in London of the International Congress of Anarchists on July 14, 1881. Here the leading Anarchists met to assert their belief that a revolution could be brought about only through illegal means (Fleming, 1982; Ivianski, 1985; Joll, 1972). Terrorism was to be the means for awakening people throughout the world from their tranquility.

In 1884, Johannes Most, a German Social Democrat turned anarchist, published in New York a manual entitled *Revolutionary (Urban) Warfare*, which bore the rather alarming subtitle "A Handbook of Instruction Regarding the Use and Manufacture of Nitroglycerine, Dynamite, Guncotton, Fulminating Mercury, Bombs, Arson, Poisons, etc." Most pioneered the notion of the letter bomb and argued that the liquidation of "pigs" was not murder because murder was the willful killing of a human being—a category to which policemen did not belong.

By definition, anarchism means a fixed belief in the rejection of all ruling authority. Here, as Tuchman (1966) points out, lies the fundamental paradox within anarchism that frustrated progress. Anarchism rejected the political party, as a "mere variety of absolutism"; yet to bring about a revolution, it is necessary to submit to authority, discipline, and organization. Revolution, presumably, only needed the Idea and a spark—and revolution would burst forth spontaneously from the masses.

Anarchism had its theorists, such as Bakunin and Kropotkin, who were sincere, dedicated, and humanitarian in their ideas and aims. In press and pamphlet, they "constructed marvelous paper models of the anarchist millenium; poured out tirades of hate and invective upon the ruling class and its despised ally, the bourgeoisie" (Tuchman, 1966, 72); and issued clarion calls for action to overthrow the established order.

Those who heeded the calls were men without fear and without hope, whom poverty had reduced to a nearly subhuman status—the inhabitants of Gorky's "lower depths." They had nothing to lose but their lives, and these they were ready and even eager to trade for the chance of striking a blow against their oppressors. With knife, revolver, or bomb, they provided the wherewithal for the "propaganda of the deed."

Michael Bakunin

One of the most influential anarchists was Michael Bakunin. Although he lived during the same period and appeared to espouse the same political philosophy as Karl Marx, he had little regard for the father of Communism. He once referred to Marx's *Das Kapital* as "a dreadful book of 784 pages of small print" and also as "economic metaphysics" (Pyziur, 1955, 16). Ironically enough, Bakunin, who was living in exile from Russia, lost control of the First International to Karl Marx, who did not share Bakunin's and other anarchists' contempt for organization and discipline.

In tracing the development of Bakunin's revolutionary thought, Draper (1978) observes that he was heavily influenced by Pierre-Joseph Prudhon, recognized among historians as the "father of anarchism." In fact, Bakunin was a disciple of Proudhon, although it appears that he also exerted an impact on Proudhon's views on anarchism.

One of Bakunin's contributions to anarchist action was his Pan-Slavism, the manifesto that was published in 1848 as a people's call to action. Pan-Slavism represented a hatred of the Germans and faith in the future of the Slavs. Laden with Messianic overtones, Pan-Slavism was later abandoned as unsuccessful.

Anarchism is a product of revolt against oppression and is seen more as a natural reaction than as an ideological conviction. An anarchist is perceived as a rebel without a cause or an "insurrectionist without a dogma." The target against which anarchists direct their attacks is the state itself, or some group or object that symbolizes state authority. Bakunin believed that the state will always be an instrument of the capitalist ruling class for domination and exploitation. In rejecting the tenets of parliamentary democracy, Bakunin declared: "One must be a donkey, ignorant, crazy, to hope that any constitution, even the most liberal, most democratic one, can improve the relationship of the state to people" (Pyziur, 1955, 66).

Bakunin summarized the sentiments of the oppressed masses and the organization of their revolt in his work *Golos Truda*:

> In moments of great political and economic crisis, when the instincts of the masses are sharpened to the utmost keenness and are open to all worthwhile suggestions, at a time when these herds of human slaves, crushed and enslaved but still unresigned, rise up at last to throw off their yoke, but feeling bewildered and powerless because of being completely disorganized—then ten, twenty, or thirty well-organized persons, acting in concert and knowing where they are going and what they want, can easily carry along one, two or three hundred people or even more. (quoted by Pyziur, 1955, 67)

A recurrent theme throughout Bakunin's doctrine of anarchism is the notion of "pan-destruction." This nihilistic approach to revolution was to begin in Europe and spread outward, engulfing all nations in its path. This concept can be likened to Trotsky's idea of communism enveloping the world or, as we shall see later, Ernesto "Che" Guevara's idea of establishing a revolutionary guerrilla base in Bolivia in the hope that revolution would radiate outward from this central point into surrounding countries. Bakunin advocated a sweeping revolution that would encompass both the urban industrial workers and the rural peasants. Only by this means would Bakunin and his followers be able to overpower the state.

Peter Kropotkin

The most eminent anarchist after Bakunin was Prince Peter Kropotkin, a revolutionist. During the course of his wanderings throughout the world, Kropotkin aligned himself with a secret revolutionary committee, which led to his imprisonment when its existence was discovered. Kropotkin is credited with having maintained that the perfection of the human condition was impeded by the inertia of those who have a vested interest in existing conditions. He believed that progress required a violent spark "to hurl mankind out of its ruts into new roads . . . Revolution becomes a peremptory necessity" (Tuchman, 1966, 71). Revolutionary consciousness has to be stimulated in the masses by repeated "propaganda of the deed," that is, anarchist violence. To Kropotkin, a single deed was better propaganda than a thousand pamphlets.

Propaganda of the Deed

Although contemporary acts of terrorism occur within a wide range of contexts, anarchist violence at the turn of the century was principally confined to bombings and assassinations. One of the first major anarchist bombings was a domestic incident that occurred in May of 1885, during the Haymarket Square riot in Chicago.

The riot started as a strikers' meeting; during the course of the meeting, there was a clash between the strikers and strikebreakers. Called in to quell the disturbance, the police fired into the crowd, killing two people. The next day, August Spies, editor of Chicago's German-language anarchist newspaper, *Arbeiter-Zeitung*, called a protest meeting in Haymarket Square. The police responded to disperse the crowd, and a bomb of unknown origin was thrown. The eight men who participated in the bombing were sentenced to death. Three later had their sentences commuted to prison terms, one committed suicide on the eve of his execution, and the remaining four, including August Spies, were hanged on November 11, 1887.

At the Opera House in Barcelona, Spain, on November 8, 1893, during a performance of *William Tell*, the theme of which deals with revolt against tyranny, two bombs were tossed over the balcony into the crowd. Twenty-two people were killed and fifty injured. In January of the following year, a man named Santiago Salvador claimed responsibility for the bombing and was arrested and subsequently executed. Salvador's arrest was immediately followed by another bombing, for which his fellow anarchists of Barcelona took credit. This pattern follows the contemporary cycle of action-reaction (Shaw, Hazelwood, Hayes, & Harris, 1977), in which terrorists and governments engage in a series of exchanges of force, each seeking to emerge the victor in the struggle for public support.

One of the most notorious bombing incidents occurred in March 1893, when August Vaillant detonated a homemade explosive device in the French Parliament's Chambre des Deputes in Paris. Vaillant hurled his bomb onto the debate floor from his seat in the public gallery. Fortunately, although several people were injured, the explosive charge was nonlethal. Vaillant's motivation was simply to end his life so that he would not have to see his family suffer in a society ruled by a government that was rife with scandal and corruption. During his trial, Vaillant stated that if he had really wanted to kill, he would have used a heavier explosive charge and bullets instead of nails. Nevertheless, he was given the death penalty. This incident was the first time in the nineteenth century that anyone was sentenced to capital punishment for a crime that did not result in the death of a victim.

A number of anarchist-inspired assassinations occurred in Europe during this period. The first, and most important, was the assassination of President Sadi Carnot of France, who was fatally stabbed by an Italian named Santo Caserio on June 24, 1894. Caserio was Italian-born; and after aligning himself with anarchist factions in Milan, a center of anarchist activity, he eventually emigrated to France, where he befriended a group of anarchists who called themselves "Les Coeurs de Chene" (Hearts of Oak).

Caserio was angered by Carnot's refusal to pardon Vaillant for his bombing of the Chambre des Deputes. When Caserio learned that Carnot would be arriving in Lyons shortly, he made arrangements to be in that city during Carnot's visit. While riding in an open carriage through the crowds that had assembled for the Exhibition, Carnot was approached by a man holding a rolled-up newspaper, which the guards assumed contained flowers. Concealed in the newspaper was the knife that Caserio used in the fatal stabbing. Obsessed with anarchist philosophy, Caserio described the assassination as "propaganda of the deed."

There followed the assassination of Premier Antonio Canovas del Castillo of Spain in 1897; of Empress Elizabeth of Austria in 1898; of King Umberto of Italy in 1900; of President McKinley of the United States in 1901; and of Premier Jose Canejas of Spain in 1912, all at the hands of avowed anarchists.

There is an interesting link between the assassinations of King Umberto and of President McKinley. The American newspaper accounts of Umberto's murder were read avidly by a twenty-year-old Polish-American, Leon Czolgosz. After having been laid off during a strike, Czolgosz aligned himself with a group of workers dedicated to socialism, anarchism, and political radicalism. Among the topics discussed in their meetings was "Presidents and that they were no good." In 1898, Czolgosz contracted an illness that left him depressed. On September 6, 1901, at the Pan-American Exposition in Buffalo,

New York, he passed through the receiving line in front of McKinley and shot the President with a gun concealed in a handkerchief wrapped around his hand. In his confession, Czolgosz stated: "I killed President McKinley because I done my duty, because he was an enemy of the good working people." He also indicated that he had been inspired by a lecture given by anarchist leader Emma Goldman, whose central theme was that "all rulers should be extermi- nated." Czolgosz went on to say that "I don't believe we should have any rulers. It is right to kill them" (Tuchman, 1966, 106).

The assassination of McKinley marked the end of anarchist political murder in the western democracies. Anarchism survived as a movement in Russia until World War I, and in Spain until the beginning of World War II, but the force of anarchist passion flowed into the more realistic combat of the syndicates or trade unions. Anarchists achieved their greatest success in the U.S. with the founding of the International Workers of the World (I.W.W.) in 1905. Labor unions were seen as the cutting edge of revolutionary struggle and the chief instrument for bringing about a stateless industrial society. As its energy passed into syndicalism, anarchism added its qualities of violence and extremism to the struggle for power of organized labor.

To Shake an Empire

For many, in the U.S. and elsewhere, the quintessential figure of terrorism is the IRA gunman or bomber, blowing up innocent shoppers in a Belfast department store or ambushing a British soldier who is trying to anesthetize his homesickness and feelings of estrangement in an off-duty pub. For others, the IRA is a trench-coated hero, carrying on a gallant fight to free Ireland's sacred soil from seven centuries of occupation and domination by foreigners. As Calton Younger puts it:

> The I.R.A. is not a gang of unprincipled thugs. Its members believe fervently in the legality of their cause and the justice of their actions. They declared war on a nation which seized their country long ago and still occupies part of it. Twenty-six of Ireland's thirty-two counties were liberated by their grandfather's genera- tion. Now it is their turn to finish the job. (1969, 524)

The origins of the IRA can be traced back to the Fenian Brotherhood, an Irish-American revolutionary secret society that was active during the 1860s. The major goal of Fenianism was to foment a revolt against British colonial rule in Ireland; at the end of the American Civil War, Irishmen who had served in armies on both sides of the conflict were urged to return to Ireland to topple British rule.

When the Fenians began a campaign of terrorism against the British (and their Irish collaborators), the movement was swiftly crushed. But the Irish Republican Brotherhood (IRB), which had been formed in the U.S. by Irish patriots in exile after the rising of 1848, breathed new vitality into the struggle for Irish independence. The IRB was dedicated to the use of force in the achievement of Irish independence, which places it in lineal descent from Wolf Tone's United Irishmen and their unsuccessful rebellion in 1798.

In 1905, *Sinn Fein* ("Ourselves") was founded by Arthur Griffith and was to become practically synonymous with revolutionary violence. Brendan Behan, author of *Borstal Boy*, tells of reaching Liverpool at the outbreak of World War II armed with a "Sinn Fein conjuror's kit" (dynamite and detonators) and orders to blow up a British battleship. (He was sixteen years old at the time.) In the beginning, however, Sinn Fein was primarily political in its orientation and closely bound up with the Gaelic League, which represented the resurgence of Irish language and culture.

But the IRB, represented by Eoin MacNeill of the Gaelic League, proposed a force of volunteers "to secure and maintain the rights and liberties common to all the people of Ireland" (Younger, 1969, 20). In the North, the Ulster Volunteers were already armed and drilling, prepared to maintain the Union with Great Britain and defeat, at any cost, the passage of Home Rule for Ireland.

The Easter Rising

From its inception, the IRB infiltrated the Irish Volunteers and finally achieved domination over its 10,000 members. Together with a second militia group, the Irish Citizen Army, the Volunteers trained and prepared for a revolt against British rule.

James Connolly, the Commandant General of the Irish Citizen Army, was a Marxist and nationalist. On Easter Sunday morning, April 24, 1916, in Dublin, Connolly and his citizen militia stormed through the main thoroughfare of downtown Dublin (Sackville Street, subsequently renamed O'Farrell Street) and seized the General Post Office, which they were to occupy for the next six days.

The Rising was finally ended on April 30th, when Patrick Pearse, director of the Irish Volunteers, and other members of the Provisional Government agreed to an unconditional surrender. Pearse and all the revolutionary leaders who signed the Republican proclamation were court-martialled and executed. During his trial, Pearse uttered these words:

> We seem to have lost, we have not lost. To refuse to fight would have been to lose, to fight is to win. We have kept faith with the past and handed a tradition to the future . . . if our deed has not been sufficient to win freedom, then our children will win it by a better deed. (Coffey, 1969, 262)

Although the Rising was put down by force, in 1921 the Irish agreed to a treaty in London that declared independent sovereignty for an Irish Republic composed of twenty-six of the thirty-two counties.

This partition ended more than two years of civil war, but left Ireland a divided country with an internal border between the predominantly Protestant North (Ulster) and the predominantly Catholic South (*Eire* or the Irish Republic). It is a pattern that has become tragically familiar in various parts of the world—and it is the situation that the Irish Republican Army has vowed to abolish, at any cost. The IRA doffed its uniforms and became an underground guerrilla army, dedicated to the goal of a free and united Ireland.

Violence begets violence; and the Ulster Volunteer Force, a Protestant extremist group, has sought to match the IRA in a savage tit-for-tat campaign of bloodshed and assassination, for which journalists have coined the expression "sectarian murders." The adversaries are locked in mortal embrace, and the end is nowhere in sight.

The Middle East

American students who are not familiar with the history of the Middle East are likely to assume that terrorism in this area resulted from the partition of Palestine in 1947 to create the state of Israel, thus initiating the Palestinian refugee problem, the refugee camps, the PLO, and all of the attendant ills that followed. They can scarcely be blamed for making this assumption, when it is one that is widely held in the Western world. As we will see, however, terrorism did not begin in the Middle East with the creation of a Jewish homeland by the action of the United Nations in 1948.

Palestine: Historical Background

Over many centuries, Arabs and Jews have developed both deep historical roots and strong emotional bonds in Palestine. From these entangled roots and attachments emerged, in the nineteenth century, two opposing nationalisms—Arab nationalism and political Zionism—both of which laid claim to the same land. The confrontation between these incompatible nationalisms produced the troublesome "Palestine question" of earlier years, the bitter Arab-Israeli antagonisms, disputes, and wars of more recent years, and the dangerous Arab-Israeli dilemma that challenges world peace today.

At the beginning of World War I, the area that presently includes Israel, Jordan, Syria, Lebanon, Iran, Iraq, Saudi Arabia, Yemen, Qatar, Kuwait, Oman, the United Arab Emirates, and Turkey, was part of the Ottoman Empire. Within this sprawling area of Turkish hegemony, the Arabs were a restless minority. Turkish rule, as T.E. Lawrence once observed, was gendarme rule; and Turkish attempts to suppress the Arabic language led only to a fiercer clinging to the language of the holy book of Islam, the Koran.

Deprived of constitutional outlets, the Arabs developed in a revolutionary direction. The Arab societies went underground and changed from liberal societies into conspiracies. The *Akhua*, the Arab mother society, was replaced in Mesopotamia by the dangerous *Ahad*, a secret brotherhood of Arab officers in the Turkish Army who swore to acquire the military knowledge of their masters and then to turn it against them, in the service of the Arab people, when the moment came to strike (Lawrence, 1962, 43–44). Even more significant was the *Fateh*, the society of freedom in Syria, which included writers, physicians, landowners, and public officials, who were linked together with oaths, passwords, and a press and central treasury.

When the despotic rule of the Ottoman Sultan Abdul Hamid was overthrown by the Young Turks in 1908, there was a brief surge of optimism among Arab nationalists that they would receive greater autonomy. But they quickly discovered that the Young Turks were as opposed to Arab aspirations as had been Sultan Hamid.

Britain and France had strong interests in the fate of the Ottoman Empire, one of which was the future of the resources in this oil-rich area. Once the Ottoman Empire joined the Central Powers in the war, Britain quickly saw the advantages of an Arab revolt. Not only would it weaken Turkey militarily by depriving her of Arab manpower, but Arab forces could be used to augment the Allied armies in the Near East. Arab backing could also help prevent the Sultan's proclamation of a *jihad* (holy war) by all Muslims against the Allies. Furthermore, Britain now felt the need to create an independent Arab state to serve in place of the Ottoman Empire as a bulwark for her lifeline to India.

With the help of British officers and British supplies, the Arab revolt began on June 5, 1916. Although the Arabs did not play a large role in the overall war picture, their revolt was of great military value because it diverted a considerable number of Turkish reinforcements and supplies to the Arabian peninsula (modern Saudi Arabia) and protected the right flank of the British armies as they advanced through Palestine.

Several weeks earlier, the French and British governments had signed the secret Sykes-Picot Agreement, which carved up many Arab-inhabited areas into zones of influence, areas intended for French and British administration, and which provided for the internationalization of Palestine. This agreement, which clearly conflicted with British promises to the Arabs, was one of several documents that helped pave the way toward endless conflict in the Middle East.

Another such document was the so-called "Balfour Declaration." This document, authored by British Foreign Secretary Arthur Balfour, concerned the fate of another minority living uneasily under Turkish hegemony: the Jews. The Balfour Declaration originated in a letter from Balfour to a private British subject, Lord Lionel Rothschild, an influential member of the Zionist movement.

Foreign Office
2 November 1917

Dear Lord Rothschild:

I have much pleasure in conveying to you, on behalf of His Majesty's Government, the following declaration of sympathy with Jewish Zionist aspirations which has been submitted to, and approved by, the Cabinet.

"His Majesty's Government views with favour the establishment in Palestine of a national home for the Jewish people, and will use their best

endeavours to facilitate the achievement of this object, it being clearly understood that nothing shall be done which may prejudice the civil and religious
rights of existing non-Jewish communities in Palestine, or the rights and
political status enjoyed by Jews in any other country."

I should be grateful if you would bring this declaration to the knowledge
of the the Zionist Federation.

Yours sincerely,
Arthur James Balfour

It is easy to exaggerate the importance of the Balfour Declaration, which
was only one of the series of attempts by the British government to provide
an accommodation for both Arab and Jewish aspirations toward freedom.
Perhaps Balfour himself and the members of the Cabinet believed this was
possible by the inclusion of language that expressly excluded anything to
"prejudice the civil and religious rights of existing non-Jewish communities"
in Palestine. As both contemporary and later spokesmen for the Arab position
maintained, the Arabs did not oppose the Jews as a religious entity, and they
did not object to the immigration of Jews into Palestine *as long as they came
without political motives*. What they objected to was Zionism.

The Zionist Movement

Jews had lived in Palestine for varying periods since 1800 B.C. The Macca-
bean revolt against the Syrian-Greek rule of Antiochus in 168 B.C. resulted in
a century of Jewish dominance that ended with the Roman conquest about 63
B.C. Two major Jewish revolts in 70 A.D. and 135 A.D. led to the leveling of the
Second Temple, the destruction of Jerusalem, and the expulsion of all Jews
from Jerusalem "forever." Few Jews remained in the Palestine region after that
date.

For two thousand years, Jews lived in the hope—in the dream and
belief—of returning one day to the Promised Land of the Old Testament.
Jewish prayers and rituals were built around the theme of the eventual coming
of the Messiah to unite the Jews in Israel and rule over them.

Until the latter part of the nineteenth century, Jewish interest in Palestine
was basically religious and humanitarian. Most who settled there, with the
financial assistance of wealthy European Jews, began to take a political interest
in Palestine. In Western Europe they had greatly improved their social and
political status, and the process of assimilation was well advanced; but in the
semifeudal systems characteristic of Eastern Europe, Jews had long been
considered a separate and alien ethnic group, with many still living in ghettoes.

The intensification of anti-Semitism in Russia in the 1880s, at a time when
nationalism was on the rise in Europe, led a number of Jews to conclude that
a just and lasting solution to their plight would never be found until Jews
attained their own national home, in which they could administer their own

affairs and determine their own destiny. The concept of Jewish nationalism was first expounded by Leon Pinsker in 1882; however, Theodore Herzl, an Austrian journalist, provided political Zionism with its most effective leadership.

Although Herzl thought in terms of mass migration of Jews to Palestine, he apparently did not consider the matter of future Arab-Jewish relations important. He seemed to feel that because the Arabs would benefit economically from the Jewish settlements, they would not object to the Jews taking control. At any rate, the Zionist movement gained worldwide momentum and, by the outbreak of World War II, had purchased Arab land and established new industries under a Jewish National Fund (Khouri, 1976).

Arab Nationalism and Jewish Nationalism

Although Jewish immigration was steadily promoted by Zionist organizations during the 1920s and 1930s, the Jewish population in Palestine remained fairly small until the Nazi persecution of Jews began in Germany. By 1939, the Jewish community had reached 450,000—about 30 percent of the total population of Palestine.

During this period, Palestine was administered by the British under a mandate from the League of Nations, the same mandate that had assigned administrative control of Lebanon and Syria to the French. Though moved by the distress of persecuted Jews, Palestine Arabs became alarmed at the increase in Jewish immigration and land purchases. Mounting tension and hostility between the Jewish and Arab communities led to acts of violence on both sides.

Burgeoning nationalism throughout the Arab world brought about a strong upsurge of interest in the Palestine Arabs by many Arabs outside the Holy Land. Volunteers and armaments came from neighboring Arab states.

After the outbreak of a large-scale Arab rebellion in 1936, Britain sent yet another royal commission to Palestine. The commission reported that the underlying cause of Arab unrest continued to be the desire of Arabs for national independence and their hatred and fear of Zionist political ambitions. *For the first time, an official report described the promises made to the Arabs and the Jews as irreconcilable and the mandate as unworkable.* The commission warned that the only hope of giving some satisfaction to both parties and of providing at least a chance of ultimate peace was to end the mandate and partition the country into separate Jewish and Arab states, with Britain retaining control over several enclaves to ensure uninterrupted access for everyone to the places that are holy for Christians, Jews, and Muslims alike (Kimche, 1973).

Partition did not occur until 1947, under the auspices of the United Nations. By that time, both Arabs and Jews had engaged in acts of violence against each other and the British. The Yishuv, the Jewish community in Palestine, built up an underground army called the *Haganah*. More radical elements in the Yishuv joined an organization, the Irgun Zvai Leumi, that embarked upon guerrilla warfare against the British and Arabs. The small but dangerous Stern Gang broke away from the somewhat less extreme Irgun and continued its attacks against the British mandate government for some time after the beginning of World War II.

Later, when the partition was carried out and the new state of Israel successfully fought its war of independence, the Arab refugee problem spawned the Palestine Liberation Organization and its various factions. In addition to a series of wars waged by Arab countries against Israel, terrorism became part of the continuing campaign of the Arabs against the Israelis and those who were viewed as her supporters, chiefly the United States. Israel was blamed for the existence and actions of such Arab groups as *al-Fatah*. The Arabs contended that the Israelis should be the last to complain about the tactics used by *al-Fatah*, since it was they who had first used the weapon of terrorism in the Middle East during the mandate period and had acclaimed those Jews who had participated in terrorist actions as brave patriots.

As we have mentioned, this argument, which is most facilely expressed as "One person's terrorist is another person's hero," ignores the fact that Irgun—and most Stern Gang—actions were part of guerrilla warfare directed against British military targets, not innocent civilians. But more important is the fact that Arabs and Jews are further today from a peaceful solution to their problems than they were on the eve of partition. The conflicting pledges and indecision of the British, the impatience of the Zionists to achieve their goals in complete disregard for the feelings and interests of the Palestine Arabs, and the political immaturity of the Arabs themselves at this critical stage in the history of Palestine helped forge the chain of events that produced today's Arab-Israeli dilemma.

Terrorism in the United States

Scattered episodes of political terrorism have occurred periodically in the U.S., but they have been of limited scope and duration. The size of the country, the decentralization of political power, and the nature of American social and political organization have all contributed to limit the appeal of revolutionary doctrines and insurgent organizations to the average person. American political terrorists have never captured public sympathy or produced fear that inhibited government response. A more characteristic form of terrorism in the historical American past—and a continuing phenomenon in contemporary life—is *vigilantism*.

Vigilantes

When a young man named Bernhard Goetz shot and wounded four youths who had approached him for money in a New York City subway car, he was promptly dubbed "The Subway Vigilante" by the mass media. This term was especially inappropriate; the term *vigilante*, as Richard Maxwell Brown (1975) pointed out in his study of vigilantism in American history, refers to a member of a vigilance committee—a group of people organized without legal authority to keep order and punish criminals when conventional law enforcement agencies fail to do so. Vigilantism is "a violent sanctification of the deeply cherished values of life and property" (Brown, 1975, 139). Vigilantism is a collective response that has a mandate, of sorts, from those whom it purports to protect. Goetz was essentially avenging only himself.

The tradition of vigilantism has been traced to the back country of the Carolinas in the 1760s, where legal order had broken down in the aftermath of the Indian wars and banditry had become widespread. People in the highlands began taking the law into their own hands and meting out hasty and rough justice. Along the coast, people tended to regard these self-appointed guardians of the peace—"Regulators," as they called themselves—as a cure that was as bad as the ailment. A countermovement of "Moderators" and the establishment of sheriffs and district courts to service the back country led the Regulators to disband in 1769.

Ten years later, in the colony of Virginia, a similar movement arose to deal with renegade Tories, supporters of the British Crown. Its leader, Colonel Charles Lynch, became the Tory nemesis. His name was perpetuated as a synonym for lawless violence and, in later years, acquired the sinister connotation of racially-motivated murder, the hanging of blacks by whites.

Frontier America, with a continuing pattern of lawlessness in newly settled areas, produced more than 300 documented vigilante groups between 1800 and 1900. On occasion, bitter and prolonged conflict between vigilantes and their opponents could only be resolved by outside intervention. By the end of the nineteenth century, nearly every state and territory in the country had experienced vigilante movements. According to Brown (1975), these movements contributed to the enduring tradition that communities have the right, when threatened, to act in collective self-defense.

The Ku Klux Klan

Perhaps the most notorious vigilante organization known to American history was the Ku Klux Klan. The first KKK originated in the post–Civil War South. Lasting from 1865 to 1876, it employed beating, flogging, hanging, and burning at the stake in the pursuit of its fundamental objective: "the maintenance of the supremacy of the White Race in their Republic by terror and intimidation" (Kirkham, Levy, & Crofty, 1970, 216). A Congressional investigation in 1871 established that the Klan had been responsible for thousands of violent attacks against freed slaves and their white supporters, including poor Southern whites and "carpetbaggers"—Northerners who went to the South after the Civil War for political or financial advantage.

Although the Klan voluntarily disbanded in 1872, its goals had been achieved. White Southern Democrats resumed control of state governments, and blacks were effectively resubjugated. Gurr (1988, 554) observes that its social function of regulating the white-dominated social order was continued "peaceably and legally through the segregationist policies of state and local government and violently by lynching mobs that killed a documented total of 1,985 blacks between 1882 and 1903."

The second KKK arose in the 1920s and appears to have been influenced by both romanticized versions of its predecessor and the so-called "White Cap" movement, which saw its mission as regulating poor whites and other "failures" in American society. By 1925, the Klan boasted four to five million members—ten times the number of the original Klan—and was drawing members from all over the U.S. The second KKK aimed at the social regulation of people whose conduct violated the Bible-based morality and norms of small-town America. Although Klan rhetoric was directed against Catholics and Jews, Brown (1975, 35) points out that KKK violence was directed less against Catholics, Jews, and blacks than against "ne'er-do-wells and the allegedly immoral. . . white, Anglo-Saxon Protestant." The influence and membership of the second Klan declined in the 1920s because of public revulsion against excessive violence and widely publicized scandals involving several national leaders (Chalmers, 1965).

The most recent revival of the KKK began in 1954 and followed more closely in the tradition of the original Klan. (We will discuss this revival in chapter 3, when we examine contemporary domestic right-wing terrorism.)

The Lessons of the Past

What can we glean from this chronicle of past violence that fits into contemporary efforts toward countering terrorism and alleviating some of the conditions that promote it?

Anarchism's major contribution—the "propaganda of the deed"—has gained, rather than lost, significance with the advent of electronic journalism. Acts of extraordinary violence, as the authors of the *Task Force Report on Disorders and Terrorism* (1976) pointed out, have come to serve as a form of mass entertainment. Acts of terrorism have gained immediacy and diffusion through television, which conveys the terrorist message to an audience of millions on a worldwide scale.

The modern terrorist has been quick to exploit this advantage; he has become a master of the medium in a way that shows government as a poor rival. Formerly, in countries where free speech and communication were jealously guarded rights, it would have been unthinkable for violent subversives to have seized control of the organs of mass communication. Today, this is a commonplace consequence of terrorist action. As the Task Force authors observe:

> In many ways, the modern terrorist is the very creation of the mass media. He has been magnified, enlarged beyond his own powers by others. (p. 9)

Another legacy of anarchism is its internationalism—or perhaps its anti-nationalism. Anarchists were committed in theory to the abolition of all governments; hence, they saw national boundaries as an expression of the very concept of sovereignty they were seeking to destroy. Individual anarchists who perpetrated acts of violence were "men without a country" in the expression's fullest meaning.

Today's terrorists move about on the world stage and are able to find refuge in a number of countries that subscribe to state-sponsorship of terrorism as a policy. Terrorists have profited from the anarchist example to accept the discipline and authority that are indispensable to the perpetuation of secret organizations and societies. They have also replaced the solitary figure of the lone anarchist who, like Caserio, could not afford to buy a knife and had to fashion one from a file, with a figure who is able to travel in comfort and can afford the latest in weapons that high-technology can provide.

Walter Laqueur noted that, although anarchists such as those who belonged to Narodnaya Volya did not fully comprehend the moral dilemma posed by terrorist strategy, they paid the moral price that established their reputations as noble and tragic figures—that is, they had to accept death and even seek it to justify the aura of evil that surrounds a premeditated act of violence. Laqueur maintained that the moral and intellectual distance between Narodnaya Volya and contemporary terrorists "is to be measured in light years" (1977, 4).

That may be true; nevertheless, we must point out that Russian terrorists of the period, including Narodnaya Volya, admired the rhetoric of Sergei Nechayev as set forth in his *Revolutionary Catechism*, which is generally recognized as the most cold-blooded instruction manual in the literature of terrorism. This document dramatizes the portrait of the ideal terrorist and his methods. He is devoid of humanity and moral sensitivity; he must denounce bourgeois morality, be suspicious of everyone, trust no one in friendship, and live exclusively for the sole mission and purpose of destroying "the system."

The *Catechism* proposes a plan that has become familiar to contemporary terrorists: to provoke government repression that may set the stage for a popular uprising. Favored targets of assassination are moderate political leaders, on the grounds that surviving leaders would favor a harsher form of repression.

The doctrines of Nechayev are reflected in the writings of contemporary revolutionary theorists such as Regis Debray (Huberman & Sweezy, 1968) and Che Guevara (Camejo, 1972; Harris, 1970; Hodges, 1977). Both Debray and Guevara stress the use of indiscriminate violence as the means of creating a situation of intense fear in the first stage of preparation for revolution. Thus, Guevara resorted to terrorizing Bolivian village leaders and elders in a deliberate program of mutilation and assassination when he found himself unable to influence the peasants to support his revolution.

Perhaps the best-known manual of terrorist strategy is the *Mini-Manual of Urban Guerrilla Warfare* (1970). Its author, Carlos Marighella, a Brazilian revolutionary who advocated such terrorist actions as the poisoning of water and food supplies, rehashes the ideas of Nechayev. Very little in the *Mini-Manual* is original with Marighella.

Thus, in a quite literal sense, the most significant document of the anarchist tradition survives as a legacy to present-day terrorists.

Perhaps the most important lesson of the past comes from the example of the Irish Republican Army—the oldest and probably the best-known guerrilla army in the world today. The IRA accepts no time limits on its mission; it is organized to persist as long as Ireland remains divided between the Republic and Ulster. It has shown its capacity to rise from the ashes of defeat and renew itself by splintering into factions. Thus, the IRA Provisionals (or "Provos") have added the ideological bonding of Marxism to their basic Irish patriotism; they have shown a willingness to accept help wherever they can find it, including Libya, Syria, East Germany, Soviet Russia, and the U.S.

Summary

Terrorism as an instrument of political action is not new in form or substance. The declarations of the anarchists of the last century have a strikingly modern ring. In all its forms, terrorism is a weapon of the weak against the strong; the terroristic strategy is intended to redress the imbalance of power.

Although terrorists are weaker than society in a confrontation, their real strength lies in their own recklessness or ruthlessness. The ancient, unalterable element of terrorist strategy has a Catch-22 quality about it. That is, any concession to save lives must be counted as a victory for the terrorist; any inflexibility leading to the loss of lives is, by the same token, a defeat for any but the most totalitarian society. Thus, modern terrorism, whatever other characteristics it may possess, exhibits all the basic elements of classical terrorism in their original form.

We can trace the history of terrorism as far back in time as we are willing to go. During the first and second centuries of the Roman empire, Jewish insurgents used techniques of coercion and intimidation that do not differ appreciably from those used in that part of the world today. But the term *terrorism* dates from the latter part of the eighteenth century, when thousands of French were victimized by the political convulsions of the French Revolution.

Modern terrorism can be said to have begun in the nineteenth century with the anarchists, who ascribed a political cause to poverty and social oppression and therefore sought the solution to mankind's problems in the destruction of *all* governments. This vision led to political assassinations, bombings, and other acts of violence, and provoked swift, ruthless reprisals in nearly every country in Europe and in the United States.

In Ireland, where for centuries the Irish quest for political independence had become hopelessly complicated by social, cultural, and religious factors, an insurgency identified as the Irish Republican Army (IRA) continues to the present, with few indications of an imminent solution. A struggle of at least comparable length has been going on in the Middle East, with equally few signs of negotiation or compromise forthcoming.

In the United States, terrorism has characteristically taken a different form from the political terrorism of Europe and the Middle East. America has a tradition of vigilante terrorism that originated in the Colonial period. The Ku Klux Klan, which sought to maintain white supremacy in the South during the post–Civil War period, has never captured the sympathy or support of any sizable minority of the American people.

Key Terms

Anarchists
Michael Bakunin
Easter Rising
Irish Republican Army (IRA)
Peter Kropotkin
Sicarii
Thugs
vigilantism
Zionism

Assassins
Balfour Declaration
Theodore Herzl
jihad (holy war)
Ku Klux Klan
Sykes-Picot Agreement
triad
Zealots

Questions for Discussion and Review

1. Where and when did the terms *terror* and *terrorism* acquire their contemporary meaning?
2. Identify the Sicarii and discuss the tactics they sought to use against their Roman oppressors.
3. The terms *assassin* and *thug* both originated in secret societies that employed the techniques of terrorism. Briefly describe these groups and their place in the historical background of terrorism.
4. Why did the IRA go on fighting after World War I ended and the free state of Eire was established? What is the major goal of the IRA today?
5. Discuss the rival claims of the Arabs and the Jews to the territory called Palestine. What role was played by the Balfour Declaration and the Sykes-Picot Agreement in the creation of today's Middle East problem?
6. Define *vigilantism* and indicate why the authors refer to vigilante terrorism as characteristically American.
7. Summarize the lessons we can learn from the historical study of terrorism that have application to the present and future.

References

Ahmad, E. "Radical But Wrong." In *Regis Debray and the Latin American Revolution*, edited by L. Huberman and P.M. Sweezy, pp. 70–83. New York: MR Press, 1968.

Begin, M. *The Revolt: Story of the Irgun.* New York: Schuman, 1951.

Bell, J.B. *Assassin: The Theory and Practice of Political Murder.* New York: St. Martin's Press, 1979.

Brandon, S. *Jews and the Zealots.* New York: Scribner's, 1967.

Brown, R.M. *Strain of Violence.* New York: Oxford University Press, 1975.

Bruse, G. *The Stranglers: The Cult of Thuggee and its Overthrow in India.* New York: Harcourt, Brace and World, 1969.

Camejo, P. *Guevara's Guerrilla Strategy.* New York: Pathfinder Press, 1972.

Chalmers, D.M. *Hooded Americanism: The First Century of the Ku Klux Klan 1865–1965.* Garden City, NY: Doubleday, 1965.

Chesneaux, J. *Popular Movements and Secret Societies in China, 1840–1950.* Stanford, CA: Stanford University Press, 1972.

Coffey, T.M. *Agony at Easter: The 1916 Irish Uprising.* Toronto: Macmillan, 1969.

Draper, H. *Karl Marx's Theory of Revolution (Vol.2).* New York: Monthly Review, 1978.

Fleming, M. "Propaganda by the Deed: Terrorism and Anarchist Theory in Late Nineteenth-Century Europe." In *Terrorism in Europe,* edited by Y. Alexander and K.A. Myers, pp. 8–28. New York: St. Martin's Press, 1982.

Gurr, T.R. "Political Terrorism in the United States: Historical Antecedents and Contemporary Trends." In *The Politics of Terrorism,* edited by M. Stohl, pp. 549–578. New York: Marcel Dekker, 1988.

Hacker, F.J. *Crusaders, Criminals, Crazies: Terror and Terrorism in Our Time.* New York: Norton, 1977.

Harris, R. *Death of a Revolutionary: Che Guevara's Last Mission.* New York: Norton, 1970.

Hodges, D.C. *The Legacy of Che Guevara.* London: Thames and Husson, 1977.

Hodgson, M.G.S. *The Order of Assassins.* The Hague: Morton, 1955.

Ivianski, Z. "The Blow at the Center: The Concept and Its History." In *Terrorism and Combatting Terrorism,* edited by A. Merari, pp. 53–62. Frederick, MD: University Publications of America, 1985.

Joll, J. "Anarchism: A Living Tradition." In *Anarchism Today,* edited by D.E. Apter and J. Joll, pp. 212–225. New York: Anchor Books, 1972.

Khouri, F.J. *The Arab-Israeli Dilemma.* Syracuse, NY: Syracuse University Press, 1976.

Kimche, J. *There Could Have Been Peace.* New York: Dial Press, 1973.

Kirkham, J.F., Levy, S., and Crofty, W.J. *Assassination and Political Violence.* Staff Report to the National Commission on the Causes and Prevention of Violence. Washington, DC: U.S. Government Printing Office, 1970.

Laqueur, W. *Terrorism.* Boston: Little, Brown, 1977.

Laqueur, W. *The Age of Terrorism.* Boston: Little, Brown, 1987.

Lawrence, T.E. *Seven Pillars of Wisdom: A Triumph.* New York: Dell, 1962.

Lewis, B. *The Assassins: A Radical Sect in Islam.* London: Weidenfeld and Nicolson, 1967.

Lynch, E.A. "International Terrorism: The Search for a Policy." *Terrorism: An International Journal* 9 (1987): 1–85.

Mosse, W.E. *Alexander II and the Modernization of Russia*. New York: Macmillan, 1958.

National Advisory Committee on Criminal Justice Standards and Goals. *Disorders and Terrorism: Report of the Task Force on Disorders and Terrorism*. Washington, DC: Law Enforcement Assistance Administration, Department of Justice, 1976.

Neldhardt, W. *Fenianism in North America*. University Park: Pennsylvania State University Press, 1975.

Newman, G. *Understanding Violence*. New York: Harper & Row/ Lippincott, 1979.

O'Farrell, P. *Ireland's English Question*. New York: Schocken, 1972.

Pyziur, E. *The Doctrine of Anarchism of Michael A. Bakunin*. Milwaukee, WI: Marquette University Press, 1955.

Rapoport, D.C. "Messianic Sanctions for Terror." *Comparative Politics*, 1988, 20, 195–213.

Rapoport, D.C., and Alexander, Y. (eds.) *The Morality of Terrorism: Religious and Secular Justifications*. New York: Pergamon, 1983.

Saltman, R.B. *The Social and Political Thought of Michael Bakunin*. Westport, CT: Greenwood, 1983.

Seth, R. *The Russian Terrorists: The Story of the Narodniki*. London: Barrie and Rockcliffe, 1967.

Smallwood, E.M. *The Jews Under Roman Rule*. Leyden, England: Brill, 1976.

Thomas, H. *The Spanish Civil War*. New York: Harper & Row, 1961.

Tuchman, B.W. *The Proud Tower: A Portrait of the World Before the War, 1890–1914*. New York: Macmillan, 1966.

Venturi, F. *Roots of Revolution: A History of the Populist and Socialist Movements in 19th Century Russia*. New York: Knopf, 1960.

Younger, C. *Ireland's Civil War*. New York: Taplinger, 1969.

3
Domestic Terrorism U.S.A.

Although American diplomats, military personnel, business executives, and even tourists have been the targets of terrorism abroad, the continental United States has been comparatively free from much of the violence that seems to be endemic to other parts of the world. This is not to deny, however, that the 1960s and 1970s were turbulent decades dominated by extremist political activity and violence. It was a period during which the nation experienced major social and cultural changes. The civil rights revolution broke up the caste system and changed relationships among racial and ethnic groups; there was a decline in respect for tradition and a weakening of informal social controls; and there was growing disenchantment with, if not outright rejection of, authority (Silberman, 1980).

Blacks made some progress in their efforts to achieve full equality in American society. In 1954, the Supreme Court's landmark *Brown v. Board of Education* decision struck down the "separate but equal" doctrine. The growing size of the northern black vote made civil rights a primary issue in national elections and ultimately resulted in the establishment of the Federal Civil Rights Commission in 1957.

Martin Luther King, Jr., rose to national prominence and achieved a great deal of support for the civil rights movement through his nonviolent but direct action protests against segregation and discrimination. His successes included the Montgomery city bus boycott of 1955 and 1956, the 1963 march on Washington, and the battle that same year for voting rights in Selma, Alabama. But these victories also intensified blacks' expectations and made them more dissatisfied with their current circumstances. This resulted in a rising tempo of nonviolent action that culminated in the student sit-ins of the 1960s and the birth of the civil rights revolution.

By 1963, the protest movement had achieved a new sense of urgency. Blacks were no longer willing to wait, but began to demand complete "freedom now." The National Advisory Commission on Civil Disorders (1968) suggests that the meteoric rise of the Black Muslims to national prominence during this period was a major factor in awakening black protest. Black people made their demands known through massive protests in northern cities against inequities in housing, education, and employment and also through demonstrations in the South. But it became evident by 1964 that nonviolent direct action was of limited usefulness. At this point, despite major victories, most blacks were still treated as second-class citizens, were relegated to separate and inferior schools and slum housing, suffered disproportionately high unemployment and underemployment, and still experienced discrimination within the criminal justice system. Feeling as though the nation was moving toward two societies—one black and one white—that were separate and unequal, blacks took to the streets to express dissatisfaction with their circumstances.

For a period of three years, beginning with the Watts riot in Los Angeles in the summer of 1965 and continuing to the disturbances that were touched off by the murder of Martin Luther King, Jr., our cities, particularly during the summer, exploded on a regular basis. Forty-three disorders and riots were reported during 1966; in 1967, 164 civil disorders were reported, of which twenty-five percent were labeled either serious or major in terms of violence and damage. In examining the causes of these disturbances, the National Advisory Commission on Civil Disorders (1968) suggests that, in addition to pervasive segregation, discrimination, and poverty, which had served to catalyze the volatile nature of this mixture, other factors included frustration over unfulfilled expectations engendered by major judicial and legislative victories; an atmosphere created by white terrorism directed against nonviolent protests in which violence was approved and encouraged; the open defiance of federal and judicial authority by state and local officials resisting desegregation; frustrations of powerlessness that led some blacks to believe there was no other effective alternative to violence as a means of expressing and redressing grievances; and a new mood among blacks, particularly the young, in which apathy and submission to the system were replaced by enhanced self-esteem and racial pride.

Also, during the 1960s, our country experienced both violent and nonviolent reactions to the Vietnam War. This opposition was without precedent because it involved such a wide variety of individuals and social groups, including youths and students, prestigious leaders, academic and literary figures, radical groups, and segments of various ethnic and racial and religious groups. Resistance to the war began with questions about the need for tactics such as the use of napalm, saturation bombing, and defoliation, but it escalated to a point where a large minority of the population began to question the justice of the war itself. Some of the more radical opponents began to question the legitimacy of the political system that was conducting the war and to manifest willingness to use violence to oppose it. This group went on to be critical of our society in general and, particularly, of certain types of social arrangements such as those involving racism and sexism. Composed of New Left activists, racial minorities, middle-class and middle-aged liberals, and even some upper-class "radical chic" patrons, the group constituted an assertive, active, and, in some instances, aggressive minority that disrupted conventional activities while at the same time silencing and shaming more conventional and conservative citizens. Many Americans viewed this group as a serious threat to existing society and feared that it would eventually accomplish its objectives of radically transforming the country.

Some of the groups on today's ideological left and ideological right that are identified with terrorism have roots in the social activism of this earlier period. Other groups have coalesced as activist supporters of single issues, such as the pro-lifers and pro-choice activists, gay rights activists, feminism advocates, animal rights activists, environmental preservationists, and the militant Jewish Defense League (JDL). Still other groups reflect nationalistic concerns: the Puerto Rican independence movement supporters; the anti-Castro Cubans; the Croatian separatists; and the Armenian nationalists.

It is easy to get lost in this bewildering welter of names, acronyms, and initials, many of which closely resemble one another. The specific groups and their nomenclature are less important, in our judgment, than is the underlying ideological or psychological motivation that allows them to resort to terrorist methods to achieve their objectives.

The Ideological Left

In the late 1960s and into the 1970s, according to FBI Special Agent Thomas Strentz (1988), most American terrorist groups were composed of urban, college-educated, middle-class young people. They were disciplined, well-trained, and sophisticated enough to deal with last-minute alterations in plans; they could adjust to change and still complete the mission. Strentz provides a demographic profile of the 1960s and 1970s leftist groups, as shown in Table 3–1. This profile shows a blend of highly motivated and well-educated members, with the additional involvement of a criminal element.

White Leftists

A prototypical organization of this period was the Weather Underground (WU), which originated at a May 1969 meeting of the Students for a Democratic Society (SDS) Convention in Chicago. The group called itself the Weathermen (after a line in Bob Dylan's "Subterranean Homesick Blues"). Later it changed its name to the Weather Underground because of the sexist connotations of the original name. The expressed views of the Weather Underground delineate their ideological position on the extreme left: "Our intention is to disrupt the empire. . . to incapacitate it, to put pressure on the cracks, to make it hard to carry out its bloody functioning against the people of the world, to join the world struggle, to attack from the inside" (Homer, 1983, 149). During October 1969, the Weather Underground staged demonstrations in Chicago, where they had several encounters with the police. The demonstrations were denounced by both the Students for a Democratic Society and the Black Panthers as counterproductive (Parry, 1976, 334). In December 1969, they decided to turn the WU into an elite, paramilitary organization to carry out urban guerrilla warfare; thus, according to Marsha McKnight Trick (1976, 519), it became "the grandperson of American revolutionary organizations." Activities shifted to bombing police buildings and courthouses in California,

New York, and other cities. In September 1970, they arranged the escape of Timothy Leary from prison in San Luis Obispo, California, and helped him to reach Algeria. The Weather Underground continued to publish magazines and took credit for bombings through the mid-1970s. The Weather Underground had hoped to start a revolution, but, like most ideological terrorist groups, failed to reach its objectives.

Although these ideological terrorists professed a desire to transform society, they lacked a coherent concept of what they wished as its replacement. A dialogue between Herbert Marcuse and a student offers a graphic illustration of the nihilistic strain of this type of ideological terrorist.

> *Student:* But, Dr. Marcuse, what system of life will there be after the System is destroyed?
>
> *Marcuse [with some surprise]:* You know, I've never given thought to this. I just want to see what the damned thing looks like when it is destroyed. (Parry, 1976, 528)

Table 3-1
Demographic Profile of the 1960s and 1970s Leftist Groups

Leader	*Opportunist or Criminal Element*	*Follower*
Male or female	Male	Male or female
No specific race or religion	No specific race or religion	No specific race or religion
College education or attendance	Limited education	College education or attendance
25–40	20–30	20–25
Middle class	Lower class	Middle class
Urban/sophisticated	Urban or rural with good	Urban/sophisticated
Multilingual	street sense	Multilingual
High verbal skills	Literate in native	Good verbal skills
Well-trained perfectionist	language	Well-trained
Dedicated	High verbal skills	Dedicated
Strong personality	Learned criminal skills	Weak personality
Politically active prior to terrorist/criminal activity	Selfish	Politically active prior to terrorist/criminal activity
	Strong personality	
	Years of criminal activity recruited from prison/ politics are peripheral	

SOURCE: Strentz, T. "A terrorist psychosocial profile, past and present." 57 *FBI Law Enforcement Bulletin* (1988), 13–19. Reproduced by permission of the author and publisher.

Another leftist group with techniques similar to those of the Weather Underground was the New World Liberation Front, a San Francisco–based group that published Marighella's *Minimanual of the Urban Guerrilla* in 1970. The NWLF espoused a variety of leftist causes and directed its attacks primarily against major corporations or government buildings. Trick (1976) identified it as the most active revolutionary group in the United States and noted that the NWLF was seen as an umbrella for other terrorist groups in California, such as the Chicano Liberation Front and the Red Guerrilla Family.

By the end of the 1970s, terrorist activities by such organizations as the Weather Underground had subsided to the point where law enforcement officials concluded that left-wing terrorism had all but ceased to be a problem. As things turned out, this judgment was premature; during the 1980s, white leftist terrorism once again became a factor after several years of relative inactivity.

According to Harris (1987), the most active New Left terrorist organization during the 1980s was the United Freedom Front (UFF). This group was quite small—four white males, three white females, and one black male who left the group when they began to participate in bombings—and had ties to radical movements of the 1960s and 1970s. In addition to a series of bombing incidents, UFF members were involved in the 1981 murder of a New Jersey State Police officer and the attempted murders of two Massachusetts State Police officers in 1982. The group also reportedly committed armed bank robberies from Connecticut to Virginia to sustain themselves. They lived under a variety of false identities and usually resided in rural areas, moving frequently. Prior to a criminal act—a bombing or robbery—group members conducted a lengthy and extensive surveillance of the target and surrounding areas.

Five UFF members were arrested in Cleveland, Ohio, in November 1984. The remaining two white members were arrested in Norfolk, Virginia, in April 1985. Automatic shoulder weapons, handguns, bomb components, and printed communiques were found in the group's safehouses. Group members were tried and convicted in New York and Massachusetts on a number of criminal charges, including murder, assault, and armed robbery.

Black Leftists

During the early 1970s, prisons were a source of recruitment for the black radical movement. Many inmates came to view themselves as "political prisoners," although they had not been convicted of offenses that had political motives or significance. They took the position that responsibility for their criminal behavior lay not with them, but with the society that had failed to provide them with equal educational opportunities, adequate housing, and the chance to compete effectively in American society. These inmates saw themselves not as aggressors, but as victims of a society that failed to provide all its members with the same kinds of opportunities and resources. They claimed that the public was misdirected in its attempts to rehabilitate them when it was really society that needed reforming.

But although many inmates felt themselves victims of society, most did not endorse the revolutionary ideology that called for the overthrow of society. The majority of inmates subscribed to a position that called for working within the existing socioeconomic structure to make the system share some of its power and influence. Although devoid of revolutionary intent, these inmates did employ strong rhetoric and even violence to pressure the system into meeting their demands.

A much smaller group adopted a class-oriented Marxist position that embraced a revolutionary political ideology (Berkman, 1979). This position was more attractive to blacks and other minorities because it provided an explanation for their current social and economic circumstances. This ideology maintains that racism is a phenomenon that is historically rooted in our capitalistic economic system. According to this position, racism is an economic strategy that is a means of keeping a "reserve army" of labor and preventing the rise of the working class. It is also a tool to keep the labor force divided. Therefore no meaningful change can occur as long as our economic and political system is based on capitalism.

An excerpt from the writings of George Jackson, one of the more articulate of the Marxist/Leninist black militants, shows how this position viewed the effects of capitalism on the black population:

> The new slavery, the modern variety of chattel slavery updated to disguise itself, places the victim in the factory or in the case of most blacks in subordinate roles inside and around the factory system (service trades), working for a wage. However, if work cannot be found in or around the factory complex, today's neoslavery does not allow even for a modicum of food and shelter. You are free—to starve. The sense in the meaning of slavery comes through as a result of our ties to the wage. You must have it, without it you would starve or expose yourself to the elements. (Jackson, 1970, 251)

This ideology also explains the conflicts among ethnic and racial minorities in our society. It argues that the ruling elite, by virtue of its control of the government and the work place, are able to effectively set one group of exploited people against another in the same way that the prison administration is able to turn blacks against whites as a method of maintaining control. In both instances, racial differences provide a basis for dividing these populations (Berkman, 1979).

It follows that blacks were not the only group viewed as oppressed by the capitalist system. Other minorities, including chicanos, Puerto Ricans, Indians, women, and many white workers are also exploited under this system. This sense of exploitation provides the basis for a coalition of groups that could jointly struggle against oppression. The need for this type of coalition was recognized by black leaders as well as other radical leaders.

Radical groups were not primarily interested in either helping the inmate or changing prison conditions; instead their primary focus was on changing society (Irwin, 1980). The group's ideology considered the prison simply a further illustration of the oppression and exploitation of the poor and nonwhites by a capitalist economic system. Some, like Huey Newton of the Black Panthers, considered the prison experience of blacks similar to their experiences as slaves:

Both systems involved exploitation: the slave received no compensation for the wealth he produced, and the prisoner is expected to produce marketable goods for what amounts to no compensation. Slavery and prison life share a complete lack of freedom of movement. The power of those in authority is total, and they expect no deference from those under domination. Just as in the days of slavery, constant surveillance and observation are part of the prison experience and if inmates develop meaningful and revolutionary friendships among themselves, these ties are broken by institutional transfers, just as the slave master broke up families. . . . It is generally recognized that a system of slavery is degrading for the master and slave alike. This applies to prison, too. The atmosphere of fear has a distorting effect on the lives of everyone there—from commissioners and super-intendents to prisoners in solitary confinement. Nowhere is this more evident than among "correctional officers" as the guards are euphemistically called. (Newton, 1973, 258)

The attraction of radicals to the prison was twofold. They felt that prison provided an excellent issue that well illustrated the most negative consequences of the capitalistic system. Also, based on their early contacts with inmates, many were convinced that they could recruit inmate leaders for outside radical activities. Irwin (1980) also notes that some of the individuals involved in the movement developed an idealistic view of prisoners' sincerity and humanity.

The Black Panther party originated in Oakland, California, in 1966 in reaction to police brutality in the black community and as a means of protecting blacks against the police (Stratton, 1973). The group represented itself as a Marxist/Leninist revolutionary party that was directing its efforts toward freeing blacks from their suppression by corporate capitalism. Panther leaders saw inmates as embittered, disgruntled, and thus ripe for involvement in revolutionary political activity (Jacobs, 1976). The Panthers appealed to formerly apolitical prisoners by offering them the opportunity to adopt the more positive status of political prisoner. The Panthers took the position that both blacks and whites were oppressed by the capitalistic system and therefore did not advocate a racist position.

As of 1987, only three terrorist incidents had been ascribed to domestic black groups, all of which involved religious rivalry (Harris, 1987, 9). In addition, at least one other incident was averted by arrests in 1984. The three terrorist incidents were attributed to the group Fuqra, a black Islamic sect headquartered in Detroit, Michigan. Fuqra seeks to purify Islam by eliminating rival religious sects, such as the Ahmadiyya Movement in Islam (AMI). During August 1983, several terrorist acts were perpetrated against the AMI in Detroit: the AMI secretary was killed; firebombs were thrown at the home of the AMI treasurer; and an AMI temple was burned. Fuqra was implicated in these attacks because the bodies of the arsonists—Fuqra members—were found at the temple; they had become trapped while setting the blaze. The gun used to kill the AMI secretary was found on one of the bodies.

A possible terrorist plot involving a black street gang was prevented in August 1986, when several members of the El Rukns street gang were arrested in Chicago. Group members had in their possession numerous weapons, including an antitank weapon that had been sold to them in an undercover operation. This group, which has loose ties to Islam, is a violent criminal organization involved in drug trafficking and other illegal enterprises. Some group members allegedly met with agents of the Libyan government. The El Rukns apparently were seeking to commit a terrorist incident for hire. Thus far, nothing has happened.

Gurr (1988, 561) places black terrorism in its appropriate historical and contemporary perspective:

> Armed violence by handfuls of black militants was the last deadly derivative of a movement that won most of its victories through peaceful protest in the early 1960s. Black militancy had largely subsided by the early 1970s, in part because of the gains of the previous decades and in part because of an increasingly conservative political climate and growing skepticism among black activists about the prospects for further progress. . . Black terrorists were concerned in however distorted a way with what we have called single-issue terrorism: they sought to defend and promote the rights of black Americans. Their occasional use of revolutionary rhetoric was at best a gesture of solidarity with political and intellectual movements in the Third World, not a serious or realistic aspiration for a U.S. minority.

The Ideological Right

Right-wing terrorism became an area of focus for law enforcement during the 1980s. Harris states that "Much of the rhetoric of the extreme right is particularly volatile and corrosive" (1987, 10) and is a motivating factor in the commission of violent acts—bombings, murders, assaults, and armed robberies—to further these views.

The third revival of the Klu Klux Klan began in the 1950s in the wake of the Supreme Court's *Brown* v. *Board of Education* decision and gained momentum in the states of the old Confederacy through the 1960s. At its peak, the Klan boasted about 700 Klaverns with a membership of 17,000. Murders, beatings, cross burnings, and other acts intended to intimidate and harass civil rights workers in their attempts to enroll black voters provoked a sharp federal reaction. FBI investigations led to successful prosecutions in the federal courts, and by the late 1960s and early 1970s, many white Southerners, both officials and ordinary citizens, were alienated by the Klan's terrorist activities. The KKK has endured, however, and so does the susceptibility of some Americans to racial and religious extremism.

In 1989, former KKK Imperial Wizard David Duke was elected to the Louisiana state legislature from the New Orleans suburb of Metairie. Duke was an avowed Nazi during his college days; and although he claimed to have left the Klan in 1979, his home address still served as the local Klan office at the time he entered the Louisiana statehouse. He also heads the National Association for the Advancement of White People from the same address.

Duke insisted that his extremism was a thing of the past and, in the statehouse, espoused a line of Republican conservatism. But in March 1989, at a conference in Chicago of the extreme right-wing Populist Party, he shared the podium with Art Jones, a member of the American Nazi Party. A couple of months later, he was found selling a collection of neo-Nazi books out of his state-funded district constituents' office. Among the titles were Hitler's *Mein Kampf; Did Six Million Die? The Truth at Last*, which claims that the Holocaust was a hoax inspired by the Jewish-controlled media; *Imperium*, which argues for the preservation of Western culture through Nazi racist policies; and numerous pamphlets published by a group that supports human breeding to create a master race.

Duke waved away press questions with vague assurances, claiming that the neo-Nazi books were simply "old stock" from his book business. Such materials, he claimed, were "not part of my agenda any longer." From the Louisiana House floor, he declared: "I want to make it very clear right now that I reject categorically racial or religious intolerance or hatred. Furthermore, I am diametrically opposed to the totalitarian politics and policies of both communism and Nazism." Skeptics point out that, while Duke professes to believe in "civil rights for all people," his new organization publishes an anti-Semitic newspaper with 30,000 subscribers that advocates restricting Jews to ghettoes (Cohler, 1989; Magnuson, 1989).

A number of right-wing organizations or groups share some common ideological themes. Ranging from the United Klans of America to the Aryan Nations, a basic belief is a religious fundamentalism that asserts the superiority of the white race. According to this dogma, blacks, other nonwhites, and Jews are racially, mentally, physically, and spiritually inferior. Much of this doctrine is espoused by the racist, anti-Semitic Christian Identity Movement, which teaches that the white race is God's chosen people and that whites, not Jews, are the true descendants of Israel. Jews are considered descendants of Satan.

Theories of economic conspiracy are also widely held by members of these groups; for example, that national and international forces, led by Jewish financiers, are responsible for hardship and economic depression in rural America (Gurr, 1988, 555). Politically, the groups reject the policies and authority of the federal government, which they refer to as ZOG (the Zionist Occupational Government), as being controlled by liberals, Jews, and blacks. They also emphasize "survivalism," contending that their members should prepare to fight in the racial or nuclear Armageddon that inevitably lies ahead.

Gurr notes that despite similar beliefs, the groups differ in the extent to which they are willing to engage in various actions to support their beliefs. He identifies the principal 1980s extremist groups on a continuum from conventional to violent activity, as shown in Figure 3–1. Advocacy and recruitment are within legal limits, paramilitary training is a borderline activity, tax resistance is illegal but nonviolent, and political killings and armed clashes with law enforcement officers are a major threat to public order.

CONVENTIONAL	MILITANT		VIOLENT	
•Klu Klux Klan	•American Nazi Party	•Posse Comitatus	•The Covenant, the Sword, and the Arm of the Lord	•Aryan Nations

Figure 3-1

A Continuum of Extremist Groups

SOURCE: Gurr, T. R. *The Politics of Terrorism*, edited by M. Stohl, p. 555. New York: Marcel Dekker, 1988. Reproduced by permission of the author and publisher.

One of the leaders of this movement is the Reverend Richard Butler of the Aryan Nations, Church of Jesus Christ Christian, headquartered near Hayden Lake, Idaho. His sermons, identity propaganda, and other hate and neo-Nazi literature and materials are distributed nationally from Hayden Lake by members of the group. Some popular titles: Richard Harwood's *Did Six Million Really Die?*, an item that David Duke's bookstore also carried; Butler's own *The Aryan Warrior*; and an obscure forty-year-old pamphlet called *The Hitler We Loved and Why*. Aryan Nation members maintain contacts with other right-wing groups. Members of the Aryan Nation and other neo-Nazi extreme groups often wear swastikas, double lightning bolts, and other symbols used by Hitler's Nazis.

The most violent extremist group during the 1980s, according to Harris (1987, 11) was The Order (otherwise known as the Bruders Schweigen or Silent Brotherhood), an offshoot of the Aryan Nations. This group was founded by Aryan Nations member Robert Mathews and is loosely based on a book entitled *The Turner Diaries*—an apocalyptic account of racial warfare in the United States. In the novel, an elite clandestine force, The Order, spearheads efforts to destroy the U.S. government and replace it with one based on white supremacy.

Members of the Order have been involved in numerous criminal activities since 1983, including counterfeiting, armed robbery (with proceeds exceeding $4 million), bombings, assaults on federal officers, and the murders of a suspected informant, a Missouri state police officer, and a Denver talk-show host named Alan Berg. Between October 1984 and March 1986, thirty-eight members of the Order were arrested. On December 7, 1984, Robert Mathews was killed on Whidbey Island, Washington, while resisting arrest. Shoulder weapons, handguns, grenades and other explosives, ammunition, and potential target lists were recovered at various safehouses and other locations.

Another group that has been involved in criminal activity is the Covenant, the Sword, the Arm of the Lord (CSA). Beginning in 1980, some CSA members participated in bombings, arsons, robberies, and the murder of a black Arkansas state police officer. During April 1985, the CSA compound was raided by federal authorities, who arrested five persons, including four Order members (two of whom were fugitives) and CSA leader James Ellison. All the CSA and Order members arrested at that time or later plead guilty to charges or were convicted in federal or state courts.

Although aggressive Justice Department campaigns against white supremacist groups appeared to have significantly reduced their terrorist threat, recent events suggest that some groups may have made a comeback. Bombings that took place at the end of 1989 in Alabama, Georgia, Florida, and Maryland showed a similar pattern to earlier white supremacist incidents. The FBI is still investigating, but evidence so far suggests that a deadly campaign has begun to punish and deter members of the judiciary and civil rights advocates who have pushed school desegregation, offended the Ku Klux Klan, and respected the rights of blacks accused of assaults against whites.

Another right-wing faction that has drawn the attention of law enforcement officials includes tax protest and antigovernment groups. Organizations such as the Sheriff's Posse Comitatus (SPC) and the Arizona Patriots espouse parochial as opposed to national interests and, like the anarchists of the last century, desire as little government as possible. They advocate nonpayment of taxes and consider federal and state laws unconstitutional. The SPC, for example, regards the local sheriff as the only legitimate law enforcement authority and the justice of the peace as the highest court in the country!

Nationalistic Groups

Puerto Ricans

The independence of Puerto Rico, a former Spanish colony that the U.S. acquired at the end of the Spanish-American war in 1898, has been a burning political cause among a growing minority of Puerto Ricans for more than a century. In 1950, two nationalists attempted to assassinate President Harry S Truman at Blair House, across the street from the White House. President Truman escaped unharmed, but a District of Columbia police officer was shot and killed. On March 1, 1954, several Puerto Rican nationalists staged a shooting attack from the gallery of the U.S. House of Representatives and wounded five Congressmen. Organizations called, respectively, the *Comandos Armados de Liberacion* and the *Movimento de Independenza Revolucion en Armas* were suppressed by police action during the late 1960s and 1970s, but their surviving members formed a new organization known after 1974 as the Armed Forces of National Liberation (or FALN, after its Spanish name). This group, the most active in the continental U.S. since 1974, has been responsible for more than one-hundred terrorist attacks.

Terrorist groups in Puerto Rico, in contrast, have been far more active in the commission of acts of violence. Nearly forty of the fifty-six terrorist acts committed in Puerto Rico have been attributed to two groups: the EPB-Macheteros (Machete Wielders) and the Organization of Volunteers for the

Puerto Rican Revolution (OVRP). A majority of these actions consisted of bombings or attempted bombings; others included shootings, robberies, and two rocket attacks. Although Puerto Rican interests have been targeted in most of the incidents, U.S. government facilities and personnel have been attacked with greater frequency since 1983.

Police raids and arrests in 1985 temporarily shut down the *Macheteros*. But there is little reason to assume that terrorist actions in Puerto Rico will stop in the foreseeable future. The U.S. government, as Gurr points out, can scarcely force independence on a reluctant island to satisfy minority demands.

Émigré Nationalists

Transnational terrorism refers to terrorism that transcends national boundaries. Terrorists may originate in one country and carry out attacks in another country or may act in their own country in the name of an international cause or on behalf of a foreign government. In the United States, émigré groups nursing old grudges or fighting lost causes account for much transnational terrorism.

Armenian Nationalists

During World War I, approximately 1.5 million Armenians, an ethnic minority living in Turkey, lost their lives. Armenians have claimed that this tragic predecessor to the Holocaust of a later time was the result of a deliberate attempt at genocide carried out by the successors to the "Unspeakable Turk," Sultan Abdul-Hamid II. According to the Turks, the loss of life occurred as part of the process of deportation and resettlement of the Armenians, who were viewed as a threat to Turkish internal security (ATA-USA *Bulletin*, 1982, 4–9).

Sixty years later, young Armenian nationalists, calling themselves the Armenian Secret Army for the Liberation of Armenia (ASALA), began a campaign of terror against primarily Turkish targets. The ASALA was international and Marxist-oriented and supported the ideology of national liberation. But an ideological split led to the formation of a rival anti-Marxist group, the Justice Commandos for Armenian Genocide (JCAG), which claimed that its terrorist actions were directed exclusively against Turkish targets (Wilkinson, 1983). North American members of the latter group carried out the assassination of the Turkish Consul-General in Los Angeles in May 1982.

Armenian violence was brought to an abrupt end by the arrest of six Armenian terrorists in 1982 and the life sentence given to Hampig Sassounian, convicted of the Los Angeles murder. Experts believe there is little likelihood of future terrorism, because the actions of the ASALA and JCAG have discredited them in Armenian communities in the U.S. and in other countries.

Croatian Nationalists

In September 1976, five Americans of Croatian descent skyjacked a TWA jet, had it flown to Europe, and demanded that leaflets on behalf of Croatian independence be dropped over Chicago, London, Montreal, New York, and Paris. A manifesto issued during this media event by the "Headquarters of Croatian National Liberation Forces" contained the following language:

> National self-determination is a basic human right, universal and fundamental, recognized by all members of the UN, a right which may not be denied or withheld any nation regardless of its territorial size or number of inhabitants. . . (*New York Times*, September 12, 1976)

Behind this incident was a long, complicated tangle of ethnic and political strife between the Serbs and the Croats, the two largest republics that make up present-day Yugoslavia. Neither the Kingdom of Serbs, Croats, and Slovenes, established under the Treaty of Versailles at the end of World War I, nor Yugoslavia under the Tito government at the close of World War II were politically viable states capable of resolving centuries of hostility and violence between the contending ethnic factions.

At any rate, the skyjackers of the TWA flight were extradited by French authorities to the U.S., where they were convicted and sentenced to lengthy prison terms. The convictions appear to have ended the activities of the Croatian National Resistance against the Yugoslav government, at least within the U.S. It is doubtful whether many Americans were ever aware of their existence or of the crusading cause they represented.

Anti-Castro Cubans

Expatriate Cubans have carried on more than two decades of violence directed mainly against the Castro regime, but also against rival groups. The oldest anti-Castro group is Alpha 66, which is still led by members of the Cuban militia who participated in the ill-starred landing at the Bay of Pigs. The number 66 commemorates the year the group was formed as the beginning of an effort to wrest Cuba from the control of Fidel Castro and his Soviet-satellite Communist government.

Between 1968 and 1975, such groups as *El Poder Cubano* (Cuban Power) and the Cuban National Liberation Front were responsible for a series of bombings, assaults, and an assassination. Between 1975 and 1983, a group called Omega 7 was the main source of Cuban émigré terrorism and a serious threat to the U.S. and Latin American states that support Fidel Castro. Seven key members were arrested in 1982 and 1983, including Eduardo Arocena, the group's leader. Arocena was convicted and sentenced to life imprisonment. These law enforcement actions appear to have effectively curbed the violent activities of Omega 7.

Single-Issue Terrorists

Schmid and de Graaf (1982) designate as *single-issue terrorism* that committed by individuals or small groups attempting to exert pressure on authorities to grant some privilege to a larger group with which the terrorists sympathize.

Included in this category is a diverse collection of groups, ranging from the right-to-lifers and pro-choice activists to the Jewish Defense League. These groups display a number of common features.

Animal Rights Activists

In November 1988, in the parking lot of the U.S. Surgical Corporation in Norwalk, Connecticut, police arrested a woman who was attempting to place a pipe bomb in the bushes near the parking spot reserved for Leon Hirsch, the company's founder. Next day, New York City police found a shotgun and three more bombs in the woman's apartment amidst stacks of animal rights literature.

Fran Stephanie Trutt's arrest focused national attention on the controversial animal rights movement, estimated to comprise more than 7000 groups or organizations with membership in excess of 10 million and operating funds of more than $50 million—almost all raised by direct contributions. Taking their cue from militant British groups, some American activists have raided and ransacked labs where animals are used in tests of medical equipment. One faction, the Animal Liberation Front, claims responsibility for setting a California laboratory on fire.

In February 1989, two animal rights groups in Britain claimed responsibility for a bomb that caused severe damage to administration buildings at the University of Bristol. The activists stated that the device was intended as a protest against research on animal subjects at the university's medical and veterinary schools. Before the blast, a warning was received from a telephone caller claiming to belong to a previously unknown group, the Animal Abused Society. Although militant animal rights groups had previously used incendiary devices, the University of Bristol bombing is the first time that high explosives had been used. Predictably, the British Secretary of State for Education and Science referred to the incident as an "act of terrorism."

Many animal rights activists condemn violent protests, and most of the movement's 10 million members concentrate on lobbying and peaceful rallies. Several groups repudiated Fran Stephanie Trutt, fearing that her case would hurt their efforts; they contend that Trutt, a troubled loner obsessed with her cause, is hardly a representative of their crusade. Julie Lewin of the Fund for Animals said, "Violence toward people does not help animals." Some animal rights proponents contend that Trutt's aborted bomb attack is so damaging to their cause that it might have been instigated by an agent provocateur. Police say the bomb she planted was too sophisticated to have been made by Trutt herself, and Trutt is reputed to have told the FBI that she has no knowledge of explosives (*Time*, November 28, 1988, 24).

Pro-Life and Pro-Choice Activists

Gurr calls the series of arson and bombing attacks on abortion clinics, which began in the early 1980s and continued throughout the decade, "the most recent manifestation of vigilante terrorism in the United States" (1988, 558). Anti-abortion terrorists bombed more than forty abortion and birth control clinics between 1982 and 1986. Bombings reached a peak of twenty-five in 1984, then declined to eleven in 1985. But some of the 1985 bombings were potentially deadly, and two passersby were injured in an October 1986 bombing in New York City. (Hoffman, 1987, 238–239).

Nationwide, abortion clinics have been invaded, vandalized, burned, and bombed. Patients are harassed as they try to enter clinics, and "pregnancy clinics" have sprung up to lure unsuspecting women to anti-abortion lectures accompanied by gruesome visual details. Physicians who perform abortions receive hate mail and threats to their families; one Illinois physician and his wife were kidnapped and held for eight days (Kort, 1987, 49).

Some of those who take an active role in the pro-life movement share with right-wing groups a commitment to Christian fundamentalist doctrines, whereas some of those involved in the pro-choice movement endorse some of the basic principles identified with the ideological left. With regard to the depth and intensity of commitment displayed by people on both sides of the abortion issue, there is little room for civility and none whatever for dialogue or negotiation.

The Jewish Defense League (JDL)

The Jewish Defense League (JDL) was founded in 1968 to protest Soviet mistreatment of Jews. Its leaders were a lawyer, Bert Zweibon, and an Orthodox rabbi, Meier Kahane. Members were trained in martial arts and the use of weapons to defend themselves. They took their motto "Never Again" from the title of a book written by Kahane. During the JDL's first three years, the group carried out demonstrations and relatively harmless protest activities against Russians, Arabs, and Black Panthers.

Between 1977 and 1986, forty-three acts of terrorism have been attributed to the JDL. Although the JDL seldom claims responsibility for acts of violence, Kahane has consistently advocated the use of violence against those the League considers anti-Semitic or anti-Israel. Hoffman (1987, 5) states that more than thirty JDL members have been convicted in U.S. courts for committing, or conspiring to commit, terrorist crimes. The JDL has the somber distinction of having killed the only two victims of terrorist bombings in the U.S. in 1985.

Summary

Political terrorism of the kind that is familiar to the people of Europe and Latin America has not posed a serious danger to public order in the U.S. The number and seriousness of terrorist acts—bombings, shootings, arson, and vandalism—have shown a decade-long decline, as measured by both official and unofficial sources.

For reasons that are deeply rooted in the American history and ethos, insurgent violence from the ideological left has never proven attractive to any but a very small minority of U.S. citizens: campus radicals, intellectuals, militant blacks, and small groups of social misfits, such as the Symbionese Liberation Army and the Manson "family." Despite saturation coverage of their activities by the media, their numbers were ineffectual and their network of support extremely limited. Most important, as Gurr suggests, they were unable or unwilling to "set aside the tactical liability of their humanitarianism" (1988, 573); that is, they were willing to blow up buildings but not people, thus sharply limiting their capacity to instill real terror.

On the ideological right we find an authentic homegrown form of terrorism: vigilantism. As we saw in chapter 2, the historical antecedents of vigilantism in the U.S. can be traced to the colonial period; the Ku Klux Klan that arose in the post-Civil War South can be recognized as a familiar specimen of this phenomenon. We are currently experiencing the third revival of Klan activity, which has found its traditional theme of racial purity even less appealing to people in the most conservative rural areas from which it once drew its main support.

An emergent New Right comprises a number of groups that are relatively small in numbers and organization but are united on such themes as fundamentalist Christian identity, survivalism, and the right of communities to self-defense. Given the close surveillance and prosecution of illegal acts committed by members of such groups as the Aryan Nation, Sheriff's Posse Comitatus, and the Klan, there is little likelihood that the country will experience the widespread terrorism that scourged the rural South during the 1950s and 1960s. Gurr (1988, 573) cautions, however, that resentment about social change and economic decline are the most fertile breeding grounds for future violence on the right.

For at least two decades, émigré nationalist groups have used the U.S. as an arena to promote political causes by means of terrorist actions. For brief periods, the media stage center has been occupied by Croatian nationalists, Serb nationalists, Armenian nationalists, and anti-Castro Cubans. The most enduring and dangerous of these factions are Puerto Ricans who seek independence for their island nation. Much of the rhetoric and some of their tactics show indebtedness to Third World insurgency, but it is far from clear whether a majority of their fellow Puerto Ricans share their aspirations.

Acts of domestic terrorism in the 1980s have been committed by extremist members of single-issue groups: animal rights protesters, pro-life and pro-choice activists, and members of the Jewish Defense League (JDL). Despite bombings, arsons, vandalism, and other acts of violence, few people have been killed or injured and property damage has been relatively light. In the open warfare between the pro-life and pro-choice forces, however, there is no room for complacency when contemplating the future. Crusaders have never been known for a disposition toward tolerance in pursuing a cause. As the struggle intensifies, extremists on both sides are increasingly likely to be heard.

Key Terms

Animal Liberation Front	Armenian nationalists
Aryan Nations	Black Panthers
Croatian nationalists	Fuqra
George Jackson	Jewish Defense League (JDL)
Meier Kahane	Robert Mathews
NWLF	The Order
Puerto Rican nationalists	El Rukns
Fran Stephanie Trutt	Weather Underground
Students for a Democratic Society (SDS)	

Questions for Discussion and Review

1. What were some of the events that contributed to making the 1960s and 1970s a period of social turbulence in the U.S.?
2. How does Strentz characterize the people who made up the leftist groups of the 1960s and 1970s?
3. Why does Trick call the Weather Underground the "godperson of American revolutionary organizations"?
4. Discuss the concept of leftist insurgency among blacks and indicate why blacks in prison might have been especially responsive to revolutionary doctrines.
5. Briefly describe the main tenets held by extremists of the ideological right.
6. Identify the principal émigré nationalist groups that have made the U.S. a battleground for their causes. Which group is presently most active?
7. Who are the antagonists in the pro-life and pro-choice groups? Is it appropriate to describe the actions of the pro-life extremists as "terroristic"?
8. What are the objectives of the Jewish Defense League? Are they supported by public opinion in the U.S. and Israel?

References

ATA-USA. "Setting the record straight on Armenian propaganda against Turkey." *Bulletin of the Assembly of American Turkish Associations.* Washington, DC (Fall 1982): 4–9.

Berkman, B. *Opening the Prison Gates: The Rise of the Prisoners Movement.* Lexington, MA: Lexington Books, 1979.

Cohler, L. "Republican Racist: Dealing with the David Duke Problem." *The New Republic* 201 (1989): 11–14.

Committee on Internal Security, House of Representatives. *Staff Study on Revolutionary Activity Directed Toward the Administration of Penal or Correctional Systems.* Washington, DC: U.S. Government Printing Office, 1973.

Gurr, T.R. "Political Terrorism in the United States: Historical and Contempo-
    rary Trends." In *The Politics of Terrorism*, edited by M. Stohl, pp. 549–578.
    New York: Marcel Dekker, 1988.

Harris, J.W. "Domestic Terrorism in the 1980s." *FBI Law Enforcement Bulletin*
    56 (1987): 5–13.

Hoffman, B. "Terrorism in the United States in 1985." In *Contemporary Research
    on Terrorism*, edited by P. Wilkinson and A.M. Stewart, pp. 230–240.
    Aberdeen, U.K.: Aberdeen University Press, 1987.

Homer, F.D. "Terror in the United States: Three Perspectives." In *The Politics
    of Terrorism*, edited by M. Stohl, pp. 145–177. New York: Marcel Dekker,
    1983.

Irwin, J. *Prisons in Turmoil*. Boston, MA: Little, Brown, 1980.

Jackson, G. *Soledad Brother: The Prison Letters of George Jackson*. New York:
    Coward-McCann, 1970.

Jacobs, J. "Stratification and Conflict Among Prison Inmates." *Journal of Crim-
    inal Law and Criminology* 66 (1976): 476–482.

Kort, M. "Domestic Terrorism: On the Front Line at an Abortion Clinic." *Ms.
    Magazine* XV (May 1987): 48–53.

Magnuson, E. "An Ex-Klansman's Win Brings the G.O.P. Chickens Home to
    Roost." *Time* (March 6, 1989): 29.

National Advisory Commission on Criminal Justice Standards and Goals. *Task
    Force Report on Civil Disorders*. Washington, DC: U.S. Government Printing
    Office, 1973.

Newton, H.P. *Revolutionary Suicide*. New York: Harcourt Brace Jovanovich, 1973.

Parry, A. *Terrorism: From Robespierre to Arafat*. New York: Vanguard Press, 1976.

Reilly, S. "Life Uneasy for Woman at Center of Abortion Ruling." *The Orego-
    nian* (May 9, 1989): A2.

Schmid, A.P., and De Graaf, J. *Violence as Communication: Insurgent Terrorism
    and the Western News Media*. Beverly Hills, CA: Sage Publications, 1982.

Silberman, C. *Criminal Justice, Criminal Violence*. New York: Vintage Books, 1980.

Stratton, J. Testimony before the Committee on Internal Security, House of
    Representatives. *Staff Study on Revolutionary Activity Directed Against the
    Administration of Penal or Correctional Systems*. Washington, DC: U.S. Gov-
    ernment Printing Office, 1973.

Strentz, T. "A Terrorist Psychosocial Profile, Past and Present." *FBI Law
    Enforcement Bulletin* 57 (1988): 13–19.

Trick, M.M. "Chronology of Incidents of Terroristic, Quasi-terroristic, and
    Political Violence in the United States: January 1965 to March 1976."
    National Advisory Committee on Criminal Justice Standards and Goals.
    Disorders and Terrorism: Report of the Task Force on Disorders and Terrorism.
    Washington, DC: Law Enforcement Assistance Administration, Depart-
    ment of Justice, 1976.

Wilkinson, P. "Armenian Terrorism." *The World Today* 39 (September 1983):
    336–350.

4

Victims of Terrorism

Terrorists frequently assert that in their struggle, "there are no innocent victims." We would emphatically disagree and counter that it is exactly in the human creation of victims that the evil in terrorism resides. Many more lives may be lost in natural disasters, epidemics, or accidents, but these unfortunate people are not victims of evil. Evil is the human creation of a victim.

David A. Soskis, and Frank M. Ochberg, "Concepts of Terrorist Victimization." In *Victims of Terrorism*, edited by F.M. Ochberg and D.A. Soskis, p. 106. Boulder, CO: Westview Press, 1982.

A terrorist incident may affect a number of people: the immediate victims of the terrorist assault; their families and close friends; those in authority, who are often forced to make life or death decisions concerning the fate of hostages; the fellow countrymen of the initial victims; and, eventually, everyone in the world community of law abiding nations. We tend to restrict our use of the term *victim* to those who suffer direct assault from terrorists; we may extend the term to include families and friends of the immediate victims. But all of us—even the governments that represent us through the democratic elective process—are victimized in various ways when an act of terrorism is perpetrated anywhere in the world.

We have some understanding of the immediate effects of stress on terrorist victims from previous studies of traumatic stress induced by combat. The experiences of those who survived Nazi concentration camps, Soviet gulags, and POW camps have taught us about the more pervasive effects of captivity, and, finally, we have learned from systematic studies of victims of criminal violence, including rape, assault, and kidnapping.

A theme that has been explored at some length in the professional literature is the interaction between captives and captors that leads to victims' identifying with their aggressors—even to the extreme of trying to shield the latter from justice. The dynamics of this kind of interaction had already been explored among survivors of the Nazi death camps, but its study received additional impetus in the case of the so-called "Stockholm Syndrome." Of additional interest and concern is the strange and fateful story of the young heiress Patricia Hearst, who was kidnapped and transformed into a member of an urban terrorist group, the Symbionese Liberation Army. As we shall see, most of the questions raised about Patty Hearst's "conversion" remain unanswered, despite Hearst's autobiographical account of her captivity and its movie version.

Attention is now being given to strategies for coping with the stress imposed by terrorism. People whose work requires them to serve abroad, often in exposed and potentially vulnerable places, such as the military and the diplomatic corps, are being given "stress innoculation" through techniques intended to strengthen their emotional, physical, and psychological resources in potential confrontations with terrorist-induced stress. As our experience increases, this list will undoubtedly grow to include groups from the private sector whose geographical or occupational situation puts them at high risk for becoming hostages.

Concepts and Models of Victimization

Soskis and Ochberg (1982) have provided models based on traumatic events that can be related to terrorist victimization. These include: (1) grief; (2) death imagery; (3) encounters with bloody or terrible events; and (4) the experience of rape victims. Although each of these traumas is distinct from terrorist victimization, they offer access to a body of diverse professional literature and to a potentially illuminating perspective.

Grief

In contemporary Western society, death is an unwelcome intruder. Most people think of death as a remote event that will happen at some time in the far distant future, when their lives are all but completed. Despite the certainty of death for all of us and the inevitable loss of friends and relatives, many of us deny and ignore it—and remain unprepared. When someone close to us dies, we are psychologically upended.

Grief or bereavement is the psychological reaction to the loss of a loved one, of a cherished goal, or of a cherished aspect of one's life. Often the first reaction to loss is disbelief. Then, as we begin to realize the significance of what has happened, our feelings of sadness, despair, and even, perhaps, anger at the departed person, frequently overwhelm us.

Grief is a natural process that allows the survivors to mourn their loss and then free themselves for life without the loved one. Some individuals do not go through a normal process of grieving, perhaps because of their psychological makeup or as a consequence of the particular situation. The individual may, for example, be expected to be stoical about his or her feelings or may have to manage the affairs of the family. Others may develop exaggerated or prolonged depression after the normal grieving process should have run its course. Such pathological reactions to someone's death are more likely in persons who have a history of emotional problems and who harbor resentment and hostility toward the deceased; thus, they experience intense guilt. They are usually profoundly depressed and often have suicidal preoccupations.

Grief and mourning may be very much involved in terrorist victimization. We know that victims of terrorism can be badly beaten or injured, possibly maimed, and suffer rage at being made to feel impotent in retaliating against their terrorist aggressors. They can also grieve, however, for the loss of an image of themselves—whether that image was as potent, in control, or as whole. This grieving may be accompanied by the depressed feelings that accompany other grief reactions and may also precipitate depressive illnesses in persons who are predisposed.

The experience of terrorist victimization often represents as significant a trauma as bereavement and is often combined with it. Soskis and Ochberg observe that "Research work on and folk wisdom about grief remind us that the mourning process has a timetable of its own that should not be rushed—even if it does not coincide with the convenience of the helpers or with the convenience of the victim" (1982, 109). Various religious and cultural systems have timetables for the work of mourning (e.g., the Jewish sequence of "sitting shiva," Shaloshim, and Kaddish). Yet official helping systems usually fail to provide this kind of structured caring over time. Soskis and Ochberg suggest that such traditional practices should represent a standard for the nature and duration of helping programs for those who have been victims of terrorism.

Death Imagery

The human reaction to death imagery and its psychological importance have been explored in detail by Lifton, Kato, and Reich (1979). This phenomenon is strikingly illustrated by the comments of a woman who survived one of the worst air disasters in history, the result of a collision on the ground at the airfield in Tenerife, in the Canary Islands, of two fully loaded jumbo jets, in which 600 people were killed. One of a handful of survivors, she stated a year after the tragedy, "The problem is I know I am going to die." This was not, she explained, a feeling of fear that this would happen soon: "No, I just know I am going to die." This young woman was expressing the bleak recognition that she no longer possessed the protective veil that keeps most of us from having to constantly visualize and be aware of our mortality. For her, this veil was suddenly pulled back, and the vision was an alarming, almost devastating one to live with.

Victims of terrorism are also forcefully exposed to images of death, although in fewer numbers. The duration and quality of their exposure, however, is similar in intensity to the experience of air-disaster victims.

Inescapable Encounter with Terrible Events

A third and related model is also part of the experience of natural and man-made disaster victims, as well as of the experience of the victims of terrorism and war: the *inescapable encounter with bloody or terrible events*. It is the experience of the airline stewardess as she wandered among the bodies at

Tenerife, or the father who was forced to watch an SS man swing his two-year-old daughter by her feet and smash her head against a wall. Dori Laub, a psychiatrist who has worked extensively with Holocaust victims and their children, has pointed out the unique significance of such terrible events, which are too powerful to be tied to the ego or to objects—the terrible events themselves become the foci of symptoms and identifications (1979). Those of us fortunate enough to lead normal lives are not, and cannot be, fully prepared to encounter such events. The gory and grotesque elements in children's fairy tales and the violent or horror movies we go to see may be our attempts to desensitize ourselves to such events through small doses that we can control. For most people, encountering the real thing is so shocking and the images so overwhelming that they flood the mind, sweeping past usually effective defense mechanisms and coping strategies. In their aftermath, they haunt people when they are awake and poison their dreams for years on end. Sometimes, sadly, efforts to forget or even simply to go on with life fail.

Experience of Rape Victims

The final model for terrorist victimization is the experience of rape victims. Although terrorists use murder or the threat of murder as their basic coercive technique, the crime of murder is not as good a model as rape for terrorist victimization. By definition, all murder victims are killed; most hostages are not. Also, a significant number of murder victims have had, prior to being slain, a prolonged and/or intimate relationship with the person who killed them. This is less true in rape and seldom true in terrorist acts.

The crime of rape can serve as a model for terrorist victimization in other ways. A Palestinian terrorist who was interviewed on the ABC Television Network program "Hostage" characterized the murderous attack on Israeli athletes during the Olympiad in Munich as "a severe entry into their minds." The verbal analogy to rape is obvious—and compelling. Both rape and hostage-taking coerce the participation of the victim and force our attention, if not our understanding.

Isolation of the Victim

The special usefulness of the experience of rape victims as a model for victims of terrorism is clearest when one considers the negative consequences of victimization that have nothing to do directly with what the offender does to the victim. The most serious and far-reaching of these is *isolation of the victim*. Both hostages and rape victims are isolated by their own feelings of guilt and shame; guilt over whether they should have resisted at the cost of their lives, and shame at having been taken, used, damaged, or defiled. These feelings make it harder for victims to share their experiences with others and to work them through psychologically on a constructive, conscious level: both the subject matter and the emotions make avoidance or denial likely defenses.

Since the experience of these victims touches upon areas in which most people have some unfinished psychological business, it is not surprising that some of the guilt and shame have an unrealistic character when viewed by outsiders. This lack of "objective" reality does not, unfortunately, diminish the punitive force of the emotions themselves. Friends or relatives who try to comfort victims are often angered and saddened as they find out quickly that the guilt or shame does not go away as soon as the well-meaning helper demonstrates that, from a rational point of view, it doesn't make any sense!

In addition to being isolated by his or her own psychological reactions, the victim of rape or terrorism faces a further and related process of isolation by others. These two processes often interact in a negative spiral with more social isolation leading to more unrealistic thinking, and so on. Social isolation is particularly tragic, since friends or relatives sometimes pull away at the very time they are most needed. This distancing is often a product of the discomfort caused by the issues of brute violence or sexuality that the incident itself raises, even if the victim tries to protect friends and relatives by not talking about it. Mixed with this discomfort is a fear or suspicion that the victim has somehow been contaminated or changed irreversibly for the worse. The female victim of rape may be treated by a friend, lover, or spouse—sometimes unconsciously—as "damaged goods."

Early observers of terrorist incidents were not adequately prepared for the possibility of this social isolation, especially in light of the expressed public support and publicity the hostages seemed to be getting. The hostages also were poorly prepared, because they had believed their ordeal was finally over. Brian Jenkins (1979), who has conducted extensive studies on terrorist incidents, described a similar and subtle, yet debilitating, problem for American diplomats and executives released after terrorist captivity. It is expressed in official reports in phrases such as, "He acquitted himself well, to the best of our knowledge, during the course of his long captivity." Former hostages have described such suspicion and distancing among their friends and colleagues as if they were feared as a source of contamination.

Victim-Terrorist Interactions

In the role of controller or manipulator of information, the terrorist may have a more profound effect on the victim than through any physical abuse. A cognitive distortion or reversal of the terrorist act is one that labels the terrorist or his group as the real victims. Terrorists in many national liberation movements often come from a background of exploitation, uprooting, and sometimes poverty. Their unfortunate situation is often highlighted both in their own eyes and for the public by their battle against countries that have higher standards of living (e.g., Israel). Even in relatively developed countries, terrorists may enhance the contrast between the "ins" and the "outs" by preying on the most powerful or the most fortunate members of their society, as happened in the case of Patricia Hearst. Unfortunately for the world, disadvantaged people who gain power do not automatically behave humanely when they are in control.

The Stockholm Syndrome

On August 23, 1973, Jan-Erik Olsson attempted to rob the Sveriges Kreditbank in Stockholm, Sweden. The incident was prolonged after a rapid police response trapped the robber inside. As a result of Olsson's demand to the police, a second criminal participant named Clark Oloffsson was delivered from prison to the bank. The resulting incident lasted 131 hours.

During the initial stages of the robbery, Olsson fired an automatic weapon inside and outside the bank, wounding a police officer. He made demands and pointed his machine gun at a woman hostage, threatening to kill her. When Oloffsson arrived, the situation changed. Olsson no longer shouted, he allowed the bindings on the hostages to be loosened, and the situation became calmer.

The hostages were moved into the bank vault. There was more shooting, and another police officer was wounded. The police finally trapped the robbers in the vault and shut the door. Police decided to drill into the vault, knocking out the electricity and flooding the vault floor with water from the drill. There was more shooting. Human waste accumulated in trash baskets. Authorities stopped delivery of food and water into the vault, forcing the hostages to strain the water on the floor through cloth to filter it before drinking. Local radio stations, which were being monitored by the hostages and robbers, reported actions the police were considering, including the use of nerve gas and assault. Hostages were subsequently tied into nooses so that if they fell unconscious they would strangle.

Not surprisingly, these conditions resulted in both the hostages and the robbers fearing the actions of the police. Further, some of the hostages had favorable interactions with Oloffsson who, in at least some instances, protected them from Olsson. Throughout the incident, the hostages feared Olsson.

A positive rapport developed in this environment between the women hostages and Oloffsson. Olin and Born claim that "some of the literature and many speeches have widely misunderstood the circumstances and have suggested that the Stockholm Syndrome is a more generally occurring phenomenon than is probably the case" (1983, 22). Law enforcement literature, according to the authors, suggests that the Stockholm Syndrome occurs when hostages and hostage takers are isolated by authorities and there are:

1. Positive "feelings" from the hostages toward their captor(s)
2. Negative "feelings" toward authorities by both hostages and captor(s)
3. Positive "feelings" returned by the captor(s) to the hostages (Olin & Born, 1983, 20).

There is widespread expectation that these three conditions may be enhanced in some circumstances by the actions of authorities, although it is difficult to cite specific support for this contention on the basis of research.

Use of the term "feelings" in quotation marks reflects a concern by Olin and Born with the psychodynamically oriented explanations of the Stockholm Syndrome:

> The Stockholm Syndrome has sometimes been attributed to defense mechanisms, regression, weakness of the ego, and identification of the hostage with the aggressor. In fact, most law enforcement articles written about the Stockholm Syndrome rely on Freudian interpretations of "inner feelings" reported by the hostages and their captors. Few alternative interpretations have been offered. (Olin & Born, 1983, 20–21)

Whereas the psychoanalytic approach offers one explanation for a limited number of hostage incidents, it has not yet provided a framework to assist law enforcement personnel. In an attempt to clarify the importance of the Stockholm Syndrome for hostage incidents, Olin and Born pose a series of questions that need to be raised and answered on the basis of behavior, rather than personality dynamics and "inner feelings." They include these:

1. How often does the syndrome occur?
2. Does occurrence of the syndrome actually increase the safety of persons involved in hostage incidents?
3. Assuming that it occurs in a significant portion of hostage incidents and that it increases participant safety, under what circumstances does the syndrome occur?
4. Can it be facilitated? If so, how?
5. Is the syndrome more likely to occur in some situations, such as those involving family members, and less likely to occur in others, such as in incidents of political terrorism? (Olin & Born, 1983, 21).

Given the circumstances surrounding the original Stockholm hostage incident, it seems likely that occurrence of the syndrome depends upon specific participant interactions and, perhaps, the interactive styles of the individuals. Thus, some situations are probably more amenable to development of the Stockholm Syndrome than are others; for example, there might be less likelihood of the phenomenon's developing in kidnapping or politically motivated hostage seizures. Some terrorist incidents appear to have been deliberately structured by the terrorists to limit the possibility of interpersonal relationships developing between hostages and their captors. Such actions have been used by the South Moluccan terrorists in the Netherlands, the Japanese Red Army, and the Tupamaros. Interpersonal relationships are inhibited by hostage segregation, blindfolds, masks, language barriers, and other methods. We must emphasize that terrorists are fully as capable as anyone else of reading the professional literature and profiting from the analysis of examples drawn from previous incidents.

The Patty Hearst Case

In September 1988, a film was released under the title *Patty Hearst*. Patricia Hearst Shaw, the subject of the film, is a housewife in Westport, Connecticut. Her husband, Bernard, was one of her bodyguards while she was out on bail in the midst of a trial for armed robbery. The movie and the autobiographical book on which it is based (*Every Secret Thing*) depict Patty Hearst as a dazed captive, huddled in a dark closet for 57 days, without ever directly answering the question of whether she was a coerced victim or a willing partner.

Shaw told an interviewer, in describing what she calls a recent change in public attitude toward the Symbionese Liberation Army (SLA), a small band of self-styled revolutionaries who were among the most wanton remnants of the 1960s, that she feels vindicated. "They are no longer viewed as misguided campus activists, but sociopaths on the loose, more like the Manson Family. They raped me mentally, physically, and emotionally and they stole my reputation. For a long time people romanticized it, but that myth is finally dying" (Gross, 1988, C1, C8).

The Symbionese Liberation Army consisted of an odd coalition of white, radical, female students from the University of California (Berkeley) and black convicts serving time at California State Prison in Vacaville.

> Counting about a dozen members, it was one of the smallest and most bizarre terrorist groups. Like the Manson Family, it can perhaps be understood against that specific Californian background which has remained a riddle to most foreigners. (Laqueur, 1987, 244–245)

One might add that the Californian background to which he refers is equally enigmatic to most Americans who do not dwell in California. At any rate, the white women's participation seems to have been fueled by social guilt and sexual identity diffusion. They contributed the name "Symbionese," which was defined as "body of harmony of dissimilar bodies and organisms living in deep and loving harmony and partnership in the best interest of within the body," the SLA emblem, a seven-headed-cobra, signifying God and life, SLA slogans, and some rather turgid rhetoric culled from various radical sources (Laqueur, 1987, 244).

The motives that induced the young black men to join a terrorist group were altogether different from those that had driven white female students underground. On one side, there was the despair of the black ghetto, unemployment, poverty, and the misery of broken families; on the other, the crisis of identity, suburban boredom, the desire for excitement and action, a certain romantic streak—in short, terrorism as an antidote for personality problems. All of this, notes Laqueur, was enmeshed in intellectual confusion, the absence of values, and the conviction that anything goes. In their violent opposition to this society and its culture, in the obscenity of their language and their cruelty, the SLA members demonstrated that they were, in fact, its offspring. The young black men could point to very real social problems; the white women suffered mainly from personal hang-ups.

Patricia Hearst was kidnapped on February 4, 1974; on September 18, 1975, FBI agents arrested a young woman who called herself "Tania" and identified herself as a "self-employed urban guerrilla." On being taken into custody, she raised her clenched fist in a salute. In a subsequent chat with a friend, she said that she had nothing in common with the former Patty except physical identity.

Almost everything that happened to Patricia Hearst during the 591 days between her kidnapping and her arrest is the subject of controversy. Says Hacker,

> Patty was kidnapped, subsequently kept in complete isolation subject only to the intensive, physical, and emotional pressures of her captors who exerted total control over her. Everything that followed occurred in the sequence of these events, none of them Patty's doings or by any stretch of the imagination the result of her choice or free will. (1976, 176)

Hacker ascribes Patricia Hearst's "coerced change of mind" to the result of "concerted mind attack"—an expression he prefers to the much-abused and widely misunderstood term *brainwashing*—as the only version that is compatible with all the known facts about the case and contradicted by none.

He dismisses others' claims that the time that elapsed between Patricia Hearst's abduction and her emergence as the willing SLA accomplice was too short for a complete conversion to have taken place. According to Hacker, total control over a victim for several weeks in a situation of extreme shared danger is sufficient time. No professional training is required, only ruthlessness and single-minded determination. Donald De Freeze, former prison inmate and self-styled General Field Marshal Cinque of the SLA, had been subjected to behavior modification while serving time at Vacaville, so there is a basis for believing that he was at least familiar at firsthand with some of the techniques of contingency management (i.e., operant conditioning).

Should the the Patty Hearst case be written off as a bizarre episode in history that will never recur, or can the serious student of terrorism learn anything of value from a study of the case? The features that were unique to the case—the composition of the terrorist group and the kidnapping and mental conversion of a young heiress—seem unlikely to be repeated, but there are other features that bear closer commentary.

At the time of its occurrence, observers of the Patty Hearst kidnapping and the subsequent shootout, in which six members of the SLA lost their lives, were awed by the amount of chaos and distress created by this handful of emotionally disturbed and socially alienated young people. Their willingness, even enthusiasm, to become martyrs to a cause that was never articulated any more clearly than in the slogans it borrowed from the radical left, some of them in Spanish, was a key element in creating media attention. Television succeeded in doing the work of the SLA by magnifying this small group of maladjusted people into a genuine social revolutionary movement. As we shall see in chapter 5, we have gained a great deal of understanding of the importance of the mass media for furthering the purposes of terrorism since the Patty Hearst case.

Another noteworthy feature of the Hearst case was the absence of coordination—or even coherence—among the Hearst family members, friends, representatives of various law enforcement agencies, reporters, and others. Hacker claims there were at least three different authorities planning and acting independently, sometimes at cross purposes and always without previous consultation with one another: the FBI, the state police, and the Hearsts.

> In some cases of kidnapping, the terrorists' lack of any existing responsible command structure makes negotiations difficult or impossible. In this instance, it was the good guys, widely divergent in their views about appropriate methods, in their aims, and in their image-making interests, who had no consistent command structure. (Hacker, 1976, 147)

Possibly, even probably, nothing would have worked with a group such as the SLA. But what is more crucial in hindsight, and for possible future occasions, as Hacker points out, is that "nothing conceivably could have worked under the circumstances unless the kidnappers were not just criminal lunatics but also stupid and inept blunderers and fools." Crusading terrorists very rarely are blunderers and fools, but conventional law enforcement, according to Hacker, treats them as if they were.

Research on Terrorist Victimization

Inadequate baseline data, limited access to victims, poor documentation, and lack of funding are among the reasons that terrorist victimization has seldom been studied empirically. One investigator who has managed to conduct systematic research on victims of terrorism, Rona M. Fields, has focused on the experiences of child and adolescent torture victims and hostages, primarily in Northern Ireland and in Israel. Before we discuss Fields's conclusions, it is worthwhile to review her assessment of the difficulties that hamper an investigator who wishes to study the effects of terrorism on victims.

Barriers to Research

Terrorism has been a campaign issue in the past two presidential elections; it has been claimed that the Reagan landslide of 1980 was at least partly the result of public dissatisfaction with President Carter's handling of the Iran hostage crisis. Given the amount of intense publicity and media coverage that terrorist incidents receive—and the sensitivity of politicians to public attitudes toward terrorism—it is surprising to learn from Fields that the U.S. government had not invested major support for systematic studies of terrorist victims as of the date (1982) of publication of her report. She claims there are several reasons that requests for research support have been denied, including cost, fear of adverse reactions from subjects, and questions of reliability of data.

Lack of appropriate funding for research imposes severe limitations on the kinds of studies that can be made of terrorist victims. As Fields notes, complex studies done without funding are likely to suffer from serious obstacles to data collection, data analysis, and presentation of results. In the absence of adequate funding for large-scale studies, research on terrorist victimization has been repetitive rather than cumulative.

Problems in obtaining data from terrorist victims can scarcely be over-emphasized:

> Not every research assistant (even when funded) is eager to fly off to a war zone and, in grubby little houses and smelly alleyways, try to do psychological tests on subjects whose names, addresses, and appointment schedules are as vaporous as the mists on the Irish sea. (Fields, 1982, 141)

Hostages and kidnap victims frequently have either political or organizational reasons for seeking anonymity and rapid reabsorption into a mundane routine. The U.S. Foreign Service personnel who have been terrorist captives are almost inaccessible outside the security network, and similar factors prevail in other countries, as well.

Apart from opportunity and cost, there are several major methodological problems in doing clinical assessments of terrorism victims.

1. Time frame. If assessment is not performed within a short time after the experience, there are difficulties in evaluating the relative effects of such contingencies as starvation, imprisonment, overcrowding, and the effects of readjustment.

2. Techniques of assessment. Proper evaluation of the condition of victims requires access by the clinician to such sophisticated instruments as tests designed to detect the presence, type, and extent of organic brain dysfunction. In addition, the same tests should be given to all available victims, whenever possible, in order to build up an adequate bank of comparable data.

3. Baseline data. In order for studies of victimization to have any significance, the clinician must be given access to information on the original condition of the victims, i.e., hospital and clinic records where these are available. Lacking baseline data, accurate assessment of the effects of victimization is practically impossible. Moreover, research needs to be carried out as longitudinal studies and should include fairly large samples.

Growing Up in Terror

After a decade of examining torture victims and hostages from several countries, and after testing children between the ages of six and fifteen growing up in conditions of constant violence, Fields concluded that "little victims into big terrorists grow."

> This research substantiates what common sense and experience tell us: that people who are badly treated or unjustly punished will seek revenge. In fact, even some whose punishment is appropriate will struggle to wreak vengeance on those who imposed that punishment. It should not be surprising then that young adolescents who have themselves been terrorized may later become terrorists and that, in a situation in which they are afforded a kind of sanction by their compatriots because of the actions of an unjust government, the resort to terror tactics becomes a way of life. (1982, 146)

In their earliest years, children growing up in Northern Ireland experienced the burning down of their houses by mobs augmented by uniformed "security forces," suffered the internment and torture of family members, and lost parents who were assassinated by terror squads. Projective techniques such as the Thematic Apperception Test (TAT), a series of rather ambiguous pictures for which subjects are asked to make up stories that fit the situations depicted, consistently yielded results indicating that children saw themselves as having little or no control over their fate. Their story characters showed incomprehensible drives for destruction, and both the children and adult characters in their stories were equally helpless to combat them.

Fields also administered the Tapp-Kohlberg questions, a test of moral development in which the subject is asked to make choices for action in hypothetical situations involving complex ethical issues and choices. The final score indicates the level of moral development the subject has reached. The children and adolescents that Fields studied were stunted in their moral development, and only ten of the 350 subjects attained a normal level of moral development, that is, one commensurate with chronological age.

Children who grew into adolescence were obsessed with death and destruction and had the feeling that being helpless and afraid were commonplace. This pattern was undoubtedly aggravated when they were beaten by soldiers—supposedly the representatives of authority and justice—or experienced firsthand the death or crippling of a close relative or friend. Says Fields:

> Children growing up under conditions such as these may not achieve the level of moral development requisite to resolving legal and political conflicts nonviolently. Not surprisingly, moral development is further interrupted when the legal system is one imposed by either a foreign nation or a governing system that has goals and objectives inconsistent with those of the nationals. (1982, 146)

Fields concludes with a statement of the researcher's ultimate goal in this kind of research: to increase our understanding of how to intervene in the sequence that too often dooms innocent victims to become victimizers themselves.

Planning for the Future

If we must plan for a future in which terrorism will be a part, the least we can do is try to formulate some rational and realistic agenda. Caplan (1964, 1981) offers the useful concepts of primary, secondary, and tertiary prevention. Primary prevention reduces the incidence of disorder in a community; secondary prevention reduces the duration of a significant number of the disorders that do occur; tertiary prevention reduces the impairment that may result from the disorders that occur. We will discuss each type of prevention as it relates to programs for terrorism victims. For all three types of prevention, it is especially important to bear in mind the relationship between ends and means. Recent history has clearly shown that terrorist groups are decreasing their emphasis on political ideology and that a "terrorism for its own sake" subgroup is increasing. Thus, the means of older generations of terrorists have been transformed into ends. In planning assistance programs for victims, translating means into costs (financial and human) clarifies the issue that means are indeed used to evaluate, and often to modify, what were originally seen as ends. No planning strategy manages to avoid this interrelationship. As Ochberg and Soskis emphasize, "The only safety that we can find is in jointly determining means and ends, and in being very specific in defining the values we are for and under what conditions they apply" (1982, 174).

Primary Prevention

On the broadest level, primary prevention of terrorism consists of withdrawing its rewards and promptly punishing its perpetrators. Rewards may be withdrawn by refusing to pay or to publicize the actions of terrorists, by coopting the demands of terrorist groups, and by attempting to explore and undermine the emotional sources that nourish movements based on vengeance.

A stated aim of many terrorist groups is to provoke a wave of suppression and police-state tactics that will erode people's trust in their government. It is extremely difficult to resist this temptation, which risks the loss or subversion of our values in their very defense. Yet we must also be as clear as we can about the point at which we refuse to go any further in succumbing to terrorist demands. In the end, this may come down to choosing which side we are on and which we oppose; our choice of enemies, after all, says a great deal about who we are. Translating these concepts into programs is inseparable from the issue of national policy, which we will discuss in chapters 11 and 12. It needs to be said at this point that the specific tactics chosen should form a background of common knowledge by both hostages and hostage-takers. Thus far, several administrations have failed in this fundamental regard.

Many experts view the prospects of preparing people for possible captivity by terrorists with skepticism. They claim that captivity of any kind is an intensely personal experience to which people respond as individuals on the basis of personality resources, religious beliefs, and moral and ethical values, and that these are sufficiently idiosyncratic as to defy generalization or emulation.

Without disputing the truth of these observations, we can still recognize that steps can be taken beyond the specific context of personal meaning. For example, a person who is going to be sent abroad to live and work in a particular country needs sound education and training to become thoroughly familiar with the physical and cultural environment in which he or she will be living. This kind of detailed, specific cognitive preparation may go a long way toward helping a hostage make rational and realistic decisions about chances for escape, areas of personal vulnerability, and strengths of commitment in various dimensions. Most importantly, this kind of acquaintance can help diminish the sense of bewilderment and of dealing with the unknown that seems to have aggravated stress in a number of hostage experiences.

Reacting to the Terrorist Episode

FBI Special Agent Thomas Strentz (1986, 5) emphasizes that the most dramatic and dangerous phase of any hostage situation is the moment of abduction. At the moment of capture, victims must make an instant and correct decision regarding resistance. The potential dangerousness of resistance cannot be exaggerated. The abduction has been planned by the terrorists, who have undoubtedly tried to select the circumstances that most favor their enterprise. Thus, it may be assumed that they will have the advantage of surprise.

In addition, the terrorists will be tense and keyed to an emotional pitch for strenuous, even violent, physical action. They will be both physically and verbally abusive. Strentz warns the prospective hostage victim:

> If you try to escape, your action must be swift, fierce, and effective. Effective resistance or quick escape requires strength, knowledge of vulnerable parts of the body, a willingness to apply this strength to those parts, and the skill to succeed. Any half-hearted or ill-conceived defensive measures will only make a bad situation much worse, so do not undertake an escape unless you know you have the above qualities. (Strentz, 1986, 5)

For ordinary people lacking such qualities, the initial phase of the episode is traumatic. Because we are unable to adjust immediately to radical change, our minds use the automatic defense of denial; that is, we react by perceiving the situation as a dream or nightmare that isn't really happening.

Several studies on past hostage situations (Ford & Spaulding, 1973; Rahe, 1985; Richardson, 1985; Wesselius & DeSarno, 1983) have compared and contrasted the hostages who "survived" with those who "succumbed." These studies define survivors as those who were able to return to a meaningful existence with strong self-esteem and were able to go on living healthy and productive lives with little evidence of long-term depression, sleep disturbances, or serious stress-induced illnesses. They define those who succumbed as persons who either did not live through the ordeal or who, upon release or rescue, required extensive psychotherapy to deal with actual or imagined problems. Table 4–1 shows Strentz's (1986, 8) profile of the differences in psychological reactions between survivors and succumbers. Potential hostages are enjoined to: show subservience to their captors; cultivate faith in themselves and their government; contain their hostility toward their captors; adopt a superior attitude toward their circumstances; fantasize to fill the empty hours; rationalize the abduction (i.e., make the best of a difficult situation); keep to routines such as physical exercise; control their outward appearance and demeanor; strive to remain flexible and retain their sense of humor; and blend with their peers.

Table 4-1
Hostage Psychological Reactions

Survivors	Succumbers
Had Faith	Felt Abandoned
Contained Hostility	Acted Out Aggression
Maintained Superior Attitude	Pitied Self
Fantasized	Dwelled on Situation
Rationalized Situation	Despaired
Kept to Routines	Suspended Activities
Controlled Outward Appearance	Acted Out of Control
Sought Flexibility and Humor	Behaved Obsessive/Compulsive
Blended with Peers	Stood Out as Overcompliant or Resistant

SOURCE: Strentz, T. G. *A Hostage Psychological Survival Guide*. Paper presented at the International Society of Crime Prevention Practitioners, October 1-4, 1986, Portland, Oregon. Reproduced by permission of Special Agent Strentz.

Former hostages provide a pool of valuable experience in the planning and execution of primary prevention programs aimed at minimizing hostage-related disorders. Victims of analogous situations, such as POWs and victims of conventional violent crimes, can also contribute valuable insights into how people make the best of the worst. Ochberg and Soskis make the point that former hostages or captives should be cast in the role of advisers to experts, rather than considered experts themselves:

> This distinction is an important one, since the task of overall evaluation and planning requires that the experiences of individuals be integrated and the relevant aspects of each selected and blended into a coherent policy. Since former hostages are, correctly, highly invested in their own individual adaptations to their experiences, it is unfair to ask them to be too objective about what happened to them and how they dealt with it. (1982, 177)

One technique for improving coping skills and evaluating individual vulnerabilities is the use of simulations or "gaming" exercises. (Strentz [1986] refers to field training exercises or FTXs, which involve the training, taking, and holding of volunteer hostages for prolonged periods.) These have been used quite successfully to train hostage negotiators and may play a role in reducing the shock of an actual terrorist incident. It is important to make the exercises as realistic as possible so that potential hostages can experience at least some of the emotions they would have to deal with in an actual incident. Techniques such as evaluating escape possibilities, collecting data concerning captors, "humanization" of the hostage to captors, and the use of special communication devices or codes are mastered most effectively in a training program that combines study with practice.

Secondary Prevention

Once a terrorist incident has occurred, helping efforts must be directed toward reducing the harm it causes. The first phase of these efforts includes the attempt to resolve the situation itself as quickly as possible with minimum loss of life. Although concern for victims is a principal factor in planning intervention, many other political and situational factors influence decision makers. Options in this phase include assault, refusal to submit to demands, negotiation by governments, and the more traditional forms of hostage nego-tiation. We will deal with these procedures, which seek to resolve the incident as a whole, in Part Two. Our focus here is on measures directed specifically toward victims after the incident has been concluded.

Earlier, we mentioned analogies between victims of terrorism and rape victims. The organization of specialized helping services for rape victims may serve as a model for one approach to the same issue in terrorist incidents. Generally, these services do not attempt to replace traditional medical or legal systems, but rather to provide referral, advocacy, and often companionship to victims as they encounter the "helping" system. This particular structure can supply the kinds of specialized referral and counseling that would be nearly impossible to impart to the average medical or legal practitioner, especially regarding issues such as collecting evidence for later prosecution. In addition, staff members or volunteers in these services are frequently desensitized to the first phases of curiosity and fear with which many average people greet victims of rape or terrorism. Involving former victims adds another helpful element of peer support.

The availability of such specialized services either to victims or helping clinicians must be made known to the target groups. This raises the issue of how far such outreach should go—an issue of particular concern to a group that has been used and publicized as part of the actual victimization. It seems clear that helping services for victims should advertise, but not go knocking on doors. The right to privacy and to say "no" to helping services is particu-larly significant for former hostages and other victims of terrorism and justifies a less aggressive helping stance on both moral and clinical grounds.

Tertiary Prevention

Our knowledge of effective techniques in the tertiary prevention of disability resulting from terrorist victimization is still in an embryonic state. What we do know from studying analogous victimization situations, especially POWs and Nazi concentration camp victims, is that late effects and residual disability occur in a significant proportion of victims. Clinicians' experience in dealing with American hostages released from Iran supports a cautionary perspective. Although clinicians agreed that the amount of psychopathology observed was less than expected, there was concern over the possible negative effects that could have resulted from the highly publicized speculations about post-captivity disorders that were made as the hostages were being released. Helping efforts that are least likely to produce negative results may be those that support internal or subjective resolution of the event and its aftermath. Bard and Sangrey (1979) explored the process of attribution in victims of conventional crimes and the various pathways this process can take in both the victim and the victim's family. It may be safer and more prudent for former victims to make peace and reach closure and a sense of purpose about the event on an internal, cognitive basis.

Summary

The victim of terrorism holds a special place among victims of premeditated human violence. Victims represent the government that terrorists are challenging when they take hostages. One of the core functions of government is to provide basic security. When this function fails, as it does in a successful terrorist assault, a strong argument can be made that the government itself should assume responsibility for restitutive care. More than half the states currently have crime victim compensation laws, usually providing payments for lost work time and medical expenses. These programs function imperfectly, but they do function; and they may provide some models for planning services to victims of terrorism.

Professional studies of traumatic stress and its consequences in a variety of circumstances and situations help us understand the effects of terrorist victimization. From the experiences of those who have lived through modern combat, survived imprisonment in POW or concentration camps, or have been victims of criminal violence, we have learned a great deal that is potentially relevant to dealing more effectively with victims of terrorist assault.

Conceptual models based on traumatic events that can be related to terrorist victimization include grief, death imagery, encounters with terrible events, and the experience of forcible rape. The psychological isolation suffered by the rape victim offers an especially meaningful source of insights into the needs of the victim of terrorism.

People who have been seized and held as hostages for a prolonged period may develop unexpected positive feelings toward their captors, a phenomenon called the Stockholm Syndrome, based on an incident that occurred in Stockholm, Sweden, during a bank robbery in 1973. The Stockholm Syndrome seems to occur with sufficient frequency during kidnappings and hostage-takings that terrorist groups have begun to apply tactics to prevent it.

An extreme example of victim identification with the aggressor occurred in the case of Patricia Campbell Hearst, who was kidnapped and "converted" by members of the Symbionese Liberation Army, a small, pseudo-revolutionary band of former convicts and radical students. The truth of the conversion and its extent are only part of the mystery that still surrounds the Patty Hearst case.

Research on terrorist victimization faces formidable obstacles, including lack of funding support, fear of adverse reactions from subjects, and difficulties of access to victims. Despite these barriers, a few researchers have managed to conduct studies that have contributed significantly to our knowledge of the effects of terrorist victimization, especially among those who are forced to grow up in terror.

Coping strategies that people have used in traumatic incidents with varying degrees of success include keeping one's anxiety level within tolerable limits, maintaining self-esteem, and preserving relationships with fellow victims.

Key Terms

death imagery	field training exercises (FTXs)
grief	Patty Hearst
primary prevention	secondary prevention
Symbionese Liberation Army (SLA)	Stockholm Syndrome
tertiary prevention	traumatic stress

Questions for Discussion and Review

1. What can we learn from studying the normal process of grief or bereavement that might help us to gain insight into the plight of terrorist victims?
2. Why are the experiences of rape victims especially relevant to understanding the ordeal of terrorist victimization?
3. Briefly define the Stockholm Syndrome and evaluate its significance for analyzing terrorist/victim interactions. What major factor appear to promote its occurrence in a hostage situation?
4. Who was Patty Hearst? What occurred during the period she was involved with the Symbionese Liberation Army?
5. Indicate some of the obstacles that confront the researcher who wishes to systematically study terrorist victimization.
6. Cite some of the features that seem to distinguish between those who survive and those who succumb to terrorism. What advice would you give a family member or close friend who is taking a trip to a part of the world where terrorism is a real danger?
7. How should our society attempt to provide compensation for terrorist victims?

References

Bard, M., and Sangrey, D. *The Crime Victim's Book*. New York: Basic Books, 1979.

Caplan, G. *Principles of Preventive Psychiatry*. London: Tavistock Publications, 1964.

Caplan, G. "Mastery of Stress: Psychosocial Aspects." *American Journal of Psychiatry* 138 (1981): 413–420.

Fields, R. "Research on the Victims of Terrorism." In *Victims of Terrorism*, edited by F.M. Ochberg and D.A. Soskis, pp. 137–148. Boulder, CO: Westview Press, 1982.

Ford, C.V., and Spaulding, R.C. "The Pueblo Incident: A Comparison of Factors Related to Coping with Extreme Stress." *Archives of General Psychiatry* 28 (1973): 340–343.

Gross, J. "Full Circle: The New Life of Patty Hearst." *The Oregonian* (September 19, 1988): C1, C8.

Hacker, F.J. *Crusaders, Criminals, Crazies: Terror and Terrorism in Our Time*. New York: Norton, 1976.

Jenkins, B.M. *A Scenario for Simulation in Negotiating with Terrorists Holding Hostages*. Santa Monica, CA: Rand Corporation, 1979.

Laqueur, W. *The Age of Terrorism*. Boston: Little, Brown, 1987.

Laub, D. "The Traumatic Neurosis Revisited: Traumas Experienced During the Yom Kippur War by Children of Concentration Camp Survivors." Paper presented to the Association for Mental Health Affiliation with Israel, Eastern Pennsylvania Chapter, Elkins Park, Pennsylvania, May 20, 1979.

Lifton, R.J., Kato, S., and Reich, M.R. *Six Lives/Six Deaths: Portraits from Modern Japan*. New Haven, CT: Yale University Press, 1979.

Ochberg, F.M., and Soskis, D.A. "Planning for the Future: Means and Ends." In *Victims of Terrorism*, edited by F.M. Ochberg and D.A. Soskis, pp. 173–190. Boulder, CO: Westview Press, 1982.

Olin, W.R., and Born, D.G. "A Behavioral Approach to Hostage Situations." *FBI Law Enforcement Bulletin* 52 (1983): 18–24.

Rahe, R.H. "Coping with Captivity." Unpublished article, Uniform Services University of the Health Sciences, Bethesda, MD, 1985.

Richardson, L.D. "Surviving Captivity: A Hundred Days." In *Terrorism and Personal Protection*, edited by B.M. Jenkins, pp. 407–422. Stoneham, MA: Butterworth, 1985.

Soskis, D.A., and Ochberg, F.M. "Concepts of Terrorist Victimization." In *Victims of Terrorism*, edited by F.M. Ochberg and D.A. Soskis, pp. 105–135. Boulder, CO: Westview Press, 1982.

Strentz, T. "A Hostage Psychological Survival Guide." Paper presented at the International Society of Crime Prevention Practitioners, October 1–4, 1986, Portland, Oregon.

Wesselius, C.L., and DeSarno, J.V. "The Anatomy of a Hostage Situation." *Behavioral Science and the Law* 1 (1983): 33–45.

5

Terrorism and the Media

We want to shock people, everywhere.... It is our only way of communication
with the people.

Member of the Japanese United Red Army quoted in Gerard McKnight, *The Mind of the
Terrorist*, 1974, p. 168

In the past, when incidents of violence were reported by word of mouth, town
crier, correspondence, or newspapers, the impact of a given incident was
deadened by the sheer inertia of communications processes as they existed in
a primitive form. All of that has changed. Within hours or even minutes, the
seizure of an airplane with its passengers as hostages, the car bombing of a
crowded market, an attack on a government official—all are subjected to
immediate saturation by the broadcast media. The details are dished up for
consumption on the televised evening news.

The present economic and political alignment of democratic/liberal capitalist states, totalitarian/Marxist states, and the Third World provides unpar-
alleled opportunities for terrorists and terrorist movements to play one side
against the other for various advantages. Thus, a PLO "freedom fighter" can
claim and receive the cynical blessing of the Soviets for attacks against colonial
powers (e.g., the U.S. and Britain) and, at the same time, appeal to Islamic
fundamentalism, which is antithetical to the kind of society represented by
the USSR.

As noted in chapter 2, terrorist groups since the early anarchists have
realized the importance of the media to their goals. In the late 1880s, John Most
expressed the anarchist sentiment of "propaganda by the deed":

> We have said a hundred times or more that when modern revolutionaries
> carry out actions, what is important is not solely these actions themselves but also
> the propagandistic effect they are able to achieve. Hence we preach not only action
> in and for itself, but also action as propaganda. (Laqueur, 1978, 105)

Technological advances in communications, such as satellites, microwave
relays, and portable cameras and recorders, have made the media an even
more important weapon in the terrorist arsenal. The terrorist act is not meant
to be a battle that will win the war, but simply a method of getting the media
to publicize a group's objectives. Jenkins also observed this phenomenon:

> Terrorism is violence for effect—not primarily, and sometimes not at all for
> the physical effect on the actual target, but rather for its dramatic impact on an
> audience. Developments in world communciations, particularly the news media,

have expanded the potential audience to national and, more recently, to international proportions. (1978, 101)

Laqueur has claimed that "The media are the terrorist's best friend" (1976, 104). This position is surely an oversimplification. Schmid and De Graaf offer the more balanced appraisal that the media are unwitting allies of the terrorist. Both terrorists and the media have a common interest in reaching a large audience; both want attention, and it is on this basis that collaboration occurs.

Does media portrayal of violence produce more of the same? This is an easy question to pose, but extremely difficult to answer and fraught with controversy. Jenkins claims that "the news media are responsible for terrorism to about the same extent that commercial aviation is responsible for airline hijackings" (1978, 4). Schmid and De Graaf (1982), on the other hand, explore evidence of the contagion or imitation effects of media coverage as a potential direct cause of subsequent acts of terrorism.

It is already apparent that much of the voluminous literature dealing with mass media and terrorism is polemical, with adversaries confronting one another over various issues from well-polarized viewpoints and perspectives. One can expect public officials (including law enforcement executives, representatives of various agencies, and elected members of local, state, and federal government) to differ sharply with media representatives on nearly every specific issue. There are some interesting exceptions; for example, Patrick Murphy, a law enforcement official, who argues for a generally unrestricted press, and journalist and editor John O'Sullivan favors certain prohibitions on media coverage of terrorists and terrorism (Murphy, 1977; Koppel et al., 1986).

Inevitably, before discussions of terrorism and the mass media have gone very far, the question of censorship is raised. Terrorism, as Laqueur (1987) has observed, is almost entirely a problem for permissive democratic societies and ineffective authoritarian regimes; there is no future in challenging effective dictatorships. But this is precisely where we encounter the ineluctable dilemma of controls: there is an inherent contradiction in restricting a society's civil liberties in the interest or hope of preserving the liberal basis of that society.

We do not believe that a plausible argument can be made at present for imposing official controls (i.e., censorship) on media coverage of domestic terrorist events. On the other hand, case law decisions have placed constraints on unrestricted media coverage, despite well-intentioned and pious invocations of the public's "need to know" and real or imagined threats to First Amendment freedoms by some media representatives. It seems more than probable that the only kinds of controls we are likely to see on media coverage of international terrorist incidents are those that the media themselves impose in the form of voluntary "guidelines."

Presentation of the Event

A terrorist incident is obviously a newsworthy event and deserves media coverage. There is a constant risk, however, that instead of an objective presentation of the news, media representatives may be manipulated into merely presenting propaganda. Fitzpatrick points out the danger:

> The media must not be the dupes of the radical scriptwriters, nor should they be the mouthpiece of government. There is a mean. Law enforcement and the media cannot be locked in combat. Law enforcement has to realize the function of the media is to report the news, and hopefully, not alter it. The media must be cognizant of the very real danger of glorifying the terrorist. (1974, 23)

The Hanafi Muslim Siege

The media coverage of the Hanafi Muslim siege in Washington, DC, is a good example of how the media can be used to make a big story out of a relatively minor terrorist incident. On March 9, 1977, twelve members of a Muslim sect took 134 hostages. A reporter was shot, and other hostages were injured. Their leader, Hamaas Abdul Khaalis, wanted the murderers of his family handed over to him so that he could personally administer justice. He also demanded that a movie, *Mohammad, Messenger of God*, be banned from American movie screens because it was blasphemous. Television reporters began to broadcast live from the scene, and journalists tied up telephone lines by interviewing the terrorists. During the three days that the hostage situation lasted, NBC spent over 53 percent of its evening news time on the story, CBS spent over 31 percent, and ABC spent 40 percent (Schmid & De Graaf, 1982, 77). One reporter, seeing the police bringing food to the terrorists, broadcast that this was the preparation for an assault. The police were able to convince the Hanafis that the reporter was incorrect, and the situation was calmed (Miller, 1980, 87). In another instance, a reporter called Khaalis and suggested that the police were trying to trick him. The terrorist leader picked ten older hostages to execute, and the police withdrew some of their sharpshooters to put the Hanafis at ease (Schmid & De Graaf, 1982, 77).

A great deal of criticism was directed toward the media because of the intensity of their reporting and their interference with the hostage negotiation process. One of the hostages, a reporter, made the following observation:

> As hostages, many of us felt that the Hanafi takeover was a happening, a guerrilla theater, a high impact propaganda exercise programmed for the TV screen, and secondarily for the front pages of newspapers around the world. . . . Beneath the resentment and the anger of my fellow hostages toward the press is a conviction gained. . . that the news media and terrorism feed on each other, that the news media and particularly TV, create a thirst for fame and recognition. Reporters do not simply report the news. They help create it. They are not objective observers, but subjective participants—actors, scriptwriters and idea men. (Schmid & De Graaf, 1982, 42)

TWA Flight 847

The hijacking of TWA Flight 847 in June 1985 by Shiite terrorists is another extremely disturbing example of how media representatives may cross the line from *portrayal* into *advocacy* when covering acts of terrorist violence. Beginning with the exclusive focus of the networks on only one of the terrorists' demands—the release of more than 700 Lebanese detainees in Israel—to the total exclusion of all others, and culminating in the depiction of Amal chief Nabih Berri as a moderate negotiator and impartial go-between striving to save the lives of both the American hostages in Beirut and the Arab "hostages" in Israel, media involvement was intensive, detailed, and thoroughly distorted in its partisan interpretations of the meaning of events for the American television public.

The hijackers had begun by making a number of demands that included (in addition to the release of the more than 700 Lebanese held by the Israelis): the release of seventeen Shiite prisoners held in Kuwait; the release of prisoners held in Greece; the release of two Shiite terrorists held by the Spanish; the overthrow of King Hussein of Jordan and Mubarak of Egypt; an end to American aid to Israel; and the reversal of American policies in the Middle East, that is, a switch in support from Israel to support for the Arab states.

When it became apparent to the hijackers that the television networks were interested only in the quid pro quo transaction of swapping 700 Lebanese for thirty-nine Americans, excluding American Navy diver Robert Dean Stethem, who was brutally murdered by the Shiite terrorists, the hijackers dropped the other demands. Said Israeli journalist Bar-Illan:

> So the familiar scene was set: on one side persecuted Arabs, "understandably enraged" by horrible injustices, making "reasonable demands"... and on the other side, intransigent Israelis cold-bloodedly disregarding the fate of innocent people. ... Over and over again, television commentators, anchormen, and reporters, alternating hints with accusations, and assuming the roles of negotiators, arbiters, and moralizers, portrayed Israel as an ungrateful ally which had freed 1,150 convicted murderers in return for three Israeli soldiers, but would not free over 700 innocent Lebanese ("not charged with any crime") to save the lives of 39 American tourists. (1986, 111)

Throughout the seventeen-day ordeal, the media uncritically adopted the Shiite interpretations of events. The TWA plane had been hijacked by men desperate to free their "relatives" held captive in Israel, thus creating a parallel with the families of the American hostages. Allyn Conwell, who became the spokesman for the hostages, said: "If my wife and children were abducted and taken illegally across the border, I guess I, too, would have resorted to anything at all to free them."

As Bar-Illan observes, there were no "wives and children" in Israeli custody—only young men of military age, a piece of information that should have been known to even the most ignorant reporter in Lebanon. This is the kind of "moral symmetry" all too similar to that invoked by the media in speaking of the U.S. and the Soviet Union: the Soviets invaded Afghanistan, we invaded Grenada; the Red Air Force shot down KAL Flight 007, we shot down a civilian aircraft from Iran in the Persian Gulf.

In addition to the correspondents on the scene, anchormen and talk-show hosts in the U.S. provided nearly unlimited coverage of the hijackers and their apologists. When asked why they had been given so much air-time, the answer was that the American population needed the education and that it was only fair to give the hijackers an opportunity to present their point of view. On July 10, New York Times columnist Tom Wicker wrote: "Was television 'used' by Amal? Of course, just as it is being used all the time by the Reagan administration for its own purposes."

Here, said Bar-Illan, we have ultimate evenhandedness: a "godfather" of cutthroats, kidnappers, and assassins linked with the democratically elected President of the U.S. Given the kind of philosophical orientation and political ideology that supports and makes possible this kind of "moral symmetry," it is not difficult to account for the smugness, complacency, and self-adulation that characterized a posthijacking program on "Nightline," on which all the senior ABC correspondents in Beirut agreed that they had advanced the cause of peace and justice in the Middle East by exposing the defects of American policy! Barbara Rosen, the wife of a man who had been held hostage, told of the education she received in how the news is produced at CBS. She draws a sharp picture of the ways technological expertise is employed in creating the image of the anchorperson as omniscient.

> I never asked to become an "expert" on television and terrorism, but I did, the way anyone who undergoes a unique experience is an "expert." I was a teacher, wife, and mother when my husband was taken hostage in Iran in 1979, and because I was living in Brooklyn—about 12 miles from the networks' corporate headquarters—I got a lot of coverage. It was an education. Here is some of what I learned.
>
> On "Nightline" the guests sat in separate studios with their microphones turned off. They are summoned by Ted Koppel to appear on his monitor and to answer questions at his beck and call. Guests are at times unable to comment on or refute certain misstatements of fact because there is no dialogue. The audience gets the information and perspective on the news that Ted Koppel and ABC News decide to show.
>
> On the day the hostages returned from Iran, CBS asked me to join Dan Rather in the studio. At one point I remarked that while we were happy for the hostages, we should also remember the eight who gave their lives in the aborted rescue attempt. Mr. Rather did not recall their names. However, since the camera was on me, he turned to an assistant off camera and mouthed the words "get me their names." In less than a minute the eight names appeared on a monitor. Mr. Rather continued, "Let us not forget. . .," and he not only named each man but also included his branch of service and rank. I was shocked. I realized how all these years anchormen had impressed me as tremendously knowing; I never considered how the aura of savant is created.
>
> I have nothing against the technology that made the exchange possible, but I felt like Dorothy exposing the Wizard of Oz. It wasn't honest and the public has the right to know how the magic happens. If the audience does not understand the process, then news organizations exercise control and power without the audience's knowledge.
>
> One day during the crisis, I accompanied a local TV newsman on a story—a scandal of faulty Grumman buses acquired by New York City. He and his camera

crew gathered their film—interviews and shots of buses—then returned to the studio to record his voice-over. His producer selected the film and coordinated it with the audio. I was appalled at the speed at which the pictures changed. With my educational background, I observed that people are unable to filter both visual and audio information at that rate. My host said that television, being a visual medium, is intended to report through pictures and that the audience needed and wanted that rapidly paced visual stimulation. But I said that no one can remember the story. Finally, I understood why I could never remember what I saw on TV. Unlike reading, it does not let the viewer reflect, reread, underline, and develop comprehension. I said I thought that there should be a balance between the visual and the auditory, a balance that furthers understanding rather than confusion.

I learned how editing and splicing can destroy an interview. I learned how, if you are interviewed and do not want your face and words used their way, request that that interview be live. I found it most interesting (amusing?) that after the hijacking of TWA 847, the networks were self-critical about televising the messy "press conference" at the Beirut airport when, oddly, that was perhaps television at its best: showing the emotions of all those involved, including for once those of the reporters—live, spontaneous, real, unrehearsed moments in the whole sorry affair, un-stage-managed by the kidnappers and their allies at "Amal Broadcasting Co.," "Nabih Berry Co.," and others.

Television journalists see "stories" as dramas. Being employees of a medium whose prime time products are soap operas, sitcoms and cop shows, reporters focus on the feelings of the hostages and their families. To the medium, it's all emotion, which must be restructured as entertainment. Thus, the journalists' embarrassment of seeing themselves as they usually show others.

The criticism of journalistic ethics and behavior is important, but no more so than the issue of quality and content in reporting. TV anchormen and journalists are expected by the networks to be generalists. They have little expertise in the areas they are expected to cover—the Middle East, Africa, and elsewhere. They flit around from country to country, like gossips at a cocktail party. Wouldn't the quality of their reportage improve if they stayed put in one area learning the language, customs, and history?

Worse, they all seem afflicted by historical amnesia (possibly induced by staring at their ever-changing monitors). They want to know who the hijackers are and what they want over and over again. They want to know how it feels ad nauseam. Without an understanding of the area's history, and political and social fabric, reporters consistently fail in reporting the whole story.

The comparison between the Israeli prisoners and the hostages in Beirut was wrong—factually, as well as morally. Presenting Lebanese families in juxtaposition to American families only served to cloud and confuse the primary issue—the hijacking, murder and terrorism of American citizens.

Have television journalists forgotten they are Americans? Everyone knew that terrorists want publicity for their cause, yet no less do they want to inflate their personal status in their communities. They don't care that they look like barbarians to us when among their friends they are heroes. Therefore, each time the media afford terrorists the right to speak, they award them a victory. Giving in to violent extremists who engage in the most deviant behavior reduces the ability of moderates to pursue other, more acceptable avenues to reach their goals. If the U.S. would like to promote democracy and human rights, then those individuals or groups who wantonly suppress the rights and liberties of others through terrorism should not be afforded the public airways to advance their own "careers."

I respectfully request the networks to rethink what they are doing. (Barbara Rosen, *Wall Street Journal*, September 12, 1985)

The Iranian Hostage Crisis

The seizure of U.S. Embassy personnel in Tehran on November 4, 1979, by young Iranian militants and the ensuing efforts to secure their release provide a textbook illustration of what Friedlander calls the "incestuous relationship" between terrorism and the media (1982, 50). The author denies that the media were unaware of "their operative role in the terror syndrome" and offers an insightful analysis of how the media coverage of the hostage ordeal was generally characterized by a flouting of most of the codes promulgated by the media themselves for dealing with terrorism.

In the hostage drama that was played out in Iran, the terrorists used a gimmick that is hoary with tradition in law enforcement circles: the "hard cop/soft cop" routine in which the accused is placed off balance by the differences between the hard cop, who wants to throw the book at him, versus the soft cop, who wants to make things easier for the accused. Thus, in Iran, it was Bani-Sadr and Ghotbzadeh (good guys) against the Ayatollah Khomeini and the "militants," or terrorists (bad guys).

Bar-Illan (1986, 115–116) notes that a few of the hostages were astute enough to recognize what the journalists ignored: namely, that all the various groups involved had been in cahoots and that there were no differences among them.

Media-Induced Contagion of Terrorist Violence

One of the longest-running controversies among social scientists, nearly ranking in longevity with the nature-nurture controversy or the deterrence effects of capital punishment, is the effect of media presentations on aggressive or violent behavior. If one were to include the arguments pro and con about the consumption of pornography (i.e., the effects of literary or graphic presentations of sexually provocative material on sexual behavior), the controversy could be viewed as preceding the advent of movies and television. But it is primarily with the broadcast media, especially television, that most researchers have been concerned.

Modeling and Aggressive Behavior

We are obviously affected by what we see others do; by observing others, one may form ideas of how to perform various acts, including aggressive and violent acts. Bandura points out that one can learn general strategies that provide guides for action beyond those associated with a particular model.

The observer must be able to pick out the essentials of a model's behavior and remember them:

> When an observer witnesses a model exhibit a sequence of responses the observer acquires, through contiguous association of the sensory events, perceptual and symbolic responses possessing cue properties that are capable of eliciting, at some time after a demonstration, overt responses corresponding to those that had been modeled. (1971, 14)

In the most widely publicized phase of Bandura's work, groups of children were exposed to adult models who either exhibited aggressive or nonaggressive behavior toward a large Bobo doll. The children were then subjected to a mildly frustrating experience, then a record was made of their actions. Children who had been exposed to the aggressive model showed a greater number of imitative aggressive responses than did the children who were exposed to the nonaggressive model. These same results occurred when children were exposed to the aggressive and nonaggressive models by means of television. In view of the amount of time the average American child spends in front of the television set, the implications of these experimental findings were quickly recognized.

Protests by concerned parents and educators prompted a series of Congressional hearings, in which representatives of NBC, ABC, and CBS gave conflicting testimony regarding the effects of television on behavior in general and in particular. The network executives, under sharp questioning by legislators, appeared to be agreeing to diametrically opposite propositions: "Yes, television affects people in a variety of ways, including their purchasing habits, appetites, product preferences, and brand-name recognition; no, television does not influence people to emulate aggressive or violent behavior portrayed on televised programs." Said Schmid and De Graaf,

> A strange kind of schizophrenia seems to affect television producers. On the one hand, they suggest to the sponsors of advertisements that television has massive effects, that the public copies consuming behavior suggested in alluring commercials. On the other hand, they tend to discard the possibility that the public learns the lessons of television violence which they use to attract large audiences. (1982, 121)

There is overwhelming anecdotal evidence that various types of media portrayals are immediately followed by "copycat" commission of the events portrayed. When a television crime show depicted the sadistic murder of a skid-row derelict by several young thugs who drenched the victim with gasoline and set him afire, the grisly act was emulated by youths in areas as widely separated as Boston and Los Angeles. Heller and Polsky (1971) found that sixty-three of the one hundred institutionalized delinquents they examined reported having imitated characters they had seen on television; twenty-two said they had tried criminal techniques they had seen on television; another twenty-two stated that they had contemplated committing crimes they had seen on television.

Schmid and De Graaf reviewed twenty-six parachute hijackings and concluded that the media "must have played a decisive role" in fostering copycat emulations: "Had the media not reported the detail about the parachutes, most of these imitations would not in all likelihood have taken place" (1982, 136).

Media and Terrorism Motivation

Although researchers agree that the media might encourage violence by providing models of violent behavior and even specific know-how necessary for committing particular acts of violence, there tends to be less agreement on whether the media can provide the motivation for commission of violent acts. Schmid and De Graaf suggest six ways in which the media can motivate potential terrorists.

1. The mass media extend experience, present models, stimulate aspirations, and indicate goals.
2. The media-fostered overestimation of great personalities has given rise to the star cult, which implies that history can be changed by the elimination of "big people"—that is, political assassination.
3. Akin to the above, visibility provided by the mass media has created a new category of people—the celebrities, people who are known to be known.
4. The media can motivate terrorists by inciting them, wittingly or unwittingly, to a terroristic deed.
5. There is a "built-in escalation imperative" that requires that terrorists must commit more and more bizarre and cruel acts to gain media attention.
6. The high news value that violence has in the Western media is, for some people, motivation enough to engage in the kind of violence to which the media are highly responsive. (1982, 137—142)

With regard to the last item, which the authors consider the most important, Schmid and De Graaf emphasize the competitive pressures that drive journalists to report such news and note that "there is something paradoxical and perverse in this relationship."

The First Amendment and Media Access

Do the media have a privileged right under the First Amendment to unrestricted access to news? Will restrictions on a journalist's access to information cut off the search for truth or its expression and consequently create a despotic state? Is unrestricted access so intrinsic to the process of democratic government that there can be no restrictions on the gathering of information?

Miller (1982) reviewed a series of case law decisions (*Environmental Protection Agency v. Mink*, 1974; *Zurcher v. Stanford Daily*, 1978; *Branzburg v. Hayes et al.*, 1972; *Pell v. Procunier*, 1974; *Saxbe v. Washington Post*, 1974; *Houchins v. KQED Inc.*, 1978; *KQED, Inc. v. Houchins*, 1976) that indicate that the U.S. Supreme Court during Burger's tenure as Chief Justice did not regard the media right to access as superior to that of the general public. In *Pell*, the Court noted specifically that when the public is excluded from the scene of a crime or disaster, the media may also be excluded.

In *EPA v. Mink*, the Supreme Court ruled that the stamp of "classified" on a government file exempted everything in that file from disclosure. Even a U.S. District Court in closed chambers was not permitted to study classified documents for the purpose of extracting nonsecret information from them. A Congressional amendment to the Freedom of Information Act (Section 552, Title 5, U.S. Code) was necessary to override the *Mink* decision to permit the district courts to penetrate the exclusionary executive branch classification to ascertain whether documents are properly classified.

The Court has refused to give the media special status or accord them immunities from warrants. In *Zurcher v. Stanford Daily*, the Supreme Court rejected the notion that searches of newspaper offices for purposes of seeking criminal evidence based on probable cause will jeopardize the ability of the press to perform its functions of gathering, analyzing, and disseminating news.

Miller observes that the Burger Court's rulings also imply that access to the perimeter between the tactical squad and the public—the kind often established by the police in hostage-taking and siege situations for the purposes of allowing media access—is not a First Amendment right, but a privilege granted at the discretion of the law enforcement agency.

> Access to the site where news is being made cannot be claimed by the press if the general public is also being excluded. Press access, largely a privilege under the most sanguine circumstances, can be revoked, and where the situation is fraught with imminent danger of people being injured or killed, the media's claim to special access rings especially hollow. (Miller, 1982, 43)

The present, and likely future, composition of the U.S. Supreme Court makes it difficult to imagine the Court's moving to a more liberal position.

Censorship v. Guidelines: Curbing Media Excesses

Complaints about media excesses inevitably raise the issue of censorship. Whereas the concept of a free press is held in high esteem in the U.S., the same is not the case in many other countries. Terrorism has led to government censorship of the media in some countries, such as Uruguay and Argentina (Schmid & De Graaf, 1982; Timmerman, 1981).

We even find censorship of the media in some of the Western democracies. The Irish state broadcasting authority in the Republic of Ireland censors interviews with members of the Ulster Defence Association, the IRA, and the Provisional Sinn Fein. Conor Cruise O'Brien has stated that "We in the Irish state regard the appearance of terrorists on television as an incitement to murder." In Great Britain, the Home Secretary was able to pressure the BBC into banning the documentary "Real Lives: At the Edge of the Union," which was an accurate portrayal of Northern Ireland extremism (Wilkinson, 1986). Schmid and De Graaf summarize arguments for and against censorship of terrorist news reporting in Table 5–1. They warn that the list offers nothing more or less than a series of plausible hypotheses whose validity is unproven. They add that even if the validity of some of them could be established, they would not be automatically valid in all places at all times.

Table 5.1
Arguments for a Censorship Debate

Arguments for Censorship	Arguments against Censorship
1. Insurgent terrorists use the media as a platform for political propaganda which also helps them to recruit new members to their movement	1. If the media would keep quiet on terrorist atrocities, the violent men might be judged less negatively by sections of the public
2. Since publicity is a major, and in some cases the unique reward sought by terrorists, censorship would make terrorism a less desirable strategy	2. With psychotic terrorists publicity can be a substitute for violence. Without media attention their threats might be translated into acts
3. Detailed coverage of incidents by the media provides potential terrorists with a model that increases their success chance in their own acts	3. Political terrorists boycotted by the media might step up their level of violence until the media have to cover their deeds
4. Information broadcast during incidents can be useful to terrorists	4. If the media did not report on terrorism, rumors would spread, which might be worse than the worst media reporting
5. Media presence during acts of hostage-taking can endanger hostages	5. During siege situations, media presence can prevent the police from engaging in indefensible tactics, causing unnecessary loss of lives among hostages and terrorists
6. Reporting on acts of terrorism can produce imitative acts	6. If terrorism would be treated with silence, governments could label all sort of quasi- or non-terroristic activities by political dissenters terroristic; uncontrolled government actions might be the result

(continued)

Table 5-1 (continued)

Arguments for Censorship	Arguments against Censorship
7. In cases of kidnappings, media reports can cause panic with the kidnapper so that he kills the victim	7. If the media would censor terrorism the public would suspect that other things are censored as well; credibility in the media will decline
8. People who have so little respect for other people's lives as terrorists do, should not be enabled to command public attention only because they use violence	8. Suppression of news on terrorism might leave the public with a false sense of security. People would be unporepared to deal with terrorism when directly faced with it
9. Sadism in the public might be activated by reporting terrorist acts	9. The lack of public awareness of certain terroristic activities would keep the public from fully understanding the political situation.
10. Media reports on terrorist outrages might lead to vigilantism and uncontrolled revenge acts against the group the terrorists claim to speak for	10. The feeling of being deprived of vital information might create a public distrust in the political authorities
11. Negative news demoralizes the public while "good news makes us good"	11. The assertion of insurgent terrorists that democratic states are not really free would gain added credibility if the freedom of the press were suspended

SOURCE: A.P. Schmid, & J. De Graaf, *Violence as Communication*. Newbury Park, CA: Sage, 1982, p. 172. Reproduced by permission of the authors and publisher.

An alternative to censorship is self-imposed "guidelines," which are usually the product of deliberations by media representatives themselves. An exception is the study and guidelines reported in the National Advisory Committee on Criminal Justice Standards and Goals *Report of the Task Force on Disorders and Terrorism* (1977). These guidelines are reproduced below.

Table 5-2
Standard 10.8   News Media Self-Regulation in Contemporaneous Coverage of Terrorism and Disorder

When an incident involving a confrontation between law enforcement officers and participants in mass disorder, terrorism, or quasi-terrorism is in progress, the role of the news media is an important and controversial one. The manner in which information about the incident is collected, and the form of its presentation to the public, will necessarily affect the conduct of the agencies and persons involved. In addition, these factors will be critical influences on the growth or spread, if any, of the incident. Finally, the approach taken by the media to news gathering and reporting on an incident-by-incident basis will have an important cumulative effect on public attitudes toward the phenomenon of extraordinary violence, the groups and persons who participate in it, and the official measures taken against it.   *(continued)*

Table 5-2 (continued)

No hard rules can be prescribed to govern media performance during incidents of extraordinary violence. Whatever principles are adopted must be generated by the media themselves, out of a recognition of special public responsibility. But in general, the essence of an appropriate approach to news gathering is summarized in the principle of minimum intrusiveness: Representatives of the media should avoid creating any obvious media presence at an incident scene that is greater than that required to collect full, accurate, and balanced information on the actions of participants and the official response to them. Similarly, the essence of an appropriate approach to contemporaneous reporting of extraordinary violence lies in the principle of complete, noninflammatory coverage; the public is best served by reporting that omits no important detail and that attempts to place all details in context.

Putting these general principles into practice, however, requires hard choices for the media, both at the organizational policy level and by the working reporter. In particular:

1. News media organizations and representatives wishing to adopt the principle of minimum intrusiveness in their gathering of news relating to incidents of extraordinary violence should consider the following devices, among others:
   a. Use of pool reporters to cover activities at incident scenes or within police lines;
   b. Self-imposed limitations on the use of high-intensity television lighting, obtrusive camera equipment, and other special news-gathering technologies at incident scenes;
   c. Limitations on media solicitation of interviews with barricaded or hostage-holding suspects and other incident participants;
   d. Primary reliance on officially designated spokesmen as sources of information concerning law enforcement operations and plans; and
   e. Avoidance of inquiries designed to yield tactical information that would prejudice law enforcement operations if subsequently disclosed.
2. News media organizations and representatives wishing to follow the principle of complete, noninflammatory coverage in contemporaneous reporting of incidents of extraordinary violence should consider the following devices, among others:
   a. Delayed reporting of details believed to have a potential for inflammation or aggravation of an incident that significantly outweighs their interest to the general public;
   b. Delayed disclosure of information relating to incident location, when that information is not likely to become public knowledge otherwise and when the potential for incident growth or spread is obviously high;
   c. Delayed disclosure of information concerning official tactical planning that, if known to incident participants, would seriously compromise law enforcement efforts;
   d. Balancing of reports incorporating self-serving statements by incident participants with contrasting information from official sources and with data reflecting the risks that the incident has created to noninvolved persons;

(continued)

Table 5-2 (continued)

e. Systematic predisclosure verification of all information concerning incident-related injuries, deaths, and property destruction.

f. Avoidance, to the extent possible, of coverage that tends to emphasize the spectacular qualities of an incident or the presence of spectators at an incident scene.

SOURCE: The National Advisory Commission on Criminal Justice Standards and Goals, *Disorders and Terrorism: Report of the National Task Force on Disorders and Terrorism*. Washington, DC: U.S. Department of Justice, 1976, pp. 387–388. Reproduced by permission of the U.S. Department of Justice.

The National News Council "Paper on Terrorism" lists six recommendations of a Maryland psychologist who works with the police:

1. Do not name the individual (terrorist); naming gives credit and strengthens what he/she is doing. Do not print the methods; this prevents imitation. Do not print anything the terrorists say. This takes away from what they want to accomplish.
2. If media coverage is part of the demands, it should be done in as limited a manner as possible with as few people involved as possible. Take care not to be manipulated.
3. The act itself should be shown as a despicable act by losers.
4. The point should be made that no hostage situation has been successful.
5. No direct calls should be made to the terrorists: that draws out the process.
6. Continuing on-site coverage should not be used: it gives away intelligence to the terrorists. (Miller, 1982)

The fourth item is patently false; the Iran terrorists' seizure of the U.S. Embassy personnel is difficult to see as anything other than a smashing success for the terrorists and a major diplomatic defeat for the U.S. Authorities might approve the first item, but it would reduce the news to meaningless babble for the average reader or television viewer.

The internal guidelines developed by some members of the media have not put an end to complaints that the media spend too much time, space, and effort sensationalizing terrorism. A Gallup survey conducted for the Times Mirror Company found that the media's credibility and public image have suffered because of the heavy coverage of the Iran-Contra story (cited in Aeppel, 1987, A7).

Sullivan made an interesting distinction between terrorist coverage by the popular press and by what he called the "quality" press. O'Sullivan illustrated the difference between the reporting of a terrorist incident (an IRA bombing involving an innocent victim) by a popular newspaper like the *New York Post* and a quality newspaper like the *New York Times*:

> *Popular newspaper:* "A shy 21-year-old girl, whose only interest in life is tennis, is fighting for her life in a London hospital after being blown up in a restaurant by

an IRA bomb. By her bedside was her fiance, Gordon Williamson, 23. 'She didn't have an enemy in the world,' he said."

Quality newspaper: "Two people were killed and one injured in an IRA explosion last night in London. Government sources interpreted the explosion as a response to the government's decision to introduce a bill increasing parliamentary representation for Ulster. Sources in Belfast believed to be close to the IRA said that the attack was the start of a major campaign in which targets on the British mainland would not be exempt." (Koppel et al., 1986, 103)

The assumption of the popular press, according to O'Sullivan, is that terrorists are important for what they *do*, whereas the quality press assumes that terrorists are important for what they *say*. He suggests that the first assumption is much more sensible.

One of the Koppel panelists, Lord Alan Chalfont, a former minister in the British Foreign Office, responded by noting the tendency of the quality press— and we would argue for including under this category the major television network commentators—to adopt a position of magisterial objectivity between our society and those attacking it. This leads to the subtle excuse of certain terrorist acts by implying that they arise out of intolerable social conditions or oppression—thus, the media tendency to equate the actions of legitimate governments in fighting terrorists with the actions of the terrorists themselves. "Can we not," Chalfont asks, "simply accept the fact that we are at war with international terrorism, that there are two sides, ours and theirs? If their side prevails, our freedoms will disappear, and the first freedom to go will be freedom of the press."

Summary

Progress in communications technology has greatly increased the importance of the media for terrorists. Whether the media are the terrorist's "best friend" or "unwitting ally" is a matter for debate, but there is little doubt that many, if not most, terrorist incidents are committed with a view to their dramatic impact on a target audience.

A number of incidents—the Hanafi Muslim siege, the hijacking of TWA Flight 847, the Iran hostage crisis—have demonstrated how easily media representatives may cross the line from portrayer of terrorism events to advocate for the terrorists.

One area of sharpest controversy in media/terrorism relations is the extent to which coverage of terrorist incidents such as skyjackings produces "copycat" emulations. Research on the effects of televised violence on the behavior of child viewers indicates that aggressive behavior can be learned (modeled); anecdotal evidence also suggests that violent behavior depicted on television can lead to emulation by delinquent youths.

Another controversial topic is the unrestricted access of media representatives to coverage of terrorist incidents. The U.S. Supreme Court under Chief

Justice Burger refused to assign special status to the media and chose to view media access as a privilege granted at the discretion of law enforcement authorities rather than a right guaranteed under the First Amendment. Still another area of controversy involves imposition of government censorship on media coverage of terrorist incidents. Terrorist news reporting is censored in a number of countries, including the Irish Republic and the United Kingdom.

Government imposition of censorship restrictions in the U.S. on media coverage of terrorist events is remote enough to verge upon the improbable. On the other hand, guidelines of some kind seem desirable; the question is who should formulate such guidelines.

> If the media do it themselves, they might be too self-serving, steering in the direction that they still want to use the exciting news terrorists provide without allowing themselves to be used by the terrorists. If the government establishes such guidelines they will tend to serve the government first and this might be even more harmful. (Schmid & De Graaf, 1982, 174)

Schmid and De Graaf propose, as a possible alternative, a council with members drawn from both the government and the media to formulate joint guidelines in matters of media coverage of terrorism.

There is no greater challenge in the struggle against terrorism, as Edward Lynch (1987) has stated, than finding a policy that is compatible with the long tradition in America of a free and vigorous press. We are accustomed to electing bodies of legislators that make laws by which we govern ourselves. Schmid and De Graaf ask whether we should not, in this Age of Communication, also elect a media council to decide issues affecting the coverage of terrorism. If some news on terrorist incidents has to be censored, perhaps it is best done by such a publicly elected body.

Key Terms

advocacy v. portrayal	censorship
"copycat" emulations	First Amendment
guidelines	Hanafi Muslim siege
"hard cop/soft cop" routine	Hamaas Abdul Khaalis
media access	media-induced contagion
modeling	TWA Flight 847

Questions for Discussion and Review

1. Are the communications media more fairly described as the terrorist's "best friends" or "unwitting allies"?
2. What occurred during the Hanafi Muslim siege in Washington, DC, that made it so important in the study of media coverage of terrorist incidents?
3. Discuss the hijacking of TWA Flight 847 and how it was handled by the media, especially by television.

4. How did Mrs. Barbara Rosen, wife of a hostage taken in the Embassy seizure in Iran, become an "expert" on television and terrorism? What did she learn?
5. What is the consensus of research findings regarding the effects of television violence on aggressive behavior?
6. Identify some of the ways, according to Schmid and De Graaf, that the media may motivate potential terrorists?
7. Is media access to terrorism a privilege or a right guaranteed by the First Amendment?
8. Summarize the pros and cons of imposing censorship on media coverage of terrorist incidents.

References

Aeppel, T. "News Media Hit from All Sides for Iran-Contra Affair Stories." *The Oregonian* (January 25, 1987): A7.

Bandura, A. *Psychological Modeling: Conflicting Theories.* Chicago: Aldine-Atherton, 1971.

Bar-Illan, D. "Israel, the Hostages, and the Networks." In *Terrorism,* edited by S. Anzovin, pp. 108–120. New York: Wilson, 1986.

Bell, J.B. *A Time of Terror: How Democratic Societies Respond to Revolutionary Violence.* New York: Basic Books, 1978.

"Die Hatten Alles Metzeln Konnen." *Der Spiegel,* 34 (August 29, 1988): 16–31.

Fitzpatrick, T.K. "The Semantics of Terror," *Security Register* 1, no. 14 (November 4, 1974): 21–23.

Friedlander, R.A. "Iran: The Hostage Seizure, the Media, and International Law." In *Terrorism, the Media and the Law,* edited by A.H. Miller, pp. 13–50. Dobbs Ferry, NY: Transnational Publishers, 1982.

Heller, M.S. and Polsky, S. "Television Violence—Guidelines for Evaluation." *Archives of General Psychiatry* 24, 3 (1971): 279–285.

Jenkins, B.M. "High Technology Terrorism and Surrogate War: The Impact of New Technology on Low-Level Violence." In *Contemporary Terrorism: Selected Readings,* edited by J.D. Elliott and L.K. Gibson, pp. 99–116. Gaithersburg, MD: International Association of Chiefs of Police, 1978.

Koppel, T., Podhoretz, N., Krauthammer, C., Besancon, A., O'Sullivan, J., Schorr, D., Will, G., and Woodward, B. "Terrorism and the Media: A Discussion." In *Terrorism,* edited by S. Anzovin, pp. 96–108. New York: Wilson, 1986.

Laqueur, W. "The Futility of Terrorism." *Harpers* 252, no. 1510 (March 1976): 99–105.

Laqueur, W. *The Terrorism Reader: A Historical Anthology.* New York: New American Library, 1978.

Livingstone, W.D. "Terrorism and the Media Revolution." In *Fighting Back: Winning the War Against Terrorism,* edited by N.C. Livingstone and T.E. Arnold, pp. 213–227. Lexington, MA: D.C. Heath, 1986.

McKnight, G. *The Mind of the Terrorist.* London: Michael Joseph, 1974.

Miller, A.H. *Terrorism and Hostage Negotiations.* Boulder, CO: Westview Press, 1980.

Miller, A.H. "Terrorism, the Media, and the Law: A Discussion of the Issues." In *Terrorism, the Media and the Law,* edited by A.H. Miller, pp. 13–50. Dobbs Ferry, NY: Transnational Publishers, 1982.

Murphy, P.V. "The Police Perspective." In *The Media and Terrorism,* pp. 10–12. Chicago: Field Enterprises, 1977.

National Advisory Committee on Criminal Justice Standards and Goals. *Report of the Task Force on Disorders and Terrorism.* Washington, DC: U.S. Government Printing Office, 1977.

Schmid, A.P., and De Graaf, J. *Violence as Communication: Insurgent Terrorism and the Western News Media.* Beverly Hills, CA: Sage Publications, 1982.

Timmerman, J. *Prisoner Without a Name, Cell Without a Number.* New York: Knopf, 1981.

Wilkinson, P. *Terrorism and the Liberal State.* New York: New York University Press, 1986.

Case Law Citations

Branzburg v. *Hayes et al,* 408 U.S. 605 (1972).

Environmental Protection Agency v. *Mink,* 410 U.S. 73 (1973).

Houchins v. *KQED, Inc.,* 438 U.S. 1 (1978).

KQED, Inc. v. *Houchins,* 546 F.2d 284, 9th Circuit (1976).

Pell v. *Procunier,* 417 U.S. 817 (1974).

Saxbe v. *Washington Post,* 417 U.S. 843 (1974).

Zurcher v. *Stanford Daily,* 436 U.S. 547 (1978).

6
Women and Terrorism

When a colleague learned that we planned to include a chapter on women in terrorism in this book, she asked why we considered it necessary to devote separate coverage to this topic. Her question deserves and requires a comprehensive answer, and this chapter represents our somewhat extended reply.

One reason is the emergence of women as full-fledged members and leaders of terrorist groups. The March 11, 1978, raid by PLO terrorists on Israel that left more than thirty dead and seventy injured was unusual for that period because it was carried out by an eleven-member team that included two women and was commanded by a young Palestinian woman, Dalal Mughrabi, who was subsequently killed in the fighting. Once relegated to support roles, such as collecting intelligence and smuggling arms, women have acquired increasing prominence in the highest councils of terrorist movements and organizations.

Whereas women, with some notable exceptions, have usually been excluded from top leadership positions and still constitute a minority of the membership of most terrorist organizations, they have nonetheless increased in both numbers and influence. One of the most feared terrorists in the world is Fusako Shigenobu, who helped plan the massacre at Lod Airport in Israel. Samira, as she was known to her Arab colleagues, is reputed to have run a global network of trained terrorists available to allied movements around the world.

A second reason for devoting a separate discussion to women and terrorism is to acquaint the reader with the remarkable profusion of stereotypes, caricatures, simplifications, distortions, and gender-biases that one encounters in much of the literature on women and terrorism. Rather than begin with the working hypothesis that women become involved in terrorism for largely the same or similar reasons that men do and examine the empirical evidence that supports or refutes the hypothesis, some writers have made "female terrorism" the focus of "explanations" ranging from penis envy to the premenstrual stress syndrome. One finds the nearest resemblance to these kinds of dubious interpretations in the literature on "female crime," which exhibits many of the same biases and distortions. Indeed, some writers have not hesitated to treat women's participation in terrorism as a subcategory of female criminality. To the extent that these perceptions are shared by personnel in social-control agencies (a euphemism for agencies concerned with the administration of criminal justice), they influence official conduct toward terrorists and terrorism. Despite our personal aversion toward this disreputable body of material, we consider it important that the reader become acquainted with enough of it to be able to understand its significance and the issues it raises in the systematic study of terrorism.

Finally, as we told our colleague, we welcomed an opportunity to discuss the small but growing body of serious work that reflects an attempt to establish an adequate empirical and theoretical basis for understanding the participation of women in terrorism in countries of widely varying historical, economic, political, and cultural backgrounds. As a result of similarities in the acculturation and education of men and women in the more industrially advanced countries, it should be no surprise that women have become more and more politicized, and that a growing number of them have sought violent solutions to political problems, just as some men have done. Of greater potential interest is the increasing involvement of women in societies that have traditionally relegated women to subordinate positions—for example, the Arab Middle East and Central and South America.

Women and Terrorism in the Past

Gaucher (1968) points out that women played an important role in all Russian revolutionary organizations, and not only in the areas of propaganda, liaison, information, and assistance; some took a direct part in terrorism. Almost a quarter of Russian terrorists were women, whose devotion and courage are described in the work of many contemporary authors.

Tatiana Leontiev, the attractive and wealthy daughter of the Vice Governor of Yakutsk, was to be named Lady-in-Waiting to the Czarina. Under an agreement with the Social Revolutionaries, she planned to present the Czar with a bouquet at a court ball and, taking advantage of the occasion, to shoot him with a revolver concealed in the flowers. She was arrested. Her family was able to pass her off as insane and sent her to Switzerland. There, in the hotel where she resided, she shot and killed a seventy-year-old man, whom she mistook for Durnovo, the Russian Minister of the Interior. Through an extraordinary coincidence, not only did he closely resemble Durnovo in appearance, but his name—Muller—was the one that Durnovo used as an alias whenever he travelled abroad.

Tatiana Leontiev, who was no more than twenty, was sentenced to a long prison term. This was also the fate of twenty-three-year-old Marie Spiridonova, who fired five shots at counsellor Luzhanovsky because he had led an expedition to repress the peasants at Tambov in 1907. Said to have been raped by police, Marie Spiridonova was destined to play an important role after the Revolution of 1917, then to experience Bolshevik prisons as well as those of the Czar. She was arrested and imprisoned repeatedly by the Bolsheviks, but after her final arrest in October 1920, she disappeared and nothing is known of her fate (Gaucher, 1968).

Another young woman named Lydia Sture was hanged. Together with nine comrades, she was stopped in the street in St. Petersburg by the police. Just as they were about to arrest her, she drew a revolver and fired on the policemen who were trying to seize her. She and the old terrorist Anna Rasputin were among seven who awaited execution together, inspiring Leonid Andreyev with material for his famous story *Seven Who Were Hanged*, which was made into a film in Russia in 1920 (Laqueur, 1987, 189).

We can add the names of Vera Zasulich, one of the Narodniki, who attempted to assassinate Governor-General Trepov of St. Petersburg in 1878, and Vera Figne, who laid mines along a route to be taken by the Czar. According to Georges-Abeyie, these represent "isolated instances of primarily middle-class women engaged in revolutionary or terrorist violence" (1983, 76). He maintains that the class variable holds in the contemporary period if we exclude the predominantly lower-class nationalistic struggles of such groups as the Irish Catholics in Northern Ireland, the Basque separatists in Spain, and the other revolutionary groups in Africa (FRELIMO in Mozambique, UNITA and MPLA in Angola, and the Patriotic Front in Zimbabwe).

Georges-Abeyie refers to an undated and apparently unpublished work by W. Middendorff and D. Middendorff entitled "Changing Patterns of Female Criminality," which compared Russian revolutionary women of the pre–World War I period and contemporary German terrorists. Georges-Abeyie notes that this comparison brings out three points: (1) both groups of terrorists were ideologists and tried to change the course of history, although without success; (2) both groups were from middle- and upper-class families; and (3) the Russian terrorists' demeanor in court was refined, courageous, and dignified, while the German terrorist in court exhibited extreme hostility, profanity, and discourtesy.

If the Middendorfs are referring to Ulrike Meinhof and her companions, one should know that these terrorists have been identified as self-acknowledged nihilists; that is, they have espoused the doctrine that destruction of existing political or social institutions is necessary to ensure future improvement. In our opinion, it may be stretching the definition of ideology to impermissible limits to include nihilism.

With regard to the impact of the acts attributed to terrorists of the later nineteenth and early twentieth centuries on the Russian revolution in 1917, it hardly seems a matter of contention that those acts did, in fact, help change the course of history.

Women and Contemporary Terrorism

Urban terrorism (as contrasted with rurally-based guerrilla and revolutionary movements) has been a predominantly male phenomenon. Prior to the late 1970s or early 1980s, almost all significant terrorist operations were directed, led, and carried out by males. Within Latin American terrorist organizations (the Argentine Montoneros and ERP, the Brazilian successors to Marighella, and the Tupamaros of Uruguay), female membership was less than 16 percent, based on arrest-identified cadres (Russell & Miller, 1983). Among these organizations, the Tupamaros made the greatest use of women; however, with few exceptions, the women's roles were confined to intelligence collection, operations as couriers, duties as nurses and medical personnel, and in the maintenance of safe houses for terrorists sought by police and for storage of weapons, propaganda materials, false documents, funds, and other supplies. This same predominantly support role for women has been noted with respect to Spanish, Italian, Turkish, and Iranian terrorist groups.

There have been notable exceptions to the relatively low-level participation of women as members of terrorist groups.

Twenty-four Sandinista guerrillas struck Nicaragua's National Palace in Managua at midday in late August 1979. The second in command appeared to be twenty-two-year-old Dora Maria Telles Arguello. Earlier in that year, a woman terrorist, who took over the leadership of an ill-fated El Fatah raid when its male commander was lost before setting foot on Israeli territory, was killed in a gun battle on the outskirts of Tel Aviv. The previous year was highlighted by a hostage situation in which the U.S. Ambassador to Colombia, along with other high-ranking diplomats, was held captive by M-19 guerrillas. A woman guerrilla appeared to play a major role in the actual hostage negotiations.

Georges-Abeyie notes other exceptions:

1. Leila Khalid and Fusako Shigenobu, leaders in the Popular Front for the Liberation of Palestine (PFLP) and the Japanese Red Army (JRA), respectively. Together they were instrumental in arranging the initial training of Japanese Red Army and West German cadres in Lebanon, under PFLP direction, during the early 1970s.
2. Ellen Mary Margaret McKearney, a runner for the IRA bombers operating in England.
3. Norma Esther Arostito, cofounder of the Argentine Montoneros. She also served as their chief ideologue until her death in 1976.
4. Genoveve Forest Tarat, who played a key role in the December 12, 1973, operation by the Basque Fatherland and Liberty Movement (ETA-V) that resulted in the assassination of Spanish Premier Admiral Carrero Blanco. She also participated in the September 13, 1974, bombing of a Madrid restaurant, the Cafe Rolando, that resulted in eleven dead and seventy wounded.
5. Margherita Cagol, the now-deceased wife of the Italian Red Brigades leader Renato Curcio, who occupied a major place in the organization and quite possibly led the Red Brigades commando team that freed Curcio from Rome's Casale Monferrato jail on February 8, 1975.
6. Maria Torres, wife of Carlo Torres, of the Armed Forces of National Liberation (FALN). They were possibly co-leaders and co-founders of this Puerto Rican movement.

7. In the U.S., the short-lived Symbionese Liberation Army (SLA) included
    Angela Atwood, Camilla Hall, Emily Harris, Nancy Ling Perry, Mary
    Alice Landles, and Patrician Solytsik (alias Mizmoon-Zoya).

The Weather Underground, a group splintered from the Students for a
Democratic Society (SDS), included Bernadine Dohrn, one of America's most
sought-after terrorists (Jacobs, 1971; U.S. Senate, 94th Congress, 1975). Inter-
estingly, female factions within the WU became quite powerful and, in fact,
moved into the organization's leadership.

Table 6–1 reveals by region and country terrorist groups that had either
female leadership or a sizable female component in their cadres. All of these
groups were Marxist or anarchist in orientation, even when primarily nationalistic with regard to propaganda. Considerable feminine input in terrorist
groups, though often apparent in nations with strong feminist movements, is
not confined to such nations. Spain, Argentina, Uruguay, Italy, and Northern
Ireland lack a strong feminist tradition, yet they have had considerable female
participation in terrorist organizations.

Table 6-1
Terrorist Organizations with Women as Leaders or Sizable Numbers
of Women as Cadre

North America		
United States		
Symbionese Liberation Army (SLA)	Extremist	Inactive after May 1974
Armed Forces of National Liberation (FALN)	Puerto Rican Separatist	Active
Weather Underground (WU)	Extremist	Active
South America		
Argentina		
Fuerzas Armed Revolutionaries (FAR)	Peronist	Merged with Montoneros in 1973 making strongest Peronist group
Montoneros	Peronist	Active with FAR
Uruguay		
Tupamaros or Movimento de Liberaction Nacional (MLN)	Castroite, now eclectic	Broken up by security forces but formed links with guerrillas in neigh-boring communities— Inactive in 1976
Europe		
Great Britain		
Angry Brigade	Extremist	Defunct

(continued)

Table 6-1 (continued)

Ireland		
Irish Republican Army (IRA) Provisional wings	Catholic nationalist but officially under Marxist control	Active in shootings and bombings
Italy		
Red Brigades or Brigate Rosse	Maoist	Active in street violence
Spain		
Euzkadita Azkatasuna (ETA)	Basque Separatist	Active (approximate strength 200)
West Germany		
Movement Two June	Left-Wing Anarchist	Active
Red Army Faction	Left-Wing Anarchist	Active

SOURCE: Georges-Abeyie, Daniel E. "Women as Terrorists." In L.Z. Freedman, and Y. Alexander (Eds.), *Perspectives on Terrorism*. Wilmington, DE: Scholarly Resources, 1983, pp. 74–75. Copyright 1983 by Scholarly Resources Inc. Reprinted by permission of Scholarly Resources Inc.

Female Terrorism and Female Criminality

Georges-Abeyie (1983) observes that many different and, at times, extreme explanations have been offered for female involvement in terrorist activities. He lists these as the most common:

- Revolutionary and terrorist activity provides excitement
- Danger is both an attraction and a repellant
- Terrorist violence is tied to causes that initially may appear legitimate
- Terrorist organizations provide an opportunity for upward mobility, in leadership and in an active role in formulating the group's policies, opportunities that are absent or extremely limited in the white male-dominated world of legitimate activity
- Terrorist organizations offer change and a renunciation of the current male-dominated chauvinistic mores
- The traditional American stereotype of women as weak, supportive, submissive, silent, and of lower intelligence and drive is absent in the philosophies of many terrorist organizations
- Membership in a terrorist organization is the natural outgrowth of membership in extreme feminist organizations
- Women are by nature more violent and dangerous than men, and terrorist organizations provide an outlet for this tendency
- Women are rejecting stereotypic roles and thus adopting traditional male roles that include revolutionary and terrorist violence

- Hormonal disturbances, caused by excessive sexual freedom and particularly by having sexual relations before maturity, affect these women
- Economic, political, and familial liberation due to the trend toward greater justice and equality for women plays a role
- Continuation of natural selection (survival of the fittest) has an influence
- Middle-class white Anglo-Saxon Protestant (WASP) restraints, in regard to mind-sets (ideas and attitudes) as well as behavior, are rejected

Georges-Abeyie states that "many of these explanations appear extreme and even laughable," but points out that nevertheless, such interpretations are reflected in beliefs found among criminal justice agency personnel. Both female terrorists and female criminals are viewed as committing acts that are likely to be regarded as "emotive rather than instrumental, i.e., emotional rather than well-thought-out acts with a rational program of action not tied to a love interest, such as an attempt to free a captured husband or lover from police or army custody" (1983, 78). Law enforcement agents, according to Georges-Abeyie, often state that female terrorists are more likely to engage in acts of senseless or non-goal-oriented violence than are their male counterparts, a factor that would place a disproportionately large number of female terrorists into Hacker's category of crazies.

Apart from noting an overlap between explanations of female terrorism and explanations of female criminality, we do not consider that a detailed review and critique of research and theorizing on female criminality would serve any useful purpose. Georges-Abeyie has conveniently summarized the major theoretical orientations in table 6–2.

Table 6-2
Theoretical Perspectives on Female Criminality

Theorist	Orientation	Title of Major Work
Cesare Lombroso	Crime as an atavism (survival of primitive traits in individuals, e.g., considerable body hair) Lower intelligence Lack of passion	The Female Offender (New York, 1897)
W.I. Thomas	Psychological passivity Physiological immobility Women are cold and calculating Female amorality Women driven by basic wishes to manipulate the male sex Drive to achieve ulterior motives Individual accommodation to social surroundings	The Unadjusted Girl (New York, 1923)

(continued)

Table 6-2 (continued)

Theorist	Orientation	Title of Major Work
Sigmund Freud	Psychological passivity Physiological immobility Penis envy Women are anatomically inferior The deviant is attempting to be a man	"Anatomy is Destiny," Lectures on Psychoanalysis (New York, 1933)
E. Kingsley Davis	Demands for sexual novelty are not fulfilled in marriage Some males are cut off from sexual partners because they are unmarried, ugly, and/or deformed Some males are cut off from sexual partners because of some other sexually competitive disadvantage	"The Sociology of Prostitutes," *American Sociological Review* 2 (October 1937): 744-55
Otto Pollak	Hidden female crime Rising crime rate among females is the result of sexual emancipation Women are as criminal as men When their criminality is detected, they may still avoid arrest Female crime is tied to socialization Some biological factors are tied to female criminality, e.g., lesser physical strength than men Psychological concomitants of menustruation, pregnancy, and menopause are tied to the etiology of female crime	*The Criminality of Women* (Philadelphia, 1950)
M. Rappaport	Female offenders are psychological misfits	"The Psychology of the Female Off ender," *NPAA Journal* 3 (January 1957): 7–12.
G. Gisela Konopka	Emotional problem: loneliness and dependency	*Adolescent Girls in Conflict* (Englewood Cliffs, NJ, 1966)
J. Cowie, V. Cowie, and E. Slater	Chromosomal explanation of female delinquency Female offenders are different physiologically and psychologically from the normal girl Delinquent girls are more masculine than the normal girl	*Delinquency in Girls* (London, 1968)

(continued)

Table 6-2 (continued)

Theorist	Orientation	Title of Major Work
H.C. Vedder and D. Sommerville	Female delinquency seen as blocked access or maladjustment to the normal feminine role	*The Delinquent* Girl (Springfield, IL, 1970)
D. Hoffman Bustamente	Women's crimes are the result of five major factors: 1) differential sex role expectations 2) sex differences in sociological patterns and application of social control 3) differential opportunities to engage in crime 4) differential access to criminal subcultures and careers 5) sex differences built into crime categories	"The Nature of Female Criminality," *Issues in Criminology* 8 (Fall 1973): 117–36.
F. Adler	Greater female assertiveness Spinoff of the women's liberation movement Breakdown in prevailing patterns of sexual inequality	*Sisters in Crime* (New York, 1975)
R. Simon	Breakdown in prevailing patterns of sexual inequality Greater labor force participation of females has led to increased opportunities for crime Female criminality shall not increase drastically (Adler disagrees)	*Women and Crime* (Lexington, MA, 1975)

SOURCE: Daniel E. Georges-Ageyie, Women as Terrorists. In L.Z. Freedman, and Y. Alexander (Eds.), Perspectives on Terrorism. Wilmington, DE: Scholarly Resources, 1983, pp. 79–81. Copyright 1983 by Scholarly Resources Inc. Reprinted by permission of Scholarly Resources Inc.

Earlier studies that tried to account for women's participation in criminal activities on the basis of physiological factors tended to confuse biological differences with gender differences that result from social, psychological, and cultural influences. Bole and Tatro (1979) noted that four sexual functions (impregnation, lactation, menstruation, and gestation) biologically distinguish the sexes. As long as allowance is made for these basic reproductive functions, no particular sex role is unchangeable. Research that attempted to explain female crime in social, rather than biological, terms had to challenge a number of widespread myths about the nature and extent of female involvement in crime.

One of the newer myths concerning female criminality has its origins in official crime statistics. During the past twenty years, arrest rates for women charged with Crime Index offenses (i.e., the eight crimes the Federal Bureau of Investigation regards as most serious) have risen much more sharply than have rates for men (*Uniform Crime Reports*, 1988). Accounts in the popular media would seem to suggest that the nation is undergoing a female "crime wave"—a misleading impression resulting from a superficial analysis of statistics on female crime. It is true that there have been large *percentage* increases in the number of women involved in crime as compared with two decades ago, *but the increases represent relatively modest increases in actual numbers.*

Changes in the nature and volume of female crime have also been tied to female emancipation. This viewpoint raises several questions regarding changes in female involvement in the labor market. First, have there been substantial changes in the rate and pattern of female criminality? Examination of official data from the *Uniform Crime Reports* indicates quite clearly that much of the apparent change in female crime and delinquency results from a concentration on gross percentage changes without reference to their numerical significance. These data show that patterns of female crime and delinquency have not undergone any dramatic changes during the past two decades. Adult female crime continues to be primarily a matter of involvement in the offenses of larceny, embezzlement, fraud, and forgery. Official juvenile involvement has also remained relatively constant, with offenses of larceny and running away from home accounting for the vast majority of these girls being taken into custody. While the juvenile self-reporting data do show a greater trend toward convergence than is evident in official statistics, this must be interpreted in the light of other data that show that more serious and persistent delinquents are more likely to be arrested.

A second issue is whether there have been sufficient changes in the female role (i.e., expanded employment opportunities, more liberated or feminist attitudes toward self, and masculinization of female behavior) to affect female crime patterns. The attribution of crime to the masculinization of female behavior can be traced back to Lombroso; more recently, it has been linked to role convergence between the sexes. Although current research does show that female roles have become more egalitarian, other research indicates that traditional female role patterns emphasizing the wife and mother role are still dominant among both American men and women. Despite the fact that more women are entering male-dominated fields, attitudes still persist that make their active pursuit and acceptance in these areas a long way off. With respect to crime, although more women have not only become involved in but also active participants rather than accessories in male-dominated crimes, their numerical involvement is still relatively minor.

Another indication of the influence of female emancipation on crime is the extent to which female offenders subscribe to more liberal as opposed to traditional role definitions. Existing research on delinquency largely failed to find any positive relationship between these attitudes and crime, with some research actually showing a negative relationship (Eve & Edmonds, 1978). A study by James and Thornton (1980) examined the relationship of attitudes toward feminism and delinquency, while controlling for the influence of the feminist movement on delinquency-related variables. They concluded that, although increasing delinquency and reduced social controls "might contribute to the growth in rate of delinquency and crime among females, our evidence suggests that the extent of crime among feminist women is similar to, or even less frequent than, that among their more traditional counterparts" (1980, 243). Studies of adult females provide remarkably similar results. Leventhal (1977) found that female inmates were more likely to hold traditional attitudes toward the nature of women and their role expectations than were college students. The Glick and Neto (1977) study reported that the majority of incarcerated women still maintain traditional views regarding the role of women in society.

Women and Terrorism: Theoretical Perspectives

Klein (1973), in her review of theoretical approaches to female criminality, suggests that the same factors that have challenged and destabilized traditional gender roles assigned to women have also fostered terrorist activity by women. Burton (1975) and Laqueur (1977) identified a series of factors they regard as conducive to terrorism. These factors include: (1) a self-conscious, segregated, ethnic, cultural or religious minority; (2) a minority that feels itself economically deprived or politically oppressed—a feeling exacerbated by the effects of modern communication—with poor job opportunities and lacking voting rights, but encouraged to believe that change is coming and then disappointed; (3) a situation of unemployment or inflation; (4) externally encouraged; (5) blaming an historical "them"; (6) frustrated elites to provide leadership and to overcome the natural distaste, of all save the psychopathic fringe, to initiate violence by giving it an ideological justification; and (7) living in a society with at least an oral tradition of democracy and upward mobility.

In the case of female terrorism, these factors must be supplemented by the addition of feminist demands, both logical and irrational, requiring serious response and gratification by societies with a history of a lack of response to nonviolent pressure, including the so-called Western democracies. Understanding the role of women in terrorism implies a recognition that women comprise a self-conscious, dynamic sector of society that often perceives itself to be an oppressed majority—a majority oppressed not only because of religion, ethnicity, or national origin, but also because of gender.

In the Western democracies, changing role sets ascribed to women have placed them more directly into the mainstream of academia and corporate enterprise. These changes in women's expected belief and activity patterns have resulted in direct conflict with the more traditional role sets: wife, mother, and passive, gentle, noncompetitive beauties of moderate or low intelligence and low aspirations. With women entering the labor force at an accelerating rate, the system, with its limited rewards and resources, is a source of frustration for women who have attained all the socially defined attributes usually associated with success: proper speech, assertive personalities, superior technical training, and high levels of education. These highly skilled women have perceived the reality of blocked opportunity while becoming more conscious of their unique exclusion from the system of rewards, thus fostering and reinforcing demands for sociocultural change of both a socialist and feminist nature.

As new employment opportunities have opened up for women, they have acquired new skills, some of which may be used in terrorist acts. Combat or combat-supported units in the "New Army" train women to shoot guns and handle explosives, while new opportunities in various local, state, and federal-level law enforcement agencies also open up similar training. Women who are being taught to work on farms, in forests, and in mines learn skills in the storage and discharge of explosives.

Feminist organizations, or organizations with socialist principles, allow women greater opportunities for upward mobility. This upward mobility is more likely determined by a woman's innate or learned skills and leadership qualities than by the sex-linked, stereotyped characteristics often found in more traditional male-dominated organizations. Female input in groups that champion feminist or socialist objectives is likely to be considerable. If such demands should exceed society's capacity to deliver reform, then violence or the threat of violence by radical organizations is probable.

The demand for immediate change and the ability to compete forcefully in the labor market and classroom are often viewed as masculine traits. Thus, those who assert markedly radical demands for structural-functional change in regard to role sets assigned to women, or to any oppressed majority or minority, may be viewed as masculine in character. Women who lack the traits and characteristics society considers appropriate—gentleness, passivity, nonviolent personalities, seductiveness, physically attractive faces and figures—may seek success in some nonfeminine realm by displaying aggression, unadorned faces and bodies, toughness, or other masculine qualities. Masculine or feminine characteristics are often culturally defined. Future female terrorists may exhibit fewer of the characteristics usually defined as masculine because divisions between sex-linked roles are likely to become more blurred with the passage of time.

What we have said thus far regarding female membership in organizations that exhibit and espouse feminist or socialist principles applies principally to the more developed countries such as the Western democracies. In these countries, female terrorists can be expected to function in a manner similar to that of their male counterparts. No study addresses the issue of female terrorism as a general European phenomenon, but Weinberg and Eubank (1987) have supplied valuable information on the role of women in Italian terrorism.

Italian Women Terrorists

Using biographical information obtained from two major newspapers and from court records, Weinberg and Eubank were able to construct a profile of women terrorists based on 451 cases (18 percent of the total of 2512 individuals for whom biographical data were available). Their analysis suggests a number of ways in which women terrorists differed from their male counterparts: (1) the time at which women became involved in terrorist activities; (2) the routes they took prior to entry into the groups; (3) the particular terrorist organizations they joined; and (4) the roles they came to play in them.

Women were likely to become involved in terrorism later than men, both in terms of the cycle of terrorist activities in Italy and in their chronological ages when these activities came to the attention of the authorities. The paths leading to participation in terrorist groups also appear to have been somewhat different. Weinberg and Eubank speculate that the process that brought about women's participation was more likely to have involved family connections with other terrorists and less likely to have resulted from earlier experiences in other political organizations than was true for men.

The particular terrorist groups into which women were recruited also distinguishes them from men. The neo-Fascist formations held little attraction for women; instead, the preponderance of women was found in leftist revolutionary groups. Here the different ideological perspectives and social ethos that separated Left from Right terrorists, particularly their attitudes toward the appropriate role of women in society, seem to have evoked this difference.

Once inside the terrorist groups, women were found to have involved themselves in the full range of roles available to members. It is true that women were underrepresented in leadership positions, but the female-male differences were largely the product of the dramatic underrepresentation of women at the top of neo-Fascist groups.

The researchers expressed reluctance to move from a discussion of the attributes of women as terrorists to a broader focus on the linkage between this phenomenon and the status of women in Italian society. Nevertheless, Weinberg and Eubank permit themselves a few observations:

> The background for the participation of women in political terrorism was one in which there occurred a general radicalization of political life in Italy from the late 1960s throughout most of the following decade. It was in this context that a political mobilization of Italian women took place over a set of feminist issues. And it was among the leftist political parties and New Left movements that these issues were given the widest hearings and the most sympathetic responses. In turn, it was out of a pool of newly political conscious women that the leftist terrorist groups recruited some of their female members. (1987, 259–260)

They point out that these groups were out to make a revolution and establish a new society; they did not aim at completing a feminist agenda within the context of the old society.

Women in Latin American Guerrilla Movements

The analysis thus far adds to our understanding of female participation in terrorist activities in the industrialized nations; however, we need additional information on women in terrorist movements within cultures characterized by a patriarchal ideology and the structurally subordinate position of women, as in the Middle East and Latin America. Although we lack a comprehensive examination of women and terrorism in the countries of the Middle East, we are fortunate in having Linda L. Reif's analysis of female involvement in terrorism in five Latin American countries: Cuba, Nicaragua, El Salvador, Colombia, and Uruguay.

Reif's survey raised three questions with regard to women's participation in guerrilla movements:

1. What factors would prevent women from participating as frequently as men?
2. Within gender, which classes face the least barriers to participation?
3. What roles do women tend to perform?

Reif notes that her conclusions were necessarily limited by the paucity of available information about the guerrilla, a constraint encountered by anyone who tries to carry on systematic research in this area.

In all of the movements studied, women participated less extensively than men, for reasons that include: (1) structural constraints caused by women's role in reproductive activities and the patriarchal nature of Latin American society, which reflects and reinforces this role; (2) organizational characteristics of guerrilla movements, such as the lack of platforms dealing with issues important to women and inhospitable or sexist internal relations.

The three movements with substantial female participation (the Tupamaro, Sandinista, and Salvadoran) promoted routine policies of egalitarian relations between men and women within the movement. Women were to share in leadership decision making and task performance. These movements also employed platforms attractive to women, which seemed to be of two types. First, in opposition to patriarchalism, women were offered essentially feminist objectives—an end to discrimination in such areas as the work force, the polity, and education. Second, programs stressing such issues as child care, health care, and literacy, which maximized social welfare and facilitated, rather than threatened, women's commitment to the family, were advocated. The Tupamaros and Sandinistas offered women both types of platforms. In the Salvadoran case, the FMLN/FDR offer social welfare policies in conjunction with the feminist planks offered by its affiliated women's organization.

Neither the Colombian nor Cuban movements developed special programs toward women or stressed gender egalitarianism as an important component of organizational relations. There was, correspondingly, only a small degree of female involvement in these struggles. Thus, although women's role in reproductive activities and associated patriarchal attitudes certainly inhibit female participation, Reif's examination of the five movements indicates that organizations can do much themselves to eliminate barriers to recruitment.

   Within gender, the analysis of the five movements disclosed that middle-class women faced fewer barriers to participation. Where both the middle classes and working class/campesinos participated, middle-class women were more likely to be at the forefront of guerrilla activity. In Cuba, "exceptional" middle class women formed part of the 26th of July movement; and in Colombia, Torres's group had early student members. Initial organizers of the Sandinista AMPRONAC and early female recruits of the Salvadoran political-military organizations tended to be middle class. Working class and campesino women seemed to enter the movements somewhat later. The Tupamaros' middle-class base remained relatively constant throughout the life of the movement, reflecting a demographic pattern specific to Uruguay.

   Why middle-class women tended to be early participants may be linked to their higher education and perhaps greater awareness of political issues. Even campesino and working-class women who recognized the benefits of involvement, however, still faced the burdens of class as well as gender. Since these women pay the highest cost for political participation, it is not surprising that they would enter the movements only when their fundamental interests had been addressed. Hence, the Sandinista and Salvadoran groups began to recruit large numbers of working-class and campesino women through attention to their specific needs. Social welfare, for example, is critical because of the many female-headed households in the two countries.

   Women performed basically support roles in guerrilla organizations. Strategic utility rather than sexism appears to have been the major reason for placing women in support positions, though sexism was indeed apparent in accounts of the earlier movements. Women performed mainly in support capacities in the Colombian and Cuban struggles, which had limited female participation. In the three later movements, which developed policies and platforms to encourage female participation, women performed combat as well as support duties. The influx of women in the Tupamaro, Sandinista, and Salvadoran movements meant that necessary support positions could be filled at the same time that additional women would be available for combat.

   In sum, the patterns of women's participation in Latin American guerrilla movements appeared to be generally as postulated: women participated less extensively than men. Men and women came from the same class levels, and within gender, middle-class women seemed to face the fewest barriers to participation. Women tended to perform support roles, at least until large numbers of women entered guerrilla organizations. Organizational policies and platforms can greatly affect these patterns, however, as the movements that attempted to recruit women indicate.

   In the Tupamaro, Sandinista, and Salvadoran movements, females' rates of participation (though still lower) approached those of males, and women performed extensively in combat as well as support. The Sandinista and Salvadoran platforms have great appeal to campesino and working-class women and therefore have recruited large numbers of these women, despite social structural barriers.

Reif suggests reasons these later three movements have attempted to mobilize women. First, women contribute to the overall strength of a national liberation movement. The failure of Che Guevara in Bolivia and of "foquismo" throughout Latin America—and the decimation of urban movements such as the Brazilian and Tupamaro—point to the increasing necessity for popular support in the face of greater repression from the right. While subjective and objective conditions must be ripe for revolution, the guerrilla organization itself must be linked to the population. Such links have generally been absent in Latin American movements, contributing to their failure. Recruitment of women would serve to ground movements in more extensive popular support. Women's participation is thus in line with the conception of "prolonged people's war" (gradual organization of all mass sectors under a variety of organizational forms and tactics as inspired by the Vietnamese) that has been adopted as current revolutionary strategy in Central America. Further, there is considerable danger that if guerrilla movements fail to recruit women, progovernment parties may attempt to coopt feminine support—as occurred in the mobilization of middle- and upper-class women against Allende in Chile.

A second reason that later movements may have attempted to recruit women concerns the increasing awareness of feminist issues and their implications for class struggle. Although the relationship between class and gender has been explored since the time of Marx, the women's liberation movements beginning in the late 1960s (primarily in advanced capitalist nations) sensitized guerrilla leaders to feminist issues. Submission to patriarchal attitudes reinforces acceptance of the capitalist division of labor and the class structure on which it rests. The subjugation of women has historically been responsible for low levels of class consciousness and resistance toward political development. It is therefore not surprising that guerrilla leaders have advocated female recruitment and feminist platforms when sensitized to the effects of sexism.

The extensive mobilization of women in guerrilla movements indicates a new pattern in Latin American revolutionary struggles. The Cuban revolution did not have to rely on such mobilization to succeed. Only twenty years later, however, the Sandinistas demonstrated that female support could be a critical factor in achieving victory. It is likely that mobilization of women will continue, particularly since past successes and present attainments can be attributed directly to feminine involvement.

Summary

Women's role in terrorism is subject to widely differing views and interpretations. Women played a significant part in nineteenth and early twentieth century Russian revolutionary organizations. Their participation in insurgent terrorism has varied from country to country and according to a number of factors, including whether the groups have had an urban or rural base. In the U.S., women have held key leadership positions in revolutionary leftist organizations.

Attempts to relate feminine participation in terrorism to female criminality have generated a controversial body of professional literature in which the influences of gender bias are glaringly apparent. Earlier "explanations" of female crime attributed criminality to constitutional (i.e., biological) predispositions, including mental retardation and "genital deficiency." Later interpretations sought to relate female crime to social factors.

One of the more questionable interpretations ascribes a rise in female criminality to female emancipation. An analysis of official crime figures indicates that the rise in female crime is more apparent than real and is based primarily on large percentage increases in reported crime, rather than on increases in absolute numbers.

Their subordinate positions and comparatively lower membership in terrorist movements over the past three decades have largely reflected the social status and circumstances of women in both industrially advanced and more traditional societies. This situation is likely to undergo a substantial change within the immediate future, however, as women achieve egalitarian status and increasing access to participation in activities from which they have long been excluded by male domination.

Key Terms

Margherita Caghol

female criminality

female emancipation

Leila Khalid

Ulrike Meinhof

Symbionese Liberation Army

"masked crime"

Bernardine Dohrn

"genital deficiency"

Tatiana Leontiev

Samira (Fusako Shigenobu)

Questions for Discussion and Review

1. What part did women play in revolutionary organizations in Czarist Russia?
2. Did women hold positions of leadership in terrorist groups in the U.S. during the 1960s and 1970s?
3. Evaluate the attempts of early criminologists to account for female criminality. How did later theoretical approaches differ with respect to the emphasized factors?
4. Are we experiencing a real "female crime wave" in the U.S.? What do official statistics tell us about increases in female crime?
5. Is female emancipation ("Women's Lib") the cause of an increase in the rate of female participation in crime and terrorism?
6. What effect, if any, do masculinity and femininity have on involvement in terrorism?

7. Compare and contrast patterns of female participation in terrorism in Italy and Latin America.
8. Is female participation in terrorism more likely to increase or decrease in the foreseeable future? Why?

References

Adler, F. *Sisters in Crime*. New York: McGraw-Hill, 1975.

Bole, J., & Tatro, C. "The Female Offender: The 1980s and Beyond." In *Crime and Justice in America: Critical Issues for the Future*, edited by J.T. O'Brien and M. Marcus, pp. 255–282. New York: Pergamon, 1979.

Burton, A. *Urban Terrorism: Theory, Practice, and Response*. New York: Plenum, 1975.

Cohen, A.K., & Short, J.F. "Research in Delinquent Subcultures." *Journal of Social Issues* 14 (1958): 20–37.

Eve, R., & Edmonds, K.R. "Women's Liberation and Female Criminality: Or Sister Will You Give Me Back My Dime?" Paper presented at the meeting of the National Society of Social Problems, San Francisco, September 1978.

Gaucher, R. *The Terrorists: From Tsarist Russia to the OAS*. London: Secker and Warburg, 1968.

Georges-Abeyie, D.E. "Women as Terrorists." In *Perspectives on Terrorism*, edited by L.Z. Freedman and Y. Alexander, pp. 71–84. Wilmington, DE: Scholarly Resources, 1983.

Glick, R., and Neto, V.V. *National Study of Women's Correctional Programs*. U.S. Department of Justice. Washington, DC: U.S. Government Printing Office, 1977.

Glueck, S., and Glueck, E. *Five Hundred Delinquent Women*. New York: Knopf, 1934.

Jacobs, H., *Weathermen*. Palo Alto, CA: Stanford University Press, 1971.

James, J. and Thornton, W. "Women's Liberation and the Female Delinquent." *Journal of Research in Crime and Delinquency* 17, 2 (1980): 230–244.

Klein, D. "The Etiology of Female Crime: A Review of the Literature." *Issues in Criminology* 8 (1973): 3–30.

Laqueur, W. *Terrorism*. Boston: Little, Brown, 1977.

Laqueur, W. *The Age of Terrorism*. Boston: Little, Brown, 1987.

Livingstone, N.C. *The War Against Terrorism*. Lexington, MA: D.C. Heath, 1982.

Leventhal, G. "Female Criminality: Is 'Women's Lib' to Blame?" *Psychological Reports* 41 (1977): 1179–1182.

Lombroso, C., and Ferrero, W. *The Female Offender*. New York: D. Appleton, 1897.

Middendorff, W., and Middendorff, D. "Changing Patterns of Female Criminality." Mimeograph (Freiburg, no date).

Pollak, O. *The Criminality of Women*. Philadelphia, PA: University of Pennsylvania Press, 1950.

Pollock, J. "Early Theories of Female Criminality." In *Women, Crime, and the Criminal Justice System*, edited by L.H. Bowker, pp. 25–55. Lexington, MA: Lexington Books, 1978.

Rasche, C.E. "The Female Offender as an Object of Criminological Research." *Criminal Justice and Behavior* 1 (1974): 301–320.

Reif, L.L. "Women in Latin American Guerrilla Movements." *Comparative Politics* 18 (1985/86): 147–169.

Russell, C.A., and Miller, B.H. "Profile of a Terrorist." In *Perspectives on Terrorism*, edited by L.Z. Freedman and Y. Alexander, pp. 45–60. Wilmington, DE: Scholarly Resources, 1983.

U.S. Department of Justice, *Uniform Crime Reports—1987*. Washington, DC: U.S. Government Printing Office, 1988.

U.S. Senate, 94th Congress. 1st Session, January 1975. Committee on the Judiciary. *The Weather Underground: Report of the Sub-Committee to Investigate the Administration of the Internal Security Laws*. Washington, DC: U.S. Government Printing Office, 1975.

Weinberg, L., and Eubank, W.L. "Italian Women Terrorists." *Terrorism: An International Journal* 9 (1987): 241–262.

Part Two

Operational Perspectives

7
Hostage-Taking and Hostage Negotiations

As a terrorist tactic, the seizure of hostages has much to recommend it over assaults and bombings. Handled properly, a hostage incident can be stretched out for weeks, months, or even years and can be exploited to the utmost by the captors. Episodes that end in violent death, on the other hand, result in victims who are mourned by their families and friends—and are promptly forgotten by the mass media and the public. By avoiding the repugnant spectacle of slain victims, the terrorist retains room to negotiate at an obvious advantage without necessarily surrendering all the moral high ground. Also, dead victims have no value to the terrorist, whereas captives can be exchanged for money, political concessions, colleagues that are being held prisoners, or a safe conduct to freedom.

As mentioned earlier, criminals and mentally disturbed persons may also take hostages: robbers may seize hostages for the purpose of aiding their escape, and other criminal uses may include kidnapping victims for ransom or, in the turf-wars of organized crime and drug trafficking, kidnapping rivals for their potential value as counters in the bargaining process. Even more malevolent and perverse motives may compel psychopathic individuals to capture sexual victims, whose captivity ends in torture and death.

In recent years, the type of hostage-taking incident that has proven most appealing to terrorists—and the favorite of the mass media—is the seizure or hijacking of an airplane and its passengers. The advent of modern jet aircraft simplified the problems involved in large-scale seizure of hostages and led, incidentally, to the coining of a new term: *skyjacking*. Other options have included hijacking trains, buses, ships, and seizing hostages in buildings frequented in large numbers by the public, such as banks, department stores, and government offices.

For clarity and accuracy, one should distinguish between kidnapping and other forms of hostage-taking. Kidnapping usually involves the seizure of specific individuals who the kidnapper has identified as targets; after the victims are seized, they are taken to some secret and secure place that has been prepared in advance. In contrast, the hijacking of a plane, ship, or other vehicle or the seizure of a group of hostages in a barricade situation is usually played out in the full glare of intensive media coverage. Kidnappers can usually afford to take their time; hijackers are under pressure to achieve quick results.

It is practically impossible to draw a hard line between kidnapping for profit and kidnapping for political or ideological reasons, but we should be aware that terrorist groups and organizations carry out both kinds.

Once people have fallen victim to a criminal or terrorist captor, there begins a tortuous, complex, and suspenseful process of negotiation for release of the hostages. There is prima facie common sense in having a practical alternative available if negotiation fails. One terrorism expert states;

> Police departments and other law enforcement agencies face hostage-taking incidents with a twin capability: assault and negotiation. In actuality, the negotiation should be employed only when an assault or sharpshooter capability is available and the readiness for such action is apparent to the hostage-taker. (Goldaber, 1979, 22)

Hostage-Taking in Historical Perspective

The taking of hostages, like terrorism itself, is as old as the history of human conflict. Entire nations, as well as individuals, have been seized and held captive. As long as 3500 years ago, Moses led the Jewish people back from captivity in Egypt, through the wilderness of Sinai, to Canaan, where the patriarch Abraham was believed to have settled after his migration from Mesopotamia.

The city-states of ancient Greeks were constantly at war with one another—and with the "barbarians," a term that covered all peoples who were not Greek. States such as Athens and Sparta sought to secure themselves from attack by the use of hostages taken from the leading families of rival states.

Caesar subdued Gaul by requiring the Gallic tribes to furnish hostages as a pledge of good conduct. In the second book of *De Bello Gallico*, Caesar tells about receiving the tribe called the Belloraci into his protection:

> Since this tribe had such great influence among the Belgae and was the most populous of them all, I demanded the surrender of six hundred hostages. (Warner, 1960, 47)

Later, Imperial Rome relied heavily on the use of hostages as a means of suppressing rebellion among conquered peoples.

Abduction as a method of acquiring a mate dates back to ancient Rome and the rape of the Sabine women. The practice persisted well into the twentieth century in the smaller, more remote villages of Sicily and southern Italy. When a father refused to allow a man to marry his daughter, he risked the possibility of seeing her carried off against his wishes (Hobsbawm, 1959, 15).

In the Middle Ages, the capture and ransom of noblemen and royalty became a lucrative and flourishing practice. In 1193, on his way home from crusading in the Holy Land, the English king Richard I—Richard the Lion-hearted—was seized by Leopold of Austria and held incommunicado in a castle whose location was a closely guarded secret. Legend has it that Richard's minstrel, Blondel, wandered throughout Germany singing one of

Richard's favorite songs under castle windows, until at last he was rewarded by hearing Richard sing the refrain. The king was freed in 1194 by the payment of all or most of the 150,000 marks ransom that Leopold had demanded (Adams, 1905, 374–376).

During the Hundred Years War in France, the French king John II was unhorsed and captured at the battle of Poitiers by English troops under the command of Edward III and his famous son, Edward the Black Prince. John and his fourteen-year-old son Philip were taken back to England, where they were treated like royal guests rather than captives. But Philip, who was a lad of spirit, took a swing at Edward's cupbearer, a person of noble rank, for daring to serve the king of England first instead of the king of France.

Bandits and outlaws regularly extorted money as well as political concessions by seizing members of noble families and holding them hostage. Indeed, kidnapping was one of the most common crimes committed in fourteenth and fifteenth century England (McCall, 1979, 104).

As warfare was waged by professional soldiers—mercenaries and *condottieri*—in the sixteenth century, the lives of noblemen and princes were far too precious to be squandered on the field of battle. The values in ransom money of various dukes, earls, counts, and viscounts were as well established and widely known as stock market quotations or commodities futures in the twentieth century. There were occasional exceptions. The bitter religious conflict between French Catholics and Protestants left no room for amenities. A royal favorite named the Duc de Joyeuse had achieved a ferocious distinction by ordering the killing of Huguenot wounded and by hanging prisoners who had surrendered, relying on the laws of honest war for humane treatment. When Joyeuse was captured by Huguenot horsemen at the battle of Coutras, he flung down his sword and called out, "My ransom is a hundred thousand crowns." One of his captors put a bullet through his head.

Warfare became more civilized during the Age of Enlightenment, and civilian populations were spared many of the horrors that characterized the religious and ideological struggles of the seventeenth century. The dynastic wars of the eighteenth century were waged by small armies drilled to an automatonlike precision, commanded by titled officers, and extremely expensive to maintain and replace. Military tactics became as stylized as classical ballet, and strategy took on the properties of a game of chess.

All this changed as a result of the French Revolution, the emergence of the "nation in arms," and the rise of Napoleon Bonaparte. Napoleon taught his armies to live off the land across which they marched—even the French countryside. "Cause the commissary to be shot," Napoleon advised his officers, "and you will not want for supplies." The result of such policies, as practiced by the Napoleonic armies in Spain, can be seen in Goya's sketches of women raped in the broken mill, haggard peasants mutilating their captives with axe and knife, facing with despairing eyes the leveled muskets of firing squads, burning towns, and naked corpses pinned by bayonets to a charred doorway or tree.

Such atrocities did not end with the fall of Napoleon and the advent of the Industrial Age in the nineteenth century. We have already referred to the German concept of *Schrecklichkeit* (frightfulness) as a military policy endorsed by the highest levels of the German General Staff. The theory has been attributed to Roman Emperor Caligula, who is credited with the utterance: *Oderint dum metuant* (Let them hate us as long as they fear us). In World War I, according to Barbara Tuchman, "The taking and killing of hostages was practiced as systematically [by the German Army] as the requisitioning of food" (1962, 352). In Belgian towns such as Andenne and Tamines, one can find hundreds of gravestones in cemeteries inscribed *1914: Fusille par les Allemands* (Shot by the Germans).

The Germans repeated these practices in World War II, but on a much more colossal scale. The Czech village of Lidice was obliterated and its entire population killed or sent to concentration camps in reprisal for the assassination of the infamous chief of the Nazi S.D., Reinhard Heydrich. The town of Oradour-sur-Glane in France suffered a similar fate in 1944 at the hands of the 12th S.S. Panzer Division.

Kidnapping and Terrorism

The "Snatch Racket"

Although kidnapping for political reasons has always been a rare occurrence in the U.S., kidnapping for criminal purposes has been a perennial problem. The most publicized kidnapping of this century was the abduction and murder of the infant son of Colonel and Mrs. Charles Lindbergh. The baby was taken out of his bed in a second-story room of the Lindbergh house in Hopewell, New Jersey, on the night of March 1, 1932, and was never again seen alive.

Since Lindbergh's epochal transatlantic flight to Paris five years earlier, he had been admired by millions almost to the point of idolatry. He was a shy and retiring man, but despite his strenuous efforts to avoid the limelight, everything he or his wife did was a source of news. Within a few hours of the discovery that the Lindbergh baby's bed was empty, the American people became as emotionally involved in the tragedy as though the kidnapped baby had been one of their own family. About six weeks later, the discovery of the baby's body in a roadside thicket five miles from the Lindbergh home was announced in tabloid headlines: "BABY DEAD." Those two words sufficed.

On September 19, 1934, a fugitive felon from Germany named Bruno Richard Hauptmann was arrested in the Bronx, was tried at the beginning of 1935 at the Hunterdon County Court House at Flemington, New Jersey, and was convicted of kidnapping and murder. He was electrocuted on April 3, 1936.

This notorious case resulted in the passage of the Lindbergh Law in 1933, which made kidnapping a federal offense and provided for the imposition of the death penalty if the victim were injured or still missing at the time of sentencing. Before Congress passed this law, kidnapping had reached a peak of 279 recorded cases in 1931 (Clutterbuck, 1987, 38–39). Between 1933 and 1968, when the U.S. Supreme Court declared the capital punishment provision of the Lindbergh Law unconstitutional, twenty-two kidnappers were executed. The reduction in the kidnapping crime rate from the "epidemic" high of 1931 has been attributed to improved investigative techniques by the FBI and the establishment of a much closer working relationship between the FBI and local law enforcement agencies.

At the height of the kidnapping epidemic in the 1930s, the news media often referred to the "snatch racket." Terrorists appear to have devoted careful study to this chapter of criminal history, because kidnapping has provided a major source of revenue for some terrorist groups. Russell claims that approximately half of all kidnap victims from 1970 to 1985 were corporate executives or wealthy business persons who were "bought back" by their firms at a cost of approximately $250 million in ransom money (1985, 8).

One of the most successful terrorist practitioners of the snatch racket was the Argentinian People's Revolutionary Army (ERP), an extreme left-wing organization founded in 1970. Within two years, the ERP had become Latin America's most colorful and best publicized terrorist group. They had made efforts to create a "Robin Hood" image for themselves by hijacking trucks loaded with clothing or food and distributing the contents to people living in the barrios of Buenos Aires. They also pulled off a successful bank robbery that netted $300,000. In addition to assassinations of Argentinian military and political leaders, they developed ruthless proficiency in the kidnapping of wealthy business executives (Janke, 1986).

One of their abductions involved Victor Samuelson of Exxon, whose ransom netted the ERP more than $14 million. Other kidnappings included the abduction of executives representing Ford, Arrow Steel, Fiat, and Firestone. Some of these corporations are known to have paid protection money to the ERP to prevent repetition of kidnapping incidents.

The most lucrative kidnapping of the Argentinian "epidemic" of the 1970s was carried out not by the ERP, but by the Montoneros—the largest and best-known of Argentinian terrorist groups during that turbulent decade. The Montoneros were drawn mainly from the left wing of the Peronist movement. They made a much-publicized debut when they kidnapped and then killed former President Pedro Aramburu in May 1970. At their height, the Montoneros claimed a membership of 25,000. They were later denounced by Juan Peron when he returned from exile in France. Their most spectacular feat was the kidnapping of Jorge and Juan Born, sons of the owner of one of Argentina's richest corporations. The ransom amounted to a record $60 million.

The ERP and the Montoneros were ruthlessly suppressed in the "dirty war" that followed the military coup of 1976. But kidnapping of multinational corporation executives and employees for purposes of financing guerrilla and terrorist operations against the government continues to flourish elsewhere in Latin America. In 1978, in El Salvador, four kidnappings were carried out by the Armed Forces of National Resistance (FARM). Victims included the technical director of the Swedish company, Telefonico; L. M. Ericson, the manager of Phillips Corporation; the manager and assistant manager of Lloyds Bank International, and the manager of the Japanese-Salvadoran textile firm Insinca. Ransoms were paid that totaled $18 million for the release of these five men.

Kidnapping also occurs in El Salvador for strictly political concessions. In 1985, President Duarte's daughter was kidnapped, and she was released after twenty-two prisoners were freed.

In Colombia, in 1977, an American named Richard Starr was kidnapped by the Armed Revolutionary Forces of Colombia (FARC), and held for a ransom of $250,000. Because of disagreements between the U.S. government and Starr's family, Starr was not released until 1980, when the $250,000 ransom was paid through the private efforts of newspaper columnist Jack Anderson and Starr's mother (Clutterbuck, 1987, 152–153). According to Risks International, however, the majority of kidnappings that occur in Colombia today are criminally motivated, and the ransoms do not involve political concessions.[1]

Political Kidnapping

Although the techniques may appear identical, there are significant differences between kidnapping for ransom money and politically motivated kidnapping. The motivation of the political kidnapper is likely to be less simple and obvious than is that of kidnappers seeking an exchange of victims for money. Some political kidnappings are carried out for the purpose of seizing hostages for possible exchange to secure the release of prisoners held by domestic or foreign governments. Other kidnappings are perpetrated for their symbolic value, as a means of demonstrating the strength of the terrorist organization and the impotence of official authorities. Still other kidnappings can be viewed as acts of extortion intended to bring about some change in official policy that benefits the terrorists. Any of these politically motivated kidnappings may be perpetrated with the objective of securing maximum coverage by the media, whereas the practitioner of the "snatch racket" is more likely to shun the limelight.

In 1975, the IRA kidnapped Dr. Tiede Herrema, a Dutch businessman living in the Republic of Ireland. The kidnapping gave the Irish police an opportunity to use the hostage negotiation techniques developed by the New York City Police Department (which we will discuss later in this chapter). The police were able to learn where Dr. Herrema was being held, and after an eighteen-day siege, the kidnappers surrendered. Irish police have successfully employed the same techniques in other political kidnappings.

Political kidnappings have also occurred in France and the Federal Republic of Germany, but we find the highest rates of politically motivated kidnappings in Spain and Italy. In Spain the majority of kidnappings have been carried out by the ETA (Euskadi Ta Askatasuna), a Basque separatist organization. The ETA debuted in the 1960s, and originally limited itself to actions such as raising the Basque flag, but it has progressively turned to violence (Reinares, 1988). During the 1970s, the ETA carried out kidnappings for various political reasons. Using "Robin-Hood" style tactics, the group would kidnap industrialists whose employees were on strike, and the industrialists would be released only after formal announcement of wage increases was made. The ETA has also used kidnapping as a way to obtain funds to finance their activities. Some of the kidnappings resulted in the victims' murders, and the ETA has lost some popular support. Today, many of the Basque people are seeking a political solution to their problems, but kidnappings and violence by the ETA continue (Janke, 1986; Reinares, 1988).

Italy has been the site of activity for several terrorist groups: anarchists, neo-Fascists, Separatists, and groups with Marxist-Leninist ideologies have all been active (Pisano, 1986). Political kidnapping, however, has traditionally been a tactic of the Marxist-Leninist groups. The main group responsible has been the Red Brigades (Brigatte Rosse), whose avowed goal "was the construction of an armed revolutionary party which would topple the capitalist state in favor of a proletarian dictatorship" (Jamieson, 1988, 41). The Red Brigades carried out their first kidnappings in 1972 and 1973. The first three abductions were purely symbolic, and the victims were released after a few hours, with no demands made. They began making demands with the fourth kidnapping, when they kidnapped and held for eight days the personnel manager of Fiat. He was released when Fiat agreed to suspend threatened layoffs. The first kidnapping of a government official occurred in 1974 with that of the public prosecutor of Genoa. The Red Brigades claimed there had been irregularities in the trial of eight members of a left-wing organization and demanded release of the prisoners. The prisoners were never released, but the prosecutor was released a little over a month after being kidnapped. The Red Brigades did not gain materially from the kidnapping, but they embarrassed the government and gained a propaganda victory.

The two most significant political kidnappings by the Red Brigades were those of Aldo Moro and General James Dozier. Aldo Moro was a symbol of the Italian government. He had contributed to drafting the constitution and had served five times as prime minister. To the Red Brigades, Aldo Moro embodied capitalist imperialism and proletarian exploitation (Jamieson, 1988, 42). Moro was kidnapped on March 16, 1988, held for fifty-four days, and his bullet-ridden body abandoned in Rome. Moro was murdered when the Brigades realized that the government was not going to give in to their demand to release thirteen convicted terrorists. The kidnapping and murder of Aldo Moro caused the government to increase police and security force efficiency, which led to hundreds of arrests and gave the government knowledge that helped make terrorism more combatable.

The kidnapping in 1981 of General James Dozier, NATO Commander of the Allied Forces, marked a change in the activities of the Red Brigades. Dozier was the first victim of Italian terrorism who was not an Italian. His kidnapping was an attempt by the Red Brigades to internationalize their struggle, and it was the first time there was concrete evidence of a foreign power's attempting to influence Red Brigades' activities (Jamieson, 1988, 48). A direct approach was made to the Red Brigades by a Bulgarian Embassy employee in an attempt to politically control the kidnapping, but they reached no agreements. The Dozier kidnapping had a different ending than did the Aldo Moro abduction. As mentioned, the Italian police were now better equipped to deal with terrorism and launched massive police investigations. They learned where Dozier was being held, and he was rescued safely by the new Italian hostage rescue unit (Nucleo Operativo Centrale di Sicurezza) in January 1982, about one month after being kidnapped. Since the rescue of General Dozier, the Red Brigades have abandoned political kidnapping as not very profitable.

In the Middle East, most of the political kidnappings have occurred in Lebanon. Shia extremists, such as the Islamic Jihad and Hezbollah, have kidnapped American, French, British and even Soviet citizens. In November 1988 a Swiss citizen, Peter Winkler—a delegate with the International Red Cross—was kidnapped. He was freed in December, but the incident prompted the Red Cross to abandon its relief efforts in Lebanon.

Some hostages have been held captive in Lebanon for years, as shown in Table 7–1. Negotiations for the release are hampered by a number of problems, one of which is the identity of their captors. In the murky recesses of Muslim factionalism, there are few reliable cues regarding the nature, composition, and leadership of groups calling themselves the Revolutionary Justice Organization or the Organization of the Oppressed on Earth. In most instances, communication with the outside world takes place through intermediaries.

The difficulties in attempting to negotiate for the release of hostages in this kind of situation are highlighted by the recent Israeli seizure of Shiite Muslim Sheikh Abdul Karim Obeid (Williams, 1989). This individual is characterized by Israeli intelligence as a Hezbollah leader who had played a significant role in the kidnapping of U.S. Marine Corps Lt. Col. William Higgins, a member of the United Nations Truce Supervision Organization in Lebanon. The kidnapping promptly led to the execution of Higgins in retaliation for the Obeid kidnapping, from which it appears that the Israelis hoped to profit in an exchange for three Israelis held hostage by the Hezbollah (Nassar, 1989).

Hezbollah is a strongly pro-Iranian faction; within hours of Obeid's reported kidnapping, Iran's Foreign Ministry condemned the action and threatened further retaliatory measures. Shortly thereafter, threats were made against the lives of two other hostages, an American academician named Joseph Cicippio and Anglican Church representative Terry Waite of the United Kingdom. In this increasingly complicated situation, where the identity of the captors and their authority over those who act as executioners is unclear, trying to carry on meaningful negotiations is rather like trying to nail jello to the wall.

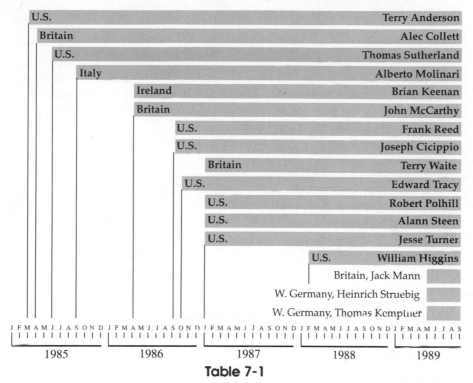

U.S.			Terry Anderson
Britain			Alec Collett
U.S.			Thomas Sutherland
Italy			Alberto Molinari
Ireland			Brian Keenan
Britain			John McCarthy
U.S.			Frank Reed
U.S.			Joseph Cicippio
Britain			Terry Waite
U.S.			Edward Tracy
U.S.			Robert Polhill
U.S.			Alann Steen
U.S.			Jesse Turner
U.S.			William Higgins
Britain, Jack Mann			
W. Germany, Heinrich Struebig			
W. Germany, Thomas Kempner			

J F M A M J J A S O N D   J F M A M J J A S O N D   J F M A M J J A S O N D   J F M A M J J A S O N D   J F M A M J J A S

1985   1986   1987   1988   1989

Table 7-1

Western Hostages Missing in Lebanon

SOURCE: From material published as an accompaniment to Nassar, F. Shiites claim Marine hanged, threaten another American. The Oregonian, August 1, 1989, A1, A8.

In Africa and Asia, the countries that suffer most from political kidnapping are Angola and Sri Lanka, respectively.[2] In Angola, the main perpetrators are members of UNITA, who have used kidnapping as a means of scaring off foreign support for the government. In Sri Lanka, Tamil separatists have kidnapped Americans who were doing development work and a British reporter (Williams, 1987).

Even though political kidnapping in the U.S. is rare, abortive attempts have been thwarted in the planning stage (Clutterbuck, 1987, 39). For instance, in 1980, eleven members of the FALN (a Puerto Rican terrorist group) were arrested, and the arrests uncovered plans to kidnap a leading businessman. In 1981, police investigations of the same group discovered dossiers of businessmen for future targeting, and a plot was uncovered to kidnap President Reagan's son and hold him for the ransom of ten members who were in jail (Dobson & Payne, 1982, 228).

Typologies of Hostage-Takers

We noted in chapter 1 that typologies represent attempts to find unity in diversity by classifying objects and events according to perceived similarities. Social scientists recognize the limitations and risks of creating typologies, but they view such classification schemas as useful analytical tools. In the case of typologies of hostage-takers, they serve the important pragmatic purpose of preparing and formulating possible negotiating responses to various kinds of hostage-takers and hostage situations. Typologies can also aid in planning counterterrorist strategies.

The several attempts by researchers to develop typologies of hostage-takers have produced classifications closely resembling Hacker's threefold typology of terrorists: crusaders, criminals, and crazies (1977, 1983). This is not surprising, since hostage-taker typologies are also based, like Hacker's typology, on the motivation of the perpetrators. Indeed, Middendorff (1975) questions whether hostage-takers can be categorized on any basis other than motives.

Miron and Goldstein (1978) have developed a typology of hostage takers based upon the offender's primary motivation: *instrumental behavior* and *expressive behavior*. Instrumental acts involve some recognizable gain for the offense. Expressive hostage-taking, on the other hand, is committed not so much for material gain as the psychological gain of significance and control. The expressive hostage-taker believes that he or she has little control over what happens and wants this to change. Media coverage of the event will achieve this change. According to Miron and Goldstein, many hostage-taking offenses may begin as instrumental acts, but change into expressive ones. An offender who originally takes a hostage for material gain may find that his original demands cannot be met, but continues anyway because of the attention and control it provides.

Stratton's typology (1978) classifies hostage-takers into three categories: (1) social, political, or religious crusaders; (2) criminals; and (3) persons who are mentally ill. Stratton points out that even though there are commonalities, one needs to be concerned with individual differences. Law enforcement authorities are obliged to keep in mind that human beings are capable of almost any kind of reaction, and therefore the police must plan for the unexpected as well as the expected.

The New York City hostage training program also divides offenders into three categories: (1) professional criminals; (2) psychotics; and (3) terrorists (Bolz, 1983, 99–116). The program claims that each requires a different approach; demands and motives vary for the three groups, so different response strategies are required.

Goldaber (1979) has developed a sophisticated and detailed typology that includes nine categories, as shown in Table 7–2. It is worth taking a closer look at how Goldaber characterizes the hostage-takers in each category.

Table 7-2

Types of Hostage-Takers

	Psychological			Criminal			Political		
	Suicidal Personality	Vengeance Seeker	Disturbed Individual	Cornered Perpetrator	Aggrieved Inmate	Felonious Extortionist	Social Protestor	Ideological Zealot	Terrorist Extremist
Who is the hostage-taker?	An unstable, hopeless, depressed individual in crisis	An otherwise ordinary person who is a disaffected former associate	An acutely or chronically unbalanced individual	Potentially any criminal	A frustrated desperate leader who can organize other inmates	An unemotional, cunning, professional criminal	An idealistic, educated young person	A fanatic, programmed cultist	An individual willing to sacrifice himself for his political philosophy
What is his distinguishing characteristic or situation?	Doesn't care if he is killed	Is driven by an irrational single purpose	Manifest lack of judgment leading to an unsound assessment of reality	Is caught unaware with no prior plan for handling predicament	Is familiar with the setting, prison authorities, and his victims	Is knowledgeable about and respectful of police power	Is an exuberant celebrant in an uplifting group experience	Is willing to sacrifice himself for his beliefs	Has realistic assessment of impact of act
When does he take the hostage?	In a severe, emotional decompensating state	After meticulous planning	When his aberrant mind seizes on the idea as a solution to his problem	In desperation when victims are available	After considerable planning, or spontaneously when pushed beyond endurance	While executing a carefully prepared plot	When he identifies the need to eliminate a social injustice	After he has sustained a wrong	When publicity potential is greatest
Where does he commit the act?	In any place, when his defenses fail	In a spot which brings him maximum satisfaction	In any setting	In the area in which he is trapped	In his own environment	In location of his selection	At the site of the unwanted entity or event or where the protest is most visible	Anywhere	Where victim is off guard
Why does he do it?	To cause someone else to fulfill his death wish	To gain revenge	To achieve mastery and to solve his problem	To effectuate escape	To bring about situational change or to obtain freedom	To obtain money	To create social change or social justice	To redress a grievance	To attain political change
How does he take the hostage?	With irrational taunts	Through overt action or furtive behavior	In an improvised, illogical manner	With weapon and as a reflexive response	With planned, overpowering, force	With a weapon in a calculated manner	In a group by massing a human thrust or blockade	With robot-like violent or non-violent conduct	With emotional and violent execution of a crafty plot
Police Response	Calm him until he can be seized	Seize him	Calm him; seize him if possible; negotiate cautiously; if unsuccessful, employ tactics	Negotiate with him; if unsuccessful, employ tactics	Negotiate with him; if unsuccessful, employ tactics	Negotiate with him; if unsuccessful, employ tactics	Negotiate with him; if unsuccessful, employ tactics	Negotiate with him; if unsuccessful, employ tactics	Negotiate with him; if unsuccessful, employ tactics

From Goldaber, I. A typology of hostage takers. *Police Chief* (June 1979), 21–23, P. 22. Reproduced by permission of the author and publisher.

The *suicidal personality* is an individual who is caught in a crisis life-style, for whom the only resolution of the crisis is ending his life. Unable to destroy himself, he creates a situation of threat in which the police officers responding to his actions are compelled to do it for him. This type of individual is not likely to react to reason and therefore must be regarded as extremely dangerous.

Time is on the side of the *vengeance seeker*, who is compulsively driven by his single purpose. This individual makes no distinction between those he believes have done him harm and innocent people trapped in his retribution scenario. His adversaries may be real or imaginary, and he is capable of holding an entire city hostage.

The *disturbed individual* may be someone who is emotionally upset over a particular situation (an enraged father who attempts to carry his child away from the home of his estranged wife) or a person with a serious personality disorder. Either type of individual is likely to engage in hostage-taking that is often improvised and always illogical. Police officers and administrators must be able to know from the hostage-taker's behavior whether they are dealing with momentary frustration or psychiatric disorder.

The *cornered perpetrator* is considered the commonest type of criminal hostage-taker—typically, a bank robber whose escape has been blocked. In this kind of situation, as noted in our discussion of the Stockholm syndrome in chapter 4, there is the possibility of a relationship developing between the perpetrator and the hostages that predisposes the hostage-taker to deal with a negotiator who offers him an acceptable way out of his predicament.

The *aggrieved inmate* is seen as extremely dangerous. As someone who is already incarcerated, he is comfortable in an adversarial relationship with law enforcement agents. In addition, he is familiar with his surroundings and his opponents, and he is capable of organizing other inmates in support of his plan.

The *felonious extortionist* has a cold-blooded, methodical approach to hostage-taking. He is aware of the kinds of things that can go wrong with his scheme and prepares himself to deal with these eventualities. Above all, he sees himself as a player for high stakes. He is capable of being bold, daring, and decisive in his actions.

The *social protester* is apt to be youthful, idealistic, and committed to a cause. The protester's actions usually involve group support from people who share his or her values and aspirations. Although social protesters can be difficult to handle, they perceive matters realistically and are susceptible to rational appeals and approaches.

The *ideological zealot* is a person who trades freedom for security of mind and considers it a fair exchange. To this type of individual, simple solutions to the complexities of life become irresistible. Anyone who fails to become a fellow convert risks being viewed as an enemy. Ideological zealots who engage in hostage-taking can become ruthless adversaries, because they can find personal validity only in serving their cause.

The *terrorist extremist* appears with increasing frequency around the world. People of this kind are trained and disciplined, and they see themselves as soldiers fighting a war in which they can give no quarter. Enemies are not entitled to humane treatment under the rules of conventional warfare. If terrorist extremists seize hostages, any approach to negotiation must be directed toward the top leaders of their organization or group.

The law enforcement response to these various hostage-takers is dictated, first and foremost, by the necessity to limit possibilities for further violence. The suicide-prone individual and the distraught or disturbed individual must be calmed and seized. The vengeance seeker should be taken into custody as quickly as possible, but negotiation might be employed to encourage him to surrender.

With respect to the other types of hostage-taker, negotiation is recommended. The question then becomes: how long should negotiations go on? Goldaber's answer is: "as long as the incident commander feels that he is able to predict with certainty the next move of the hostage-taker and that he knows that this move will not harm the hostage" (1979, 22). When the incident commander no longer feels able to predict the hostage-taker's next move with certainty, the negotiation should be terminated and an assault ordered.

This brief review of hostage-taking typologies shows disagreements among the researchers that probably result from differences in training, education, experience, and perspectives of those who developed the typology. Goldaber's typology underscores the complexity of hostage-taking situations. Authorities responsible for developing response strategies need to be aware that typologies do not necessarily facilitate effective handling of all hostage-taking situations. Captain Frank Bolz of the New York City Police Department's hostage negotiation team states that "no two cases were ever alike" (1979, 25). This recognition is probably the key to the program's success.

Hostage Negotiation

Some terrorist incidents have been successfully terminated by hostage rescue operations; others have been resolved with a minimum loss of life or property damage through skillful negotiation. In still other situations, negotiation has been used as a technique to buy time to prepare to proceed with hostage rescue.

On April 30, 1980, a group of Iranians opposed to the regime of the Ayatollah Khomeini took over the Iranian Embassy in London and took twenty-six people hostage. The terrorists demanded that ninety-one of their colleagues held prisoner in Iran be freed. The terrorists agreed to negotiate, but by the sixth day, May 5, they threatened to start killing hostages. The terrorists killed the embassy press officer. After the hostage was killed, police negotiators began stalling for time to prevent more killings and to give the SAS (Special Air Service) hostage rescue unit time to complete preparations for assaulting the embassy. "Operation Nimrod" began, and five terrorists were killed, one captured, and only one hostage was killed. The operation was considered a success.

Many people have an understandable desire to see hostages freed and hostage-takers punished—preferably at the same time. Overcoming hostage-takers by force and, if necessary, killing them in the process, has a wide appeal. It is the kind of summary justice identified with the frontier code of the Old West. Research indicates, however, that more hostages die in such assaults than are murdered by terrorists, and that the assaults do not appear to be a deterrent to further terrorist attacks (Miller, 1980, 37–38). These considerations lend support to the use of force as a last, rather than a first, resort and underscore the desirability of beginning with an attempt at negotiation with the hostage-taker.

As mentioned earlier, every hostage situation is different. There are, however, several well-accepted guidelines based on the experiences of groups like New York City's hostage negotiating team, the FBI, and European police agencies that can help us understand how the hostage negotiation process works.

The key individual in the hostage negotiating situation is the negotiator. Characteristics considered essential for a good negotiator are: good physical condition, mature appearance, ability to withstand prolonged stress, ability to observe and report, communication skills, patience, calm, and the ability to retain poise (Crelinsten & Szabo, 1977). Training and experience in dealing with violent offenders is mandatory. The negotiator must also know the kidnapper's objectives, motivations, and attitudes as well as local and national policies, so that there is an awareness of the limits within which negotiation will take place. Authorities agree that the negotiator should not also be a decision maker. Clutterbuck (1987, 136) suggests that the negotiator be a police officer of junior rank, so that he can be able to play for time saying, "I have no power to agree to that; I'll have to ask." The New York hostage negotiating team once considered using psychiatrists as front-line negotiators, but rejected the idea. Bolz explains why they believe a police officer makes the best negotiator:

> Police, on the one hand, deal with personal crises on a day-to-day basis—from fender benders to death notifications, from family arguments to interviews with sex crime victims. They can be trained and backed up by psychiatrists, sometimes at the scene of a situation when reinforcement and guidance are needed. Indeed, the control of the phenomenon of transference—the ability of one individual to relate to another's feelings—is the cornerstone of both psychiatry and constructive hostage negotiation. But it is the cop who can think like a shrink, not the shrink who can think like a cop, who is best equipped for all the possibilities of a siege. (1979, 303)

The use of a team approach instead of a single negotiator permits the negotiation process to include individuals from several specialty areas. The team approach is used by the New York City Police Department, West

Germany, and the Netherlands, as well as other police departments. This method combines the negotiator with an individual trained and educated in psychology and a person with language skills to work together to achieve the negotiation goal. This type of program also permits the use of a substitute negotiator who is already familiar and acceptable to kidnappers when psychological pressures force the primary negotiator to get some rest. The key to the success of a team program is training. All team members must train together regularly so that each knows and understands the others' strengths and weaknesses.

Talking to Terrorists

The nature of the negotiations that take place in attempts to resolve political hostage-taking, especially in incidents involving diplomatic personnel, differs substantially from the negotiation process we have already described. Jenkins (1982) has analyzed the communications problems raised by hostage-negotiation within the context of political kidnapping.

When terrorists seize American officials abroad, two governments are automatically involved: the local government and the U.S. government. The latter includes the American embassy on the scene and a task force assembled in Washington to manage the crisis. If the kidnapping takes place outside the capital of the country, the local American consul and a regional government must be added to the network. In some instances, the kidnappers contact the hostage's family, and hostages are often pressured to appear at media conferences and to make written appeals. Participation of intermediaries increases the complexity of the communications network.

The problem, as Jenkins puts it, is not that a lot of people must somehow communicate with a lot of other people; they must do so under a variety of restrictions. The local government "usually wants to cut off the terrorists, bury the crisis, remain in charge, and conduct its business in private" (1982, 3). It does not want to talk to the kidnappers (or at least not be seen talking with them); it does not want the embassy or the hostage's family to communicate with the terrorists; and it may go so far as to prohibit communications between the terrorists and the media, especially in the form of communiques.

Since the early 1970s, the U.S. has publicly espoused a no-negotiations, no-concessions policy in dealing with politically motivated kidnappings. The no-negotiations component of that policy precludes direct communication between U.S. officials and the kidnappers. In fact, the American ambassador to Tanzania was fired in 1975 when he entered into direct communication with terrorists who had kidnapped three American students. But the U.S. government holds the host or local government responsible for the safety of American diplomats assigned to it, and when an American official is seized by terrorists, it is the responsibility of the local government to negotiate for the hostage's release.

Jenkins observes that governments expend considerable effort to directly contact terrorists without addressing them publicly through the media. For a variety of reasons, the use of intermediaries poses some real dangers: intermediaries are rarely neutral; they may exploit their role to publicly criticize the government; they begin to see themselves as active arbitrators in a dispute. Entrusting communications to an intermediary almost always eventuates in concessions.

Jenkins suggests a number of "general principles" that government officials might observe to guide their communications in political hostage-taking cases. Perhaps the most important of these are the hardest for diplomats to follow: messages should be blunt and simple; committee language doesn't work; the less said in public the better; the government must speak with a single voice; and the government's public responses should be kept as low-key as possible.

Policy Issues in Hostage Negotiation

Each time a major hostage-taking incident occurs, one can expect to read a reprise of arguments for and against a "no ransom, no negotiation" policy. Although it is not our intention to exhaustively review the well-polarized positions taken by experts and authorities, it is important to consider several issues.

The "No Ransom" Policy Dilemma

Friedland (1983) has classified the various views concerning the actions governments should undertake in response to terrorists' attempts to extort ransom into two positions. One, the "no ransom" policy, holds that hostage-taking tactics are most effectively countered by a government's consistent refusal to yield to extortion attempts. As we will see in chapter 11, there is more myth than reality to the assertion that this position represents current official U.S. policy toward terrorism—or indeed that it has represented official policy in the past. The problem has existed through a series of administrations, and has caused many, both inside and outside the U.S., to ask: What is U.S. policy and who is in charge? (Celmer, 1987, 116). At any rate, adherents of the "no ransom" policy maintain that continued failure to extort ransom will convince terrorists of the futility of their efforts and encourage them to abandon further attempts.

The other position, the "flexible response" position, questions the practicality and wisdom of adhering to a single, standard policy of "no ransom." The arguments against this position can be summarized as follows:

1. Hostage incidents might be perpetrated under a wide variety of circumstances and by terrorist organizations that vary significantly in terms of

ideology, modus operandi, and the psychological makeup of their members. Therefore, strong commitment to a standard policy that fails to consider such variability is bound to be ineffective.

2. The assumption that failure to extort ransom will force terrorists to abandon hostage-taking ignores the other "fringe benefits" (e.g., media coverage, repressive government measures, undermining societal feelings of security and order) that motivate hostage tactics.

3. Consistent failure to extort ransom may prompt terrorists to escalate their attacks, either by increasing the frequency or sophistication of hostage seizures or by resorting to alternative terror tactics.

Friedland dismisses "flexible response" as a nonpolicy position. He contends that the arguments on which the "no ransom" policy is rejected reflect a basic misunderstanding of the meaning of policies. According to Friedland,

> A policy is an explicit or implicit declaration of intent to act in a certain manner under prescribed circumstances, and it is designed to affect the behavior of a defined population. It refers primarily to the future and purports to affect actions not yet taken rather than to respond to deeds done. (1983, 202)

From the standpoint of this definition, any attempt to introduce exceptions or qualifications into a stated policy in the interests of dealing with "variability" or "uniqueness" is bound to weaken the possible impact of the policy. This is especially true of the "no ransom" policy on hostage-taking, which is founded on the principle that failure to reinforce or reward a given behavior will lower the likelihood of its occurrence.

With regard to the second argument, the so-called "fringe benefits" alluded to can be gained by alternative tactics (e.g., frequent, random assassinations) that are less hazardous to the terrorist than is hostage-taking.

The third criticism seems to be based on the expectation that compliance with ransom demands will satisfy terrorists and stabilize the incidence of hostage seizures at some acceptable level. Friedland notes that this expectation is unrealistic. The actual amount of ransom received is of secondary importance to the terrorist, whose primary aim is to undermine political stability.

If a policy is to be effective, it must be credible. Here is where the "no ransom" policy creates a dilemma for democratic nations such as the U.S. The dilemma may be stated as follows: In the long run, "no ransom" is likely to be proven a most effective policy against hostage seizures; in the short run, implementing the policy and establishing its credibility may be extremely costly.

As Friedland observes, the process that is characteristic of hostage negotiations with terrorists is not one of bargaining, accommodation, and conciliation, but of brinkmanship. When faced with a hostage incident, the target government has to choose between forceful action against the perpetrators and attempts to convince them to surrender. Friedland questions whether the term *negotiations* is appropriate for this kind of transaction.

Summary

There is no foreseeable end to political hostage-taking, because it is a terrorist technique that provides a high yield at a very low risk. This rather pessimistic conclusion is underlined by the latest hostage crisis in Lebanon. Lebanon has no viable government and Iran, which has no diplomatic relations with the U.S., has proven itself largely impervious to overtures delivered through third countries.

The captors of Lt. Col. Higgins and the other hostages belong to the Organization of the Oppressed on Earth, which is believed to be a faction of Hezbollah (the Party of God), a loosely organized group of about 600 Shiite militants scattered throughout Lebanon who receive guidance and support from Iran. The Oppressed on Earth operates in southern Lebanon, and American officials believe that its leaders are separate from the various Hezbollah adherents who hold the other fourteen Western hostages in Beirut.

No one has yet proposed a realistic method to retaliate against groups whose members live among women and children in slums or refugee camps. One of the few bits of reliable intelligence from this part of the world describes the American hostages as being shuffled from apartment to apartment in the Shiite slums of southern Lebanon; even if an American hostage rescue unit such as Delta could fight their way into such an area, they would face the greatest difficulty getting out with the hostages alive.

To add to the confusion, Amal, a Shiite militia that has been fighting the Hezbollah for control of southern Lebanon, is Syrian-backed, while the Hezbollah is supported by Iran. Thus, a regional dimension must be added to the local squabble. Amal and Hezbollah are divided over the tactic of kidnapping foreigners as a tool in Lebanon's internecine warfare. Amal, which has pressed for the Israelis to withdraw from southern Lebanon, views the act as counterproductive. Hezbollah, which wants not only to drive Israel out but also to conquer historical Palestine, considers kidnapping an appropriate pressure tactic. Fierce fighting began last year between Amal and the Hezbollah after Higgins's kidnapping; the truce between them is tense and fragile.

Hostage-taking in other places around the world may present fewer complexities than are apparent in the Middle East, but it is equally devoid of opportunities for effective prevention or retaliation. Official pronouncements and bravado notwithstanding, Americans who choose to go, or are sent, to these areas must be made to appreciate the full extent of the dangers they are going to face. Official restrictions on American citizens' travel to such areas are unlikely to prevent those who are determined to seek entry for personal reasons. But they should be compelled to recognize that their decision to enter a restricted area frees their fellow citizens and the U.S. government from further responsibility for their fate. For others, whose duty requires their presence in dangerous parts of the world, the least the government can do is try to ensure that the national interests they represent or defend are important enough to justify risking lives.

Seizing persons as hostages for political advantage or profit is a practice that can be traced back to antiquity. Greek city-states and the Roman republic and empire secured hostages as a guarantee of good conduct. During the Middle Ages and the dawn of the Renaissance, noblemen and royalty captured in battle were held for ransom. The French Revolution and the Napoleonic period introduced the concept of the "nation in arms"; warfare in the twentieth century, especially as conducted by the Germans in two world wars, witnessed the large-scale seizure and murder by execution of hostages who were, for the most part, innocent noncombatants.

In the U.S., kidnapping for purposes of securing ransom money reached "epidemic" proportions in the 1930s, culminating in passage of the Lindbergh Law, which made kidnapping a federal offense and imposed the death penalty for the injury or murder of kidnap victims.

Modern terrorists in several places—Latin America, the Middle East, Africa, and Asia—have used the kidnapping of multinational corporation executives as a lucrative source of financing their insurgencies. Political kidnapping has also been a frequent practice among terrorist groups and has been employed, on occasion, by agents of official governments.

Attempts to develop meaningful typologies of hostage-takers as a useful first step toward formulating effective response and prevention strategies have concentrated primarily on the motives of individuals and groups involved in the seizure of hostages. With certain variations and amplifications, these typologies have sorted hostage-takers into three categories that reflect Hacker's triad of crusaders, criminals, and crazies.

In hostage-negotiation procedures and techniques, negotiation is likely to be most effective when backed up by a force option. The difficulties facing the U.S. government in trying to negotiate, or even communicate, directly with terrorist groups whose identity, composition, and location are extremely unclear. Private persons should be discouraged from traveling to or living in various trouble spots around the world. Military and diplomatic personnel should be regarded as serving in a combat zone, with all the physical security protections that wartime conditions require.

Key Terms

Dozier kidnapping
"flexible response" policy
hostage-taker typologies
Montoneros
"no ransom" policy dilemma
Operation Nimrod
skyjacking
Richard Starr

ERP
hijacking
Lindbergh Law
Aldo Moro
Oderint dum metuant
seige
"snatch racket"

Questions for Discussion and Review

1.   Is kidnapping a purely modern phenomenon or does it have historical precedents?
2.   How did the German practice of "frightfulness," which was followed in two world wars, involve the seizure of hostages?
3.   What events occurred in the Lindbergh case and earlier that led to passage of the Lindbergh Law? What were its provisions?
4.   How does political kidnapping differ from kidnapping for ransom? Who have been the principal targets of kidnappings for ransom perpetrated by terrorists?
5.   Typologies of hostage-takers stress the motives of individuals or groups who seize hostages. What types of hostage-taker does Goldaber consider most dangerous?
6.   Identify some of the communications problems that are apt to characterize the seizure of American diplomatic personnel.
7.   Briefly discuss the pros and cons involved in the "no ransom, no negotiations" versus "flexible reponse" policies. What is the dilemma raised by the "no ransom" policy?
8.   What kind of advice would you give a friend who is thinking about taking a job in the Middle East or Latin America?

Notes

1.   Risks International, Inc. is a consulting firm in Alexandria, Virginia, that specializes in statistical information on the worldwide terrorist problem and its direct impact on the operations of both domestic and international corporations. The present information is based on a November 17, 1988, telephone conversation.

2.   Because of the extensive media coverage, many people, when thinking about ethnoreligious conflict, think only of the problems in the Middle East or Northern Ireland. However, there are other people in the world sharing common national, religious, linguistic or cultural origins or backgrounds who are demanding separatism and use violence as a means to achieve their goals. Interested readers should be aware of the following sources: Oberst, 1988; Otis & Carr, 1988; Pisano, 1986; Reinares, 1988.

References

Adams, G.B. *The History of England: From the Norman Conquest to the Death of John (1066–1216)*. London: Longmans, Green, 1905.

Aston, C.C. "Political Hostage-Taking in Western Europe." In *Contemporary Terrorism*, edited by W. Gutteridge, pp. 57–83. New York: Facts on File, 1986.

Bolz, F. "The Hostage Situation: Law Enforcement Options." In *Terrorism: Interdisciplinary Perspectives*, edited by B. Eichelman, D.A. Soskis and W.H. Reid, pp. 99–116. Washington, DC: American Psychiatric Association, 1983.

Bolz, F., and Hershey, E. *Hostage Cop*. New York: Rawson, Wade, 1979.

Celmer, M.A. *Terrorism, U.S. Strategy, and Reagan Policies*. Westport, CT: Greenwood Press, 1987.

Clutterbuck, R. L. *Kidnap, Hijack and Extortion: The Response*. New York: St. Martin's Press, 1987.

Crelinsten, R.D., and Szabo, D. *Hostage Taking*. Lexington, MA: Lexington Books, 1977.

Dobson, C., and Payne, R. *The Terrorists: Their Weapons, Leaders and Tactics*. New York: Facts on File, 1982.

Friedland, N. "Hostage Negotiations: Dilemmas About Policy." In *Perspectives on Terrorism*, edited by L.Z. Freedman and Y. Alexander, pp. 201–211. Wilmington, DE: Scholarly Resources, 1983.

Goldaber, I. "A Typology of Hostage Takers." *Police Chief* 6 (June 1979): 21–22.

Hobsbawm, E.J. *Primitive Rebels*. New York: Norton, 1959.

Jamieson, A. "Political Kidnapping in Italy." *Conflict* 1 (1988): 41–48.

Janke, P. "Spanish Separatism: ETA's Threat to Basque Democracy." In *Contemporary Terrorism*, edited by W. Gutteridge, pp. 135–166. New York: Facts on File, 1986.

Jenkins, B.M. *Talking to Terrorists*. Santa Monica, CA: The Rand Corporation, 1982.

McCall, A. *The Medieval Underworld*. London: Hamish Hamilton, 1979.

Mickolus, E. F. "Tracking the Growth and Prevalence of International Terrorism." In *Managing Terrorism*, edited by P.J. Montana and G.S. Roukis, pp. 3–22. Westport, CT: Quorum Books, 1983.

Middendorff, W. *New Developments in the Taking of Hostages and Kidnapping: A Summary*. Washington, DC: National Criminal Justice Reference Service, 1975.

Miller, Abraham H. *Terrorism and Hostage Negotiations*. Boulder, CO: Westview Press, 1980.

Miron, M.S., and Goldstein, A.P. *Hostage*. Kalamazoo, MI: Behaviordelia, 1978.

Nassar, F. "Shiites Claim Marine Hanged, Threaten Another American." *Oregonian*. (August 1, 1989): A1, A8.

Oberst, R. C. "Sri Lanka's Tamil Tigers." *Conflict* 2/3(8) (1988): 185–202.

Otis, R., and Carr, C.D. "Sri Lanka and the Ethnic Challenge." *Conflict* 2/3 (1988): 203–216.

Pisano, V.S. "The Red Brigades: A Challenge to Italian Democracy." In *Contemporary Terrorism*, edited by W. Gutteridge, pp. 167–197. New York: Facts on File, 1986.

Pisano, V.S. "Terrorist Ethnic Separatism in France and Italy." *Conflict* 2/3 (1988): 83–95.

Reinares, F. "Nationalism and Violence in Basque Politics." *Conflict* 2/3 (1988): 141–155.

Russell, C. "Kidnapping as a Terrorist Tactic." In *Terrorism and Personal Protection*, edited by B.M. Jenkins, pp. 8–22. Stoneham, MA: Butterworth, 1985.

Stratton, J. G. "The Terrorist Act of Hostage-Taking: A View of Violence and the Perpetrators," *Journal of Police Science and Administration* 6 (1978): 1–9.

Tuchman, B.W. *Guns of August*. New York: Macmillan, 1962.

Warner, R. *War Commentaries of Caesar*. New York: Mentor Books, 1960.

Williams, D. "Israelis May Seek Exchange." *Oregonian* (July 29, 1989): A1, A14.

Williams, P. "The Tamils: Recent Events in Sri Lanka." *Asian Affairs* 18 (1987): 176–180.

8

Narcoterrorism:
Drug-Crime-Terrorism Linkage

As recently as a decade ago, the international drug trade did not figure importantly in assessments of global terrorism. Despite rumored links between the production of opium in the "golden triangle" area of Southeast Asia and various local warlords and insurgent groups, the U.S. government doubted the existence of any significant interaction between drug traffickers and terrorists. The Drug Enforcement Administration, for example, argued that, with the possible exception of the FARC (Colombian Revolutionary Armed Forces, the armed wing of the Colombian Communist Party) and the Shan United Army in the golden triangle, there was no evidence of wholesale participation by terrorist groups in drug trafficking. Ten years later, the connection between drugs and terrorism appeared to be sufficiently well-founded to columnist Jack Anderson to provide him with material on the hazards of life in Bogota, Colombia, for U.S. Embassy personnel facing the dual threat of the Medellin drug cartel and the M-19 guerrilla group (Anderson & Van Atta, 1989a).

Narcoterrorism may represent a sinister new development fraught with serious implications for counterterrorist initiatives, but we lack detailed, reliable information about the alleged connection between terrorism and drug trafficking. Apart from reports of journalists, many of whom have faced extreme hazards in pursuing story leads, the primary sources of information have been Congressional hearings and official releases by the Drug Enforcement Administration. The much-touted and highly politicized "war on drugs" that has been carried on during two Republican administrations appears to have produced more political benefits than victories; and the kind and extent of joint involvement by drug traffickers and terrorists in the manufacture, transportation, and distribution of illicit drugs remains to be adequately documented. Within the limits imposed by the available evidence, we will identify some of the major terrorist groups alleged to be participating in this traffic and how their involvement affects their capacity to conduct terrorist operations. We will also discuss the controversial matter of the international weapons trade, because it is claimed that weapons, drugs, and money form the basis for trade and negotiation among drug traffickers, terrorists, and representatives of governments that provide state support for terrorism.

Drug Abuse and Drug Demand

Any discussion of an alleged relationship between drug trafficking and terrorism must begin with the recognition that the basis of the lucrative international drug trade is the voracious American appetite for illicit drugs. The United States, a nation with 5 percent of the world's population, accounts for 50 percent of the world's drug consumption. In 1984, the House Committee on Narcotics Abuse and Control claimed that more than twenty million Americans use marijuana regularly; roughly eight to twenty million are regular users of cocaine; about half a million are heroin addicts; one million use hallucinogens; and approximately six million abuse prescription drugs. The reasons that so many people in this country indulge in drug abuse are a topic that lies outside the scope of this book; Frost suggests that the causes can perhaps be found in the breakdown of societal and family restraints, peer pressure, low tolerance for pain and hardship, media encouragement of instant gratification, and the belief that there is a quick fix for every difficulty from acne to depression.

> If neuropharmacologists and psychologists really know the answer—and this is doubtful—their knowledge has not yet been translated into a clear policy for dealing with the malaise. We would delude ourselves, however, if we attributed the drug abuse problem essentially to an external cause. With the possible exception of veterans exposed to heroin and marijuana use in Vietnam, there is little credible evidence that foreign enemies have substantially influenced Americans' demand for illicit drugs. Our national disgrace is of our own making. (Frost, 1986, 189)

The massive demand for illegal drugs puts enormous amounts of cash into the hands of drug traffickers. With multimillions in cash at their disposal, traffickers can hire lawyers and bankers to work for them; lease boats, aircraft, and real estate; and, as necessary, bribe police officers and administrators, judges, and other criminal justice personnel. It is not difficult to document drug-related corruption of foreign officials. The evidence, Laqueur (1987) noted, is overwhelming. It has come to light in reports of many governments and in court cases from a variety of countries. Corruption of the local police is claimed to have figured in the abduction and murder of Drug Enforcement Administration (DEA) Special Agent Enrique Camarena in Mexico and the escape, for a time, of the prime suspect. Before the suspect's extradition from Costa Rica, U.S. officials complained that not a single major trafficker was arrested in Mexico in eight years, despite more than $110 million in narcotics control assistance to that country.

Traficantes and Terrorists in Latin America

Seven Latin American or Caribbean countries account for the bulk of the marijuana, cocaine, and heroin illegally smuggled into the U.S. each year.

Some 90 percent of all the imported marijuana that enters the U.S. market originates in one of four Caribbean Basin countries: Mexico (35–40 percent); Colombia (20–25 percent); Jamaica (10–15 percent); and Belize (5–10 percent). The U.S. produces an additional 2,100 tons annually.

Virtually all of the cocaine is cultivated in three South American nations: Peru (50 percent); Bolivia (40–45 percent); and Colombia (5–10 percent). In the mid-1970s, Colombia emerged as the principal country for refining cocaine and for more than a decade has controlled roughly 75 percent of all the refined cocaine exported from the Andean region to the U.S. Mexico is the only country in Latin America that produces heroin. About 40 percent of the heroin smuggled into the U.S. in 1986 was produced in Mexico; the rest (50 percent) came from the golden crescent (especially Pakistan, the world's largest producer) and the golden triangle (Bagley, 1989, 163).

One must distinguish between the production of drugs and drug trafficking. Those who engage in the former are not necessarily the same people involved in the latter. Drugs such as cocaine and heroin, for example, are produced from plants grown mainly in rural areas of South America and in Southeast Asia that are not easily accessible. In both South America and Southeast Asia, guerrilla groups are known to have defended the growers of coca leaves and opium against attacks by drug law enforcement units and guarded access to private airports from which drugs were shipped.

The relationship between governments, *traficantes*, and terrorists in Latin America is complicated, subject to frequent changes, and extremely difficult—for obvious reasons—to document. If traficantes and terrorists have made common cause against the government on occasion, the fronts at times have been reversed.

Sendero Luminoso (The Shining Path)

Laqueur characterizes the Sendero Luminoso ("Shining Path") as one of the strangest, but not the least effective, of all the Latin American insurrectionist movements (1987, 255). Sendero originated in the provincial (or departmental) capital of Ayacucho in southern Peru. McClintock (1984) observes that the area of Ayacucho has two significant characteristics: it is remote and it has a university. When the Shining Path was founded by a philosophy professor, Abimael Guzman, it consisted almost exclusively of university students and junior faculty members. Almost unnoticed, these young university-educated radicals were able to forge a working alliance with the peasantry, the *campesinos*, in Ayacucho.

Strongly influenced by Castro and the Cuban experience, they proved to be ideologically more receptive to the impact of Maoism in its purest form. With the founding of the Maoist Party of Peru and aided by government neglect, the dedicated militants of the Shining Path gradually established a foothold in the Indian villages of southern Peru, where there is a tradition of radical messianic ideas. Younger peasants were discontented about the lack of economic progress and the failure of announced land reforms in the countryside.

Before 1980, while a military junta ruled Peru, Sendero guerrilla and terrorist activities were of a limited scale, confined largely to burning ballot boxes and symbolic acts such as hanging dead dogs from lamp posts in Lima and Ayacucho. When the military junta was replaced by a civilian democratic government, Sendero moved into Mao's "third stage of guerrilla struggle" and engaged in terrorist actions on a wide front. Government buildings were bombed; transportation, communications, power plants, and factories were blown up; and more than 500 murders were carried out in 1983 alone.

Early in 1986 President Garcia (elected the previous summer as head of a left-wing coalition), was forced to call upon the military to deal with a rapidly deteriorating situation that featured bomb attacks on the embassies of West Germany, Spain, India, and China. Garcia had made a number of attempts to introduce much-needed reforms in the administration of justice and to provide economic assistance to the neglected villages in the highlands. He also tried, without success, to open a dialogue with Sendero. All these efforts failed, and Lima rivaled Beirut in the level of lawlessness and violence.

Sendero Luminoso (the name purportedly came from a speech claiming that Marxism-Leninism would open "a shining path to revolution") has never actively sought collaboration with other left-wing parties in Peru and, unlike many other guerrilla or terrorist groups, has consistently shunned publicity.

Early in 1987, Shining Path rebels entered into an alliance with drug dealers, according to police and to *campesinos* involved in the trade (Hayes, 1987, 15–A). If this information is accurate, the pact seems to have brought a high level of violence to the Upper Huallaga River Valley—the world's greatest source of coca, the plant used to make cocaine. Violence is said to have included clashes between rival gangs of drug traffickers, with the Shining Path siding with kingpin figures in the drug trade. Sendero has also battled another rebel band, the pro-Cuban Tupac Amaru Revolutionary, for control of the valley.

Local residents and police call the Huallaga River the biggest cemetery in the valley and claim that barely a day passes without a bullet-riddled body floating downstream past riverfront villages. The *Carretera Marginal*, the valley's principal highway, has also been strewn with its share of the dead (Hayes, 1987).

The Upper Huallaga Valley is hemmed in by jagged peaks at its southern end, but broadens to twenty miles as the swift-flowing river drops a thousand feet by the time it reaches the town of Juanjui, 150 miles to the north. The valley floor is covered with luxuriant tropical vegetation, and the coca grown on the hillsides produces the world's best-quality cocaine.

The Colombian Connection

Practically all of the region we have referred to is filled with coca plantations. From 1980 to the present, drug traffickers have established and developed a marketing network with Colombian organizations (Smith, 1989). Tens of thousands of impoverished highland peasants poured into the valley to grow coca to meet the soaring U.S. demand for cocaine. The *campesinos* turn the coca leaves into doughlike paste in crude processing pits in the jungle. "Narcotraficantes"—local drug chieftains and their hired gunmen—collect the paste and market it to Colombian buyers, who arrive in small planes at dozens of airstrips scattered throughout the valley. In Colombia, international drug organizations refine the paste into pure cocaine for smuggling to the U.S. and Europe.

The huge profits from the cocaine trade and the *campesinos'* resentment of a U.S.-financed coca-eradication campaign combined to draw the Shining Path into the valley. In areas controlled by the Sendero, it is claimed that the rebels charge drug traffickers $3,000 to $4,000 "landing rights" for each planeload of coca paste.

The Shining Path has become the de facto government in dozens of villages in the Upper Huallaga Valley. The Sendero names "delegates" to collect taxes and maintain such essential public services as electricity and water. They have also shut down discotheques, run prostitutes out of town, and banned adultery and homosexuality. A Canadian priest in Aucayacu observed: "In a sense, they enforce a hyper-Christian morality—except they kill you if you break the rules."

M-19 (Colombia) and the Medellin Cartel

The Colombian terrorist group calling itself M-19 (which stands for "19th of April Movement") originated as a extreme right-wing youth organization headed by the dictator Roja Pinilla, who ruled Colombia in the 1950s. For reasons beyond the scope of our discussion, M-19 ended up on the opposite end of the political-ideological spectrum. The M-19 emerged in 1974, but it first gained real notoriety in 1980 when it invaded the Dominican Embassy in broad daylight and took half the diplomatic corps hostage, including the American ambassador. Negotiations for exchanging the hostages for jailed terrorists ended after more than two months, with the M-19 terrorists being flown to Cuba for asylum. In 1985, the M-19 seized the Palace of Justice and destroyed thousands of records, making the prosecution of key drug traffickers next to impossible. In the subsequent shootout with the police, eleven Supreme Court justices and many other people were killed (Fontaine, 1988, 101).

M-19 preyed on wealthy drug dealers by kidnapping their family members and demanding ransom. In 1981, more than 200 drug traffickers met at a restaurant in Medellin and plotted a war against the M-19. When the drug cartel had murdered enough terrorists to subdue the M-19, they entered into a compact that arranged for the traficantes to pay the M-19 to carry out their dirty work. It is claimed that the cartel paid M-19 $5 million to take over the Colombian Supreme Court building and destroy extradition files on cartel leaders—and that this is what led to the violence and bloodshed in the 1985 incident (Anderson & Van Atta, 1988, B9).

The cartel vowed to kill any Colombian police officer or informant working with the U.S. Drug Enforcement Administration, which has been actively engaged in Colombian efforts to cope with the corruption and violence caused by drug trafficking in that country. The cartel carried out that threat with the assassination of the DEA's most important informant, Barry Seal, in Baton Rouge, Louisiana, in 1986.

Seal was a Special Forces pilot in Vietnam, who turned to drug trafficking in 1977. He eventually flew cargoes of drugs for the Medellin cartel and amassed a private fortune said to be around $75 million. But after the DEA arrested him in 1983, he began fingering cartel members. He aided in the extradition and prosecution of cartel kingpin Carlos Lehder, who is now serving a life sentence in the U.S.

The cartel put a price on Seal's head: $1 million alive and $500,000 dead. Had Seal been brought to Colombia alive, there is no doubt that he would have been tortured to death. Emboldened by the Seal hit, the cartel has put out the word that it will pay $1 million for the murder of any DEA agent. It does not matter if the agent is working directly against the cartel or against drug traffickers from other regions. (Approximately 80 percent of the cocaine smuggled into the U.S. comes from the Medellin area.)

The previous attorney general of Colombia, Carlos Mauro Hoyos, was assassinated by the Medellin cartel on January 25, 1988. Hundreds of Colombian government officials, judges, and police officers have been gunned down or blown up for trying to enforce the drug laws. Others have been forced to flee for their lives, and at least one who fled to the U.S. has found no safe haven even here. The present attorney general of Colombia, Horacio Serpa, who is also on the cartel's hit list, told columnist Jack Anderson about a brave judge named Consuela Sanchez, who dared to indict the cartel's chief enforcer, Pablo Escobar, on a charge that he had murdered a Colombian newspaper editor (Anderson & Van Atta, 1989b).

The cartel told Judge Sanchez that every person in her family would be wiped out if she signed the arrest warrant for Escobar, boldly putting the threat in a letter to the judge: "If you call Mr. Escobar to trial, you can be sure that all the members of your family tree—ancestors and offspring—will be eliminated. We are capable of executing you anywhere on this planet. There is no place you can hide." Sanchez is living in the U.S. with her husband under an assumed name and with the protection of the State Department and DEA.

FARC (Colombia) and the Traficantes

FARC (Colombian Revolutionary Armed Forces) is the armed wing of the Colombian Communist Party. It is the oldest and largest of the country's guerrilla groups and has a rural base. Half of its "fronts" operate in coca-growing and marijuana-growing areas, where they have direct arrangements with traffickers. FARC collects protection payments from coca growers, but provides warning of the approach of antidrug law enforcement agents or military patrols. Because of their countrol of a number of strategic river points in the interior, the guerrillas can impede police travel. The FARC guarantees a number of clandestine airfields for the use of drug traffickers. In exchange, the guerrillas receive money from the traffickers to buy arms and supplies. Such goods are often smuggled in on return drug flights. The alliance between traffickers and guerrillas, however, can be turbulent at times.

Drug Trafficking and Terrorism in Asia

The Latin American experience with drug trafficking has been paralleled by developments in Southeast Asia, where the "golden triangle" has long been known as the principal source of opium growing and export. The Shan State is the major opium poppy cultivation area in the golden triangle. The Burmese Communist Party (BCP) has been trying to establish its authority and control over the Shan State almost since Burma gained its independence from Britain in 1948. For years the BCP was involved in the drug trade to a limited extent, such as collecting taxes from farmers who raised opium poppies.

During the 1960s and 1970s, the Shan United Army (SUA), the Burmese counterpart of the FARC in Colombia (i.e., the armed wing of the Burmese Communist Party) was an insurgent group, fighting for the independence of the Shan State. In the late 1970s, the Burmese Communist Party greatly expanded its involvement in drug activity and began producing heroin in its own refineries. The SUA used profits from the heroin trade to finance its insurgency. It now focuses on obtaining profits from the production, smuggling, and sale of heroin and heroin base.

So lucrative and tempting is the drug trade that it has been known to lure terrorist groups away from their original orientation (Lynch, 1987, 30). Some Communist insurgent organizations were skeptical about joining forces with drug traffickers. To orthodox Communists, drug traffickers represent the purest (i.e., worst) examples of capitalism. The SUA offers a striking case of an insurgent group that has been corrupted by drug profits and has lost its political zeal.

State-Sponsored Terrorism and Drug Trafficking

In addition to the involvement of "free-lance" terrorist organizations in drug trafficking, some states have been accused of promoting and sponsoring narcoterrorism. Chief among these are Cuba, Nicaragua, and Bulgaria. These countries have been charged with using government personnel, facilities, military bases, territorial waters, and air space to facilitate the movement of illegal drugs into the U.S., for motives claimed to be essentially the same as those that characterize other narcoterrorists: to gain hard currency for terrorist activities and to use drugs to destabilize pluralist societies. Besides smuggling drugs, narcoterrorists reputedly use the currency they acquire to buy weapons. These are then transported to the terrorists, who sometimes pay with drugs. The terrorists also gain valuable intelligence about local law enforcement efforts from the drug traffickers.

Sweeping political changes within Bulgaria would appear to have made the "Bulgarian connection" moot, and the recent election that replaced the Sandinista regime with the coalition government of Violeta Chamorro seems to have had a similar effect on a "Nicaraguan connection." These so-called "connections," if indeed they ever existed, may have become mere historical curiosities. The Cuban connection, however, may still be functioning in this hemisphere.

The Cuban Connection

The clearest evidence of a Cuban drug traffickers-terrorists link emerged in connection with the Jaime Guillot-Lara case in Federal District Court in Miami in November 1982. In that case, fourteen persons were indicted, including a former ambassador and a former deputy chief of mission of the Cuban Embassy in Bogota and Cuban Vice-Admiral Santamaria-Cuadrando. According to testimony at the trial, the admiral is supposed to have told the crew of a cargo ship smuggling $19 million worth of drugs into the U.S. that "we are going to fill Miami completely with drugs . . . so that more young Americans will die." Although information received from drug dealers may not be the most reliable evidence, and the admiral may not be speaking for Castro, it seems highly probable that this idea must have occurred to the Cuban government. It has been known for some time that the Castro regime provided a safe haven for the private navy of the infamous wanted criminal Robert Vesco.

The Guillot-Lara case documented the involvement of the Cuban government in actions to provide haven for Colombian drug smuggling vessels en route to the U.S. and the shipment of arms to the M-19 in Colombia. Lynch describes Guillot-Lara as an arms smuggler who took up drug trafficking at the suggestion of the Cuban government (1987, 34).

Before 1975, the Cuban government, and Fidel Castro himself, expressed disgust with drug trafficking and cooperated with the U.S. in disrupting the smuggling run between the north coast of South America and the southeastern coast of the U.S. Castro's aid was crucial because of Cuba's geographic location at the center of the Caribbean Sea. Then, in late 1975, some of Colombia's largest drug smugglers met with their country's Cuban ambassador to negotiate for the release of their ships, which had been seized by Cuba.

Cuban Ambassador Fernando Ravelo-Renedo, since then indicted by a U.S. federal grand jury for conspiracy to import illegal drugs, made a counteroffer to the Colombian drug lords. In return for up to $800,000 per vessel,

Cuba would not only ignore their presence in Cuban waters, but would provide refueling and repair facilities in Cuban ports. This provided the traficantes with a relatively cheap form of protection (even a modest shipment of marijuana can bring $12 million in profits) and supplied Havana with a new and steady source of hard currency.

Castro put the money to good use. In the spring of 1980, Guillot-Lara was introduced to Ambassador Ravelo-Renedo. A deal was struck through which Guillot-Lara would use his ships and connections to establish a two-way trade in drugs and arms. His ships would find safe refuge in Cuban waters and, in return, he would run guns to the M-19 terrorists in Colombia. These activities were upset in March 1981 when Colombia suspended diplomatic relations with Cuba. They resumed in the late spring, however, until Guillot-Lara's arrest in Mexico City in November 1981. Guillot-Lara escaped from a Mexican prison and fled to Europe. The DEA estimates that by the late 1970s, Guillot-Lara was delivering more than 2,000 tons of marijuana, thousands of pounds of cocaine, and 20 million methaqualone tablets each year. Since 1982, there have been tenuous indications from nautical charts and logs seized aboard smuggling vessels, as well as evidence taken from a plane that crashed in Colombia, that Cuba continues to facilitate the trans-Caribbean drug traffic. As noted earlier, Colombian officials claimed that aircraft transporting drugs out of the country returned with cargoes of weapons for the FARC.

The Bulgarian Connection

Information gathered by the DEA and its predecessor agencies over a period of fourteen years purported to show a consistent pattern of encouragement and facilitation of drug trafficking by the Bulgarian government under the corporate veil of the official Bulgarian export/import agency, KINTEX. Press coverage of Bulgaria's involvement in illicit activities began as early as 1972, when syndicated columnist Jack Anderson quoted portions of a classified CIA document that called Bulgaria "the new center for directing narcotics and arms trafficking between Western Europe and the Near East." In 1973, the Long Island newspaper *Newsday* began a 4-part series called "The Heroin Trail." An installment entitled "The Bulgaria Connection: A Throughway for Drugs" cited the Bulgarian government's use of KINTEX to smuggle arms and drugs. It was alleged that arrangements were made by KINTEX with selected Turkish traffickers, allowing morphine base to move through Bulgaria in exchange for the transport and delivery of guns and ammunition to left-wing terrorist groups in Turkey. More recently, "The Plot to Murder the Pope" and *The Time of the Assassins* by Claire Sterling; "The Plot to Kill the Pope: The Bulgarian Connection—Was the KGB Behind It?" by Paul Henze; and "Drugs for Guns: The Bulgarian Connection?" by Nathan Adams have been published; the authors contend that a complex and well-calculated Warsaw Pact conspiracy exists directed at undermining and destabilizing Western societies.

For his article, Adams interviewed an ex-Bulgarian State Security officer who stated that, in 1967, the heads of the Warsaw Pact Security Services met in Moscow to "exploit and hasten the inherent 'corruption' of Western society." According to the source, a subsequent meeting of Bulgarian State Security officers was held in Sofia, Bulgaria, to devise a three-year implementation of this strategy. The article further states that a Bulgarian State Security directive was issued in July 1970, the subject of which was "the destabilization of Western society through, among other tools, the narcotics trade." The vehicle chosen to operationally execute this strategy was KINTEX.

Sources stated that top-ranking members of the Bulgarian intelligence service and/or former heads of Bulgarian ministries comprised the directorate of KINTEX. Prior to the events that led to internal political change in Bulgaria, the Bulgarian State Security Service was the most closely aligned to the Soviet Union of all nations in the Soviet bloc.

Certain smugglers were permitted to conduct their activities within and through Bulgaria. In effect, Bulgarian officials, through KINTEX, designated "representatives" to operate as brokers who established exclusive arrangements with smugglers for bartered contraband for a fee. These representatives and smugglers were non-Bulgarians, composed primarily of Turkish nationals of Kurdish ethnicity. Selected smugglers, however, also included Syrians, Lebanese, Jordanians, Iranians, and European nationals.

KINTEX has in the past denied any knowledge of or association with these representatives. Bulgarian officials, in defense of trafficking allegations, claimed that the presence of foreign nationals on their soil constituted no crime. They further emphasized that no Bulgarian nationals have been implicated in large-scale drug trafficking either inside or outside Bulgaria.

On June 30, 1983, a DEA representative from Austria met with a high-level Bulgarian customs official in Sofia. This official responded to a question on Bulgarian arms smuggling by stating that the U.S. was "also" a major supplier of arms; by implication, this was an admission that Bulgaria dealt in arms. When countered by the distinction between U.S. weapons sales to established governments and illegal Bulgarian sales, he replied that Bulgaria sells arms to organizations representing "freedom fighters" whom it considers as legitimate as established governments.

KINTEX was described as an umbrella organization that orchestrated the trafficking of contraband through Bulgaria. Under such an arrangement, an arms dealer sold weapons to KINTEX. The weapons were then resold to drug dealers in the Middle East, who forwarded them to Middle East terrorists. The terrorists paid for the weapons with heroin. The drug dealers passed the heroin on to the Bulgarians, who sold it to other drug dealers in Europe. Between 1978 and 1980, KINTEX is alleged to have shipped as many as 25,000 Kalashnikov (AK–47) assault rifles to Kurdish separatists in eastern Turkey, for which payment was made in morphine base, the semifinal phase in the production of heroin.

The U.S. Connection

Representatives of the USSR and client states of the Soviet Union have countered charges of responsibility for terrorism by citing the involvement of Western governments—and, above all, the U.S.—in sponsorship of terrorism. Instances of Western involvement in various Third World insurgencies can be found without difficulty. The U.S. supported the Contras in Nicaragua, UNITA under Jonas Savimbi in Angola (which also received assistance from South Africa), and gave massive help to the Afghan *mujaheddin* via Pakistan. Israel has given continuing support to a militia in Lebanon; the French have intervened in Chad; and the British have given indirect aid and support to some of the minor Persian Gulf principalities.

Afghanistan has not been mentioned in official U.S. documents within the context of narcoterrorism. This appears to be a matter of convenient definition, since the Afghan *mujaheddin* were officially regarded as anti-Soviet "freedom fighters" rather than as insurgents or terrorists. When the Soviets withdrew military forces from Afghanistan, the *mujaheddin* continued to battle the pro-Soviet Najib regime, which still retains control of the government in Kabul. This omission is all the more curious because Afghan was producing, by U.S. estimates, between 400 and 575 metric tons of opium each year (*Narcotics Intelligence Estimate*, 1984). It is more than likely that a considerable proportion of this sizable tonnage was produced with the approval and encouragement of leaders of various *mujaheddin* groups. (We have already alluded to the documented involvement of the Contras in drug trafficking as a consequence of the Iran-Contra hearings and the trial of Oliver North.)

Narcoterrorism and Criminal Violence

Frost (1986) observes that the Hawkins Subcommittee hearings on drug-terrorism linkages managed to completely overlook, or failed to appreciate the significance of, the increasing use by criminal organizations of *violence for political effect*—classical terrorism. If one shifts the focus from the type of the organization or how it is defined or classified to the substance of drug-related terorist incidents, some important implications appear. Table 8–1 lists a series of incidents representing what might be considered the traditional form of struggle between trafficking organizations and government enforcement agencies. The list could have included the earlier assassinations of Supreme Court justices in Colombia and the 1982 Mafia murder in Palermo, Sicily, of General Carlo Alberto Della Chiesa, one of the highest ranking police officials in Italy. It must also be noted that the Colombian traficantes are bringing the battle to DEA's home ground.

The incidents listed in Table 8–2 reflect a startling new departure by criminal organizations: an effort to gain public sympathy for their activities. It is too early to assess the effect of such propaganda on public opinion, and one can only speculate on the expectations of those who initiate such actions. Organization leaders who are not averse to murder might welcome the opportunity to wrap their deeds in a moral cloak, as terrorists often seek to do.

Table 8-1

Terrorist Incidents Aimed Primarily at Host and U.S. Governments (Purpose: Reduce Resolve to Pursue Vigorous Law Enforcement)

Date	Event
February 1984	Murder of Eduardo Bonzalez, Colombian Justice Ministry official who actively and publicly supported implementation of the U.S.- Colombian extradition treaty
April 1984	Assassination of Colombian Justice Minister Rodrigo Lara Bonilla
14 November 1984	U.S. Embassy in Bogota reportedly received message from cocaine traffickers threatening to kill five Americans for every Colombian extradited to the United States to face drug charges
19 November 1984	Jungle coca eradication campsite in Peru is sprayed with machine gun fire, killing 15 local workers. (The $30 million U.S.-financed project was immediately suspended.)
26 November 1984	Car bomb exploded outside U.S. Embassy in Bogota, Colombia, killing a woman and wounding six others.
November 1984	(17 Embassy officials and their families withdrawn from Colombia)
1 February 1985	DEA office in Boston reported to be taking extra precautions to protect its personnel and buildings in the face of threats by Colombian drug traffickers
February 1985	DEA agent Enrique Camarena Salazar and Mexican drug eradication pilot kidnapped in Guadalajara, Mexico
February 15	(U.S. Customs initiated intensified searches at border crossings)
18 February 1985	DEA acknowledged that it had received reports Colombian traffickers were offering up to $350,000 for kidnapping Administrator Mullen or other high agency official
2 March 1985	Nine small U.S. border crossings closed on the grounds that "credible threats" against American customs agents had been received
March 1985	Tortured and beaten bodies of Camarena and Mexican pilot found under suspicious circumstances

Reprinted by permission of the publisher, from *Hydra of Carnage* by Uri Ra'anan, Robert L. Pfaltzgraff, Jr., Richard H. Schultz, Ernst Halperin, and Igor Lukes (Lexington, Mass.: Lexington Books, D.C. Health and Company), Copyright 1986, Uri Ra'anan, Robert L. Pfaltzgraff, Jr., Richard H. Shultz, Ernst Halperin, and Igor Lukes.

Table 8-2
Use of Terrorist Incident and Media Aimed at Public Opinion
(Purpose: Clothe Criminal Activity With National Interest)

Date	Event
July 1984	Bomb exploded on campus of the University of the Atlantic in Barranquilla, Colombia. The Urban Insurrection Front, a previously unknown group, claimed responsibility, stating that it was protesting the spraying of marijuana crops in the Sierra Nevada mountains.
March 1985	Filmed interview with accused Colombian drug trafficker Carlos Lehder Rivas aired on Bogota TV station. "Cocaine and marijuana," Lehder declared, "have become an arm of [the] struggle against American imperialism. We have the same responsibility in this—he who takes up a rifle, he who plants coca, [and] he who goes to the public plaza and denounces imperialism...[Justice Minister] Lara Bonilla, (American Ambassador) Tambs and (President) Betancur united to conspire against the interests of this country. Lara Bonilla was executed by the poeple."

Reprinted by permission of the publisher, from *Hydra of Carnage* by Uri Ra'anan, Robert L. Pfaltzgraff, Jr., Richard H. Schultz, Ernst Halperin, and Igor Lukes (Lexington, Mass.: Lexington Books, D.C. Health and Company), Copyright 1986, Uri Ra'anan, Robert L. Pfaltzgraff, Jr., Richard H. Shultz, Ernst Halperin, and Igor Lukes.

Table 8–3 lists incidents in which U.S. business firms operating in drug-source countries have been subjected to criminally inspired attacks. These data suggest an ominous trend toward retaliation against American businesses for losses sustained through host-government law enforcement cooperation with the U.S. U.S. overseas firms are convenient targets, and occasional attacks on them would be a logical extension of the campaign by criminal organizations against government law enforcement (Frost, 1986, 196).

Table 8-3
Terrorist Incidents Sited at U.S. Business Firms Overseas
(Purpose: Bring Indirect Pressure Against U.S. and Host Governments
to Lessen Law Enforcement Efforts)

Date	Event
January 1985	American scholar visiting Ecuador's Napo region reported that American oil company officials fear that Colombian coca traffickers will retaliate against their workers, holdings, and pipelines for losses sustained in U.S.-backed eradication on the Colombian side of the border

(continued)

Table 8-3 (continued)

9 February 1985	Bombs exploded at one-hour intervals outside the offices of IBM, Union Carbide, and Xerox in Medellin, Colombia. A private guard was killed at the IBM headquarters. The city's mayor blamed leftwing guerrillas for the bombings.

Reprinted by permission of the publisher, from *Hydra of Carnage* by Uri Ra'anan, Robert L. Pfaltzgraff, Jr., Richard H. Schultz, Ernst Halperin, and Igor Lukes (Lexington, Mass.: Lexington Books, D.C. Health and Company), Copyright 1986, Uri Ra'anan, Robert L. Pfaltzgraff, Jr., Richard H. Shultz, Ernst Halperin, and Igor Lukes.

Narcoterrorism: Some Tentative Conclusions

As we have seen, narcoterrorism comes in two forms: free-lance and state-supported. Some terrorist groups presumably enter the drug trade or muscle their way into an existing drug racket to earn money to buy weapons, bribe officials, and acquire political influence or even control of government policy. These results are made possible by the enormous profits in drug trafficking. This has typically been the pattern exhibited by Latin American involvement of terrorist groups such as Sendero Luminoso, M-19, and FARC.

State sponsorship is supposed to involve linkage among three groups: (1) revolutionary groups seeking to achieve political change; (2) drug traffickers who need the kind of protection such revolutionary groups can provide and are willing to pay for it; and (3) gunrunners, the people involved in illegal trafficking in weapons.

It is relatively uncommon for the cultivation of plants used as base materials in production of drugs or for the processing of drugs to be state-sponsored (Lynch, 1986, 32–33). But state sponsorship of the drug trade makes drug smuggling easier and thus increases the availability of drugs in the U.S.

It has not been claimed that state-sponsored narcoterrorism accounts *at present* for more than a small percentage of the illegal drugs that enter this country. In his submission to the Hawkins Subcommittee, the head of DEA acknowledged trafficker-terrorist cooperation, but minimized its importance, at least for drug traffic:

> This emerging relationship between drug trafficking and terrorism is not a reflection of any ideological coalition or conspiracy. What we find in most cases is more of an accomodation or cooperative effort for the mutual benefit of both trafficker and terrorist. Each will take advantage of the experience, equipment, and contacts of the other in order to pursue its own ends. With the possible exceptions of the FARC and the Shan United Army, there is no evidence of wholesale participation by terrorist groups in drug trafficking, or of large scale involvement by various terrorist group leaders. Although DEA believes the terrorist connection to drug trafficking is increasing, we do not believe that it has had a significant impact on drug availability in the United States. At this time,

terrorist groups are not in a position to compete with established drug smuggling organizations and are not a threat to their operations. (Mullen, 1984, 14)

The DEA is not particularly concerned with why a group or movement cooperates with drug traffickers; it looks at the entire spectrum of political violence—from agrarian revolution to separatism, urban terrorism, subversion, dissidence, and general lawlessness—but only from the standpoint of how it affects the supply of illicit drugs. One cannot fault the DEA for taking a position that reflects the priorities and agenda that constitute its official mission. But it is certainly justifiable to fault the Executive branch for its failure to adopt a broader perspective toward narcoterrorism, in which the DEA viewpoint is only one of several that need to be consulted in establishing national policy. International trafficking in weapons, ammunition, and military equipment is massive and compares with the drug trade in terms of profits.

We have already noted the impact on alleged Bulgarian sponsorship of narcoterrorism by successful moves toward democratization in Eastern Europe. Recent developments in Latin America may also portend an easing of the threat from collaboration between insurgent groups and drug traffickers in that area. On March 8, 1990, in a historic ceremony, the M-19 group turned over 65 weapons to an international committee headed by Venezuelan general Ernesto Uscategui. M-19 leader Carlos Pizarro, who ran for mayor of Bogota, pledged that his group would fight for peace as a political party. It is necessary to note, however, that M-19 is the only one of six insurgent Colombian groups to accept President Virgilio Barco's offer of amnesty. The National Liberation Army, blamed for recent kidnappings, and other groups say they will continue their armed struggle (Yarbro, 1990).

The cumulative effect of advanced weaponry and huge amounts of money is to seriously weaken the fabric of any society, especially those with an open democratic system of government. Lynch refers to a U.N. report that claims the very security of some states is threatened by the drug trade (1987, 38). Malaysia's Prime Minister has stated that drugs are the gravest security problem his government faces.

In the concluding chapters, we will explore what is involved in the search for a national policy on terrorism, and what needs to be done to implement a policy once it has been formulated. At this point, it is sufficient to note the lack of a policy regarding narcoterrorism. In some countries, drug traffickers and terrorists are literally fielding well-armed private armies. Nevertheless, it seems likely that official Washington has resisted the notion of a link between terrorism and drug trafficking on the basis of its inherent improbability. Whereas it has long been obvious that certain corrupt—or poor—governments have been involved in the drug trade, the pattern did not seem plausible for terrorist groups. Many terrorist groups are perceived as consisting of members who are motivated by an intense desire to abolish injustice and build a better world, so how would one explain their involvement in the sordid commerce of drug trafficking?

How, indeed. One answer might be that these idealistic people are not as idealistic as, or are more opportunistic than, their rhetoric and propaganda depicts them to be. A former senator claims that the portrait of the financially poor and ideologically pure terrorist is "one of the most dangerous misconceptions about terrorism" (Lynch, 1987, 29).

Summary

Many authorities and analysts perceive narcoterrorism to be a new and ominous international development. It is claimed that the enormous profits generated by the insatiable American demand for illicit drugs have led to the establishment of coalitions between drug traffickers and terrorists in several countries.

Latin American production accounts for most of the cocaine, marijuana, and heroin smuggled into the U.S. each year. For more than a decade, Colombian drug traffickers have controlled the lucrative cocaine trade. In Peru, the Sendero Luminoso (Shining Path) insurgents have become a de facto government in the highlands where coca plants are grown. The Sendero has reportedly entered into an alliance with drug traffickers to nullify official efforts at drug law enforcement. In Colombia, the M-19 guerrilla group and the insurgent FARC (Colombian Revolutionary Armed Forces) are said to have forged working relationships with the Medellin drug cartel.

Besides the involvement of "free-lance" terrorists in drug trafficking, Cuba, Nicaragua, and Bulgaria are accused of state sponsorship of drug trafficking. Evidence seems to show that Cuba has provided, and continues to provide, refuge for the drug trafficking activities of American criminal Robert Vesco. A less convincing case has been made for the charge that Bulgaria, operating through an export/import agency called KINTEX, supplied official cover for drug and arms trafficking to Europe and the Middle East. Whatever the truth of the allegations of state sponsorship in the cases of Nicaragua and Bulgaria, moves toward liberal democratic government in both countries may have made the charges academic.

Although the narcoterrorism link controls a relatively small percentage of the illicit drugs that enter the U.S. annually, this coalition brings together for mutual advantages two types of organizations noted for their propensity for criminal violence. Despite the seriousness of this threat, we still lack a coherent official policy for dealing with narcoterrorism—or, for that matter, with terrorism of any kind.

Key Terms

Drug Enforcement Administration (DEA)
FARC   "golden triangle"
Jaime Guillot-Lara   KINTEX

M-19 Group	Medellin Cartel
mujaheddin	Barry Seal
Sendero Luminoso ("Shining Path")	Shan United Army (SAU)

Questions for Discussion and Review

1. Is America's drug problem primarily the result of a conspiracy by foreign enemies? What is the evidence?
2. Why should there be a distinction between producers of drugs and drug traffickers?
3. Discuss the nature of the Sendero Luminoso insurgency in Peru. What kinds of operational linkage does the Sendero have with the Colombians?
4. Describe the relationship between the M-19 guerrilla group and the Medellin drug cartel.
5. Where is the golden triangle? What is the Shan United Army?
6. What is the evidence for a Cuban connection between drug traffickers and terrorists?
7. How does the KINTEX organization operate in the Bulgarian connection?
8. Discuss the two major types of narcoterrorism.
9. Does the U.S. have a national policy toward narcoterrorism and how to deal with it?

References

Anderson, J. and Van Atta, D. "Drug Cartel Puts $1 Million Bounty on Agents." *The Oregonian* (September 16, 1988): B9.

Anderson, J. and Van Atta, D. "U.S. Embassy Employees in Bogota Warned to be Vigilant of Ambushes." *The Oregonian* (January 24, 1989a): A7.

Anderson, J. and Van Atta, D. "Colombia Wants U.S. to Crack Down on Drug Users." *The Oregonian* (March 20, 1989b): B7.

Bagley, B.M. "The New Hundred Years War? U.S. National Security and the War on Drugs in Latin America." *Journal of InterAmerican Studies and World Affairs* 30 (1989): 161–182.

Fontaine, R.W. *Terrorism: The Cuban Connection*. New York: Crane Russak, 1988.

Frost, C.C. "Drug Trafficking, Organized Crime, and Terrorism." In *The Hydra of Carnage*, edited by U. Ra'anan, R.L. Pfaltzgraff, R.H. Shultz, E. Halperin, and I. Lukes. 189–198. Lexington, MA: Lexington Books, 1986.

Hayes, M. "Deadly Alliance Links Peru's Rebels, Drug Lords." *Tampa Tribune* (December 25, 1987): 15A.

Laqueur, W. *The Age of Terrorism*. Boston: Little, Brown, 1987.

Lee, R.W. "The Latin American Drug Connection." *Foreign Policy* 61 (1985/6 Winter): 142–159.

Llerena, M. *The Unsuspected Revolution*. Ithaca, NY: Cornell University Press, 1978.

Lynch, E.A. "International Terrorism: The Search for a Policy." *Terrorism: An International Journal* 9 (1986): 1–85.

McClintock, C. "Why Peasants Rebel: The Case of Peru's Sendero Luminoso." *World Politics* (October 1984): 48–84.

Mullen, F.M. "Testimony of DEA Administrator Francis M. Mullen." August 2, 1984 in *Drugs and Terrorism, 1984* (Hearing Report 98–1046). Washington, DC: U.S. Government Printing Office, 1984.

Palmer, D.S. "The Sendero Luminoso Rebellion in Rural Peru." In *Latin American Insurgencies*, edited by G. Fauriol. 67–96. Washington, DC: NDU Press: 1985.

Smith, J.F. "Cocaine Alliance Helps Pave Way for Shining Path." *The Oregonian* (March 6, 1989): A2.

U.S. National Narcotics Intelligence Consumers Committee. *Narcotics Intelligence Estimate: 1983.* Washington, DC: Government Printing Office, 1984.

Yarbro, S. "Colombian Guerrillas to Give Peace a Chance." *The Oregonian* (March 9, 1990): A12.

9
Weapons and Terrorism: Low-and High-Tech Options

After years of practically ignoring the use of poison gas in the Iran-Iraq war, the world finally awakened to the possibility that this indiscriminate weapon could become the weapon of choice in the Mideast and among other less developed countries. The sudden surge of alarm that led Secretary of State George Schultz to tell Congress that "The genie has gotten out of the bottle," prompting Senate demands for emergency U.N. action, was brought about by Iraq's use of poison gas in attacks on dissident Kurds. Television reports showed the sores and burns of Kurdish survivors who fled from northern Iraq into neighboring Turkey.

An Israeli source claimed that Syria and Libya, as well as Iraq, have "the means of delivery and willingness to use" chemical weapons. That, he said, "adds a new dimension to the Israeli-Arab conflict" (Corddry, 1988).

More recent concerns have been directed toward Libya, where, with the technical assistance of a West German pharmaceutical firm, the Gaddafi government completed a chemical plant with the capability of full-scale chemical weapons production. The plant at Rabta was destroyed by a mysterious fire in March, 1990. U.S. intelligence agencies believe that the Libyans are now constructing an underground high technology facility that might be a poison gas factory at Sebha. Tuohy (1989) commented that Chancellor Helmut Kohl and his aides first denied any West German complicity, but later admitted the existence of hard evidence of such involvement. In June 1990, West Germany sentenced Hippenstiel-Imhausen to five years in prison for helping Libya to build the plant at Rabta. The West German government is presently investigating other companies allegedly helping Libya build the new poison gas facility.

Until recently, most discussions about weaponry and terrorism tended to devote maximum attention to high-technology weapons. Most prominent in these discussions was the focus on nuclear weapons. The proliferation of poison gas manufacturing and the use of chemical and biological toxic agents against defenseless civilian populations (which we have defined elsewhere as a key factor in the definition of terrorism, regardless of whether the attack is state-sponsored or individual) require a radical reexamination of priorities. We will discuss a variety of high-tech and low-tech weapons that are increasingly available to terrorist organizations and individuals. The threat posed by weapons at both ends of the technology spectrum was characterized succinctly by Justice Arthur J. Goldberg: "Modern terrorism, with sophisticated technological means at its disposal and the future possibility of access to biological and nuclear weapons, presents a clear and present danger to the very existence of civilization itself" (Alexander, 1983, 226).

The sheer volume of potentially relevant information on chemical, biological, and nuclear weapons—their constituency, manufacture, transportation or delivery, and methods of use—requires discretion in what we choose to cover in this discussion. We will introduce each type of weapon with a brief sketch of its origins, development, and earlier use. Where appropriate, we will give contemporary examples of the employment or potential employment of such weapons by governments, organizations, or individuals. We also consider the feasibility and likelihood of terrorist use of chemical, biological, and nuclear weapons, and domestic and international measures to prevent their further proliferation and use. The concluding section of the chapter discusses possible attacks on the technological infrastructure of modern society, which represents a potential series of extremely important and vulnerable targets for weapons that are increasingly sophisticated—and available.

Chemical Weapons

The history of chemical warfare dates back at least as far as the Peloponnesian War, when tar pitch and sulfur were mixed to produce a suffocating gas. Twenty-three centuries later, chemical weaponry emerged as the ugly stepchild of the modern chemical industry. The great European powers, deciding that such weapons were barbaric, outlawed them in the Hague Convention of 1899.

But the peculiar language of the document was easily circumvented by the Germans, who used poison gas to devastating effect in World War I. In April 1915, German soldiers surreptitiously installed nearly 6000 cylinders of liquid chlorine in the trenches along a four-mile sector of the Western Front, near the Belgian town of Ypres. Using a heavy artillery barrage, the Germans were able to shatter cylinders and release the lethal gas. In a single afternoon, 5000 French troops were killed and an additional 10,000 injured. The carnage in Flanders was commemorated in a poem by Wilfred Owen:

> . . . the white eyes
> writhing in his face
> His hanging face, like a
> devil's sick of sin;
> If you could hear, at
> every jolt, the blood
> Come gargling from

the froth-corrupted
lungs.
Obscene as cancer, bitter as the
cud
Of vile, incurable sores on innocent
tongues. . .

German chemists subsequently introduced to the battlefield the far dead-
lier mustard gas. By the end of the war, both sides had fired about 124,000 tons
of chemicals, killing 91,000 soldiers and injuring 1.3 million more. But strategists were divided about the effectiveness of gas: advocates of chemical
warfare produced statistics showing that gas caused far more casualties per
round than explosives; opponents produced conflicting evidence that it took
a higher tonnage of chemicals to control a given area. Some claimed that gas was
a more "humane" weapon because the incidence of fatal casaulties was only one
in thirty, and even the wounded were not mutilated. Still others argued that the
figures were misleading and that gas should be outlawed forever.

At least one young German corporal who was temporarily blinded by a
retaliatory blast of British mustard gas never forgot the experience. "My eyes,"
wrote Adolf Hitler, "had turned into glowing coals; it had grown dark around
me." Hitler's memory, coupled with larger fears of retaliation, may help
explain why the Nazis never unleashed their newly developed nerve gases on
the battlefield in World War II—though they used them in the gas chambers
of the concentration camps.

Four years after World War I ended, the Washington Treaty outlawed the
use of poison gas in war. Unfortunately, the Treaty lapsed when the French
refused to become signatories. In 1925, the Geneva Protocol (similar in most
important respects to the Washington Treaty) was drafted by the U.S. delega-
tion and signed by twenty-eight countries, including the USSR. The Geneva
Protocol, however, failed to prevent the use of mustard gas by the Italians in
their conquest of Ethiopia. Nor did the Protocol deter the Japanese from
chemical warfare against both Chinese soldiers and civilians. Although the
Geneva Protocol outlawed the use of poison gas, it never forbade their
production and stockpiling.

The Nature of Chemical Weapons

The four major categories of chemical weapons are: *blood agents, choking agents,*
blistering agents, and *nerve agents.*

Blood agents (hydrogen cyanide, cyanogen chloride) are substances that,
when inhaled, block the oxygen-carrying capacity of the blood, causing tear-
ing, choking, and sometimes death.

Choking agents (chlorine, phosgene, chloropicrin) are employed in a
gaseous form. These gases, some of which smell like new-mown hay, sear the
lining of the respiratory passages. When plasma enters the lungs from the
bloodstream, victims drown in their own body fluids.

Blistering agents (sulfur mustard, nitrogen mustard, Lewisite) produce eye and skin irritation, temporary blindness, and may induce nausea and vomiting. Effects can linger for weeks, and respiratory problems can prove fatal.

Nerve agents (tabun, sarin, soman, VX) are odorless, colorless substances that disrupt the functioning of the central nervous system. The deadliest of the chemical poisons, they are absorbed through the skin and can kill within fifteen minutes.

Chemical agents are enclosed in either a *unitary* or *binary* explosive device. A unitary bomb would contain the lethal agent usually in compressed liquid form. On contact, the agent is released as an aerosol or in tiny droplets. A binary bomb includes two ingredients that are nonlethal when separate; combined in the bomb, the chemicals become lethal weapons. Thus, two canisters with chemical ingredients can be loaded into a bomb casing or an artillery shell. The force of impact or firing ruptures the canisters, allowing the ingredients to form a lethal mixture.

Chemical weapons can be delivered against a target in various ways, ranging from stationary mines to rocket-launched missiles. According to Thatcher and Aeppel (1989), fifteen tons of nerve gas (an amount that can be delivered by one strategic bomber) can act in a matter of seconds, affect an area up to 24 square miles, kill 50 percent of the exposed population, and produce contamination lasting from several days to several months.

Iraq: Return of the Silent Killer

Iraq has revived chemical warfare on a large scale and used chemical weapons against both an external enemy, Iran, and against an ethnic minority, the Kurds, within its own borders. Iraq denies that it gassed the Kurds, just as it has never acknowledged using chemical weapons—mustard gas, nerve gas, and cyanide—as weapons of last resort against attacking masses of Iranian infantry. But in 1986, Iraqi Foreign Minister Tariq Aziz told a group of U.S. Congressmen: "Our very existence is at stake. I must tell you that if we had nuclear weapons, we would probably have used them" (Watson & Barry, 1988, 30–31).

The capability of producing chemical weapons was supplied primarily by a West German company that sold millions of dollars worth of corrosion-resistant vessels and pipes, sophisticated measuring devices, and the raw materials for chemically toxic agents to the Iraqi State Enterprise for Pesticide Production (SEPP). The equipment was installed at a massive chemical manufacturing complex near Samarra, north of Baghdad, in the early 1980s.

Thatcher and Aeppel (1989, A22) observe that the transactions might have seemed routine at the time. But Western intelligence sources say this equipment gave the Iraqi government something it had pursued "with steely determination" for nearly a decade: the ability to wage chemical warfare. U.S. intelligence regards SEPP as a front for the Iraqi military and maintains that the Samarra complex is the prime production facility for mustard gas and nerve agents.

Chemical plants and their products have dual uses. A plant that turns out pesticides or fertilizers can, with minor modification, switch to nerve gas. A chemical that, in one compound, makes the ink flow freely from a ballpoint pen, can, in another mix, cause blinding, choking, agonizing death.

The companies that turned out to be Iraq's suppliers were a mixed group. Some were small specialty suppliers; others were trading companies with few fixed assets. At least one of the companies identified by Thatcher and Aeppel (1989) was the subsidiary of a U.S. corporation.

Phillips Petroleum Company, based in Bartlesville, Oklahoma, owns a small chemical plant in the Belgian industrial town of Tessenderlo. On at least three separate occasions, orders were placed with Phillips for thiodiglycol (TDG), a chemical used in textile printing, photo developing, and ink for ballpoint pens, but which is also one step away from mustard gas. Phillips shipped 500 metric tons of TDG to Iraq in 1983, but refused a second large order one year later, after reports of Iraq's use of mustard gas had begun to appear in the Western press. Phillips officials repeatedly stressed that they had no idea the chemical would be used for the production of weapons and still have no proof that it was.

In 1986, the Belgian government imposed the requirement that exports of TDG be subject to a special license. The government also took the unusual step of banning production of TDG on the Phillips property in Tessenderlo.

On at least one occasion, U.S. authorities seized an air freight shipment of a chemical bound for Iraq—potassium fluoride, a chemical that can be used to make sarin, a nerve gas. That was one of the few times authorities halted a questionable transaction before it was completed. Often, the details of transactions surface after the fact—if ever.

Iraq spent years and millions of dollars to acquire an arsenal of chemical weapons. So, for that matter, have the U.S. and the Soviet Union. But despite charges by the Afghan resistance and the U.S. that the Soviets used chemical weapons against the *mujahideen,* it is Iraq that has employed chemical weapons against both military and civilian targets. The first reported use against Iran was in November 1983, when Iranian troops were hit with blistering waves of mustard gas. Use of gas against Iran continued repeatedly throughout the Gulf war, and casualties mounted into the thousands.

Iraq used chemical weapons in March 1988, and again in September, against its own citizens. The earlier attack was directed at the Iraqi border town of Halabja, which had been occupied by Iranian troops. Iraqi authorities suspected that the townspeople, many of whom were dissident Kurds, were collaborating with the Iranians. Iraqi Air Force bombings began on the night of March 17, 1988.

In September, Iraqi chemical weapons struck again, this time against a number of predominantly Kurdish villages in northern Iraq. About 60,000 Kurds streamed into refugee camps in southern Turkey.

Iraq has not paid a high diplomatic price for its actions. For one thing, restricted press coverage of the Gulf war on both sides meant that there were few independent confirmations of the use of chemical weapons. There were also persistent reports, some buttressed by U.S. intelligence, that Iran also used chemical weapons. Iraq was irritated but unmoved by a number of United Nations resolutions, dating from 1984, that condemned the use of chemical weapons in the Gulf war. For years, the U.S. issued pro forma denunciations of the use of poison gas, but preferred to express concern through diplomatic channels. The reaction from other countries has been similarly muted. Many nations have avoided direct criticism of Iraq; none thus far has imposed sanctions.

Some diplomats claim that Iran's support for international terrorism and hostage-taking, together with its militant Islamic fundamentalism, made Iran an unsympathetic victim. In the end, Iraq's decision to use chemical weapons was a calculated one.

Chemical Weapons and the Superpowers

Other nations, especially those of the Third World, can scarcely be criticized for claiming self-interest and hypocrisy on the part of the U.S. and USSR in spearheading attempts to ban proliferation of chemical weapons, when both superpowers possess a large arsenal of such weapons and the capability of making even more. (Similar skepticism is evinced toward U.S. and Soviet efforts to curb the spread of biological and nuclear weapons.)

From the viewpoint of a nation that does not have chemical weapons (e.g., Libya) and that requires extensive foreign assistance to acquire such a capability, U.S. actions are dismissed out of hand as driven by an attempt to deny to others what is arrogated to itself. Even France, which certainly has sophisticated chemical weapons capability, once touted a proposal (since abandoned) that countries should first have the right to build up their chemical weapons stocks before destroying them.

But the situation is made far more complex by factors other than chauvinism and national pride; chief among these are economic factors. Any international treaty that seeks to accomplish chemical weapons disarmament would have a major impact on the chemistry, biotechnology, and pharmaceutical industries worldwide. It would also create a new international agency and obligate nations to foot the multimillion dollar cost of keeping the agency in business.

Last but not least, the problems of verification posed by such a treaty equal, if not outweigh, the problems involved in inspection and verification of nuclear weapons disarmament provisions.

Despite these inherent problems, representatives from 149 countries meeting in Paris called for the world community to rededicate itself to the 1925 principles of the Geneva Protocol and close the toxic loophole. Emphasis was on the necessity of concluding, at the earliest possible date, a convention on the *development, production, stockpiling, and use of chemical weapons, and on their destruction.* For whatever rhetoric is worth, the language at least of the Paris conference goes beyond anything that has thus far been uttered for international and domestic consumption. In asking for a swift conclusion to the chemical disarmament talks that have dragged on in Geneva since 1971, delegates pledged that they would abide by any agreement the forty negotiating nations reached there.

The five-day conference in Paris was convened at the summons of French President Francois Mitterand after U.N. reports that Iraq had used chemical weapons against both the Iranians and its own Kurdish minority. Without mentioning Iraq, representatives in Paris recalled "their serious concern at recent violations as established and confirmed by the competent organs of the United Nations" (Henry, 1989, A–1, A–14).

Among the areas of dispute that were not resolved was U.S. opposition to a final document that would have called on states that signed the 1925 Geneva Protocol to unilaterally withdraw their reservations, which allow states to use chemical weapons in retaliation for their first use by another nation. But there was no such call in the final declaration.

Arab states, which had argued for a declaration that would link a ban on chemical weapons with a ban on nuclear weapons, settled instead for an independent paragraph "urging general and complete disarmament" without mentioning nuclear disarmament. The Arab and Third World countries had also opposed a U.S. desire that the final register declare alarm at the spread of chemical weapons only to less developed countries without addressing the superpowers' chemical weapons capability and current modernization of the U.S. arsenal.

Until an accord on chemical disarmament is reached at Geneva, the Paris declaration has value primarily for its moral weight. The states that signed are bound only by the existing 1925 Geneva Protocol against the use of such weapons. The conference therefore avoided thorny questions such as verification that have confounded negotiators in Geneva for nearly two decades. Under the circumstances, perhaps this is as much as anyone can reasonably expect from an international conference.

Biological Weapons

Biological weapons, like chemical weaponry, have a long and disreputable history. As far back as antiquity, plague victims were deliberately smuggled into towns or cities that were under siege. The first recorded use of biological warfare was in 1343, when Caffa, a Genoese stronghold on the Black Sea, was besieged by the Tartars, who catapulted the bodies of people who had died of the plague inside the fortress. The Genoese ships sailing for Sicily spread the contagion across Europe, and, within three years, the Black Death had claimed 30 million victims.

In 1710, the Russians besieging Swedish troops at Reval emulated the Tartars of Caffa and threw bodies of plague victims over the city walls. A half-century later, the British commander at Fort Pitt, in the Ohio territory, sent two blankets and a scarf to a couple of Indian chiefs, ostensibly as a goodwill gesture. The items had been used by smallpox victims, and the result was an epidemic among the Indians, who lacked natural immunity.

In more recent times, evidence indicates that terrorists have seriously considered resorting to the use of biologically toxic agents. In 1970, for example, members of the Weather Underground were planning to steal germs from the bacteriological warfare center at Fort Detrick, Maryland, for the purpose of contaminating a city water supply (Griffith, 1975). The organizers of Rise, a group dedicated to the goal of creating a new master race, were arrested in 1972 in an abortive plot to poison Chicago's water system with typhoid bacteria (*Los Angeles Times*, January 19, 1972; *Chicago Tribune*, January 19, 1972). And in 1975, technical manuals on germ warfare were found in a San Francisco hideout of the Symbionese Liberation Army (Alexander, 1983).

For many years, the dividing line between chemical and biological warfare was clear: biological agents could reproduce themselves, chemical agents could not. But scientists point out that the line is now blurred by advances in biotechnology. Things that cannot reproduce themselves in nature can be reproduced in the laboratory. Consequently, a gray area is developing between classical chemical warfare agents, such as mustard gas and nerve agents, and biological agents, such as anthrax. Specialists have adopted an imprecise, catchall term for agents in this gray area—"novel agents," among which are these:

- Well-known biological warfare agents, including anthrax, produced by new methods such as genetic engineering.
- Toxins, such as spider venom, previously so difficult to collect that they were discounted as warfare agents.
- Unique mixtures of poisons, resulting in compounds that are potentially more lethal, virulent, or difficult to treat than the component parts.
- Substances that occur naturally in the human body, such as biological regulators and hormones, but that in abnormal quantities can have an unpredictable impact on human life.
- "Low molecular weight agents"—poisonous chemicals of such infinitesimally small proportions that they could, theoretically, slip through the activated charcoal filters of a gas mask or protective suit, as air molecules already do.
- Genetically altered microorganisms that closely resemble disease-agents but have a critical change in protein structure that renders present vaccines obsolete.

Some experts say they worry that "novel agents" could unlock a Pandora's box of new problems for arms controllers and military strategists.

Biological Weapons and the USSR

Specific information regarding the nature and extent of Soviet research and development on biological weapons is classified, but U.S. intelligence agencies claim to have confirmed the existence of two facilities where the Soviet Union is conducting biological warfare research: The Microbiology and Virology Institute in Sverdlovsk, and the Scientific Research Institute of Sanitation in Zagorsk. They have also identified at least six other "suspect" sites (see Figure 9–1). The Soviets themselves, in documents filed with the United Nations, have declared that the Ministry of Defense conducts research with various biological warfare agents at laboratories in Sverdlovsk, Zagorsk, Leningrad, Kirov, and Aralsk. But the Soviet Union maintains that all the facilities are involved in defensive research only, not offensive research, and are certainly not engaged in weapons production.

Suspicion about just what the Soviets are up to pervades the U.S. intelligence community. Official Soviet secrecy only feeds speculation. One facility that particularly intrigues U.S. experts is the Shemyakin Institute of Bioorganic Chemistry on the outskirts of Moscow. Some U.S. officials suggest that offensive biological warfare research is conducted there. But so little is known about the Institute that even the shape of the building is a matter of fascination to intelligence experts. Some think it is merely a gigantic example of architectural liberalism, others a macabre metaphor in concrete. The building, seen by satellite, resembles a huge DNA molecule!

Yevgeny Sverdlov, the head of the Institute's Laboratory of Nucleic Acids Biotechnology, claims that suspicions about the facility are unfounded. But his answer to the question of whether such research is underway elsewhere in the Soviet Union is curiously qualified: "In this place, the Academy of Sciences, I may state definitely that none of my colleagues are involved. And the Academy of Sciences is the place of work for the most distinguished scientists. So I can say that none of the really outstanding scientists of the Soviet Union are involved. This is mere logic" (Thatcher, 1989, A7).

It is also mere doubletalk.

More troubling was a 1987 statement by Valentin Falin, then head of the Soviet Union's Novosti Press Agency. He was talking about Moscow's response to new U.S. space-based weapons systems. "We won't copy you anymore, making planes to catch up with your planes, missiles to catch up with your missiles," said Falin. "We'll take asymmetrical means with new scientific principles available to us. Genetic engineering could be a hypothetical example. Things can be done for which neither side could find defenses or countermeasures, with very dangerous results. . . . These are not just words. I know what I'm saying."

Biological Weapons and the United States

Compared to that of the Soviet Union, the U.S. biological warfare defense program is a model of openness. Contracts are a matter of public record, and there is extensive documentation of the research in environmental impact

The Soviet government has declared locations of the following high–risk research centers and laboratories in compliance with the 1972 Biological Weapons Convention. The Soviets say only defensive research takes place at these sites:

1. Byelorussian Research Institute for Epidemiology and Microbiology
Minsk

2. All-Union Research Institute for Molecular Biology
Novosibirsk Oblast

3. D.I. Ivanovsky Institute for Virology
Moscow

4. N.F. Gamaleya Institute for Epidemiology and Microbiology
Moscow

5. Irkutsk Anti-Plague Scientific Research Institute of Siberia and the Far East
Irkutsk

6. Moscow Research Institute for Viral Preparations
Moscow

7. Scientific Research Institute for Poliomyelitis and Viral Encephalitis
Moscow Oblast

U.S. intelligence agencies claim the Soviets are conducting offensive biological warfare research at:

8. The Microbiology and Virology Institute
Sverdlovsk

9. The Scientific Research Institute of Sanitation
Zagorsk

In addition, the United States names six "suspect" sites where offensive research is allegedly taking place:

10. *Omutinisk*
11. *Aksu*
12. *Pokrov*
13. *Berdsk*
14. *Penza*
15. *Kurgan*
16. *and a storage facility at Malta*

17. The Pentagon says there is a biological warfare test facility on *Vozrozhdeniya Is., in the Aral Sea*

Figure 9-1

High-Risk Biological Warfare Research

SOURCE: From material originally presented in the Christian Science Monitor as reproduced in Thatcher, G., "Science opens 'Pandora's Box' of toxins," The Oregonian, January 3, 1989, A6, A7. Reproduced by permission from *The Christian Science Monitor* © 1988 The Christian Science Publishing Society. All rights reserved.

statements and other documents. In addition, the Pentagon's main biological defense research facility, the U.S. Army Medical Research Institute of Infectious Diseases at Fort Detrick, Maryland, issues an annual report detailing the research it is supporting. Nevertheless, government documents indicate that the Pentagon is also conducting secret research with both chemical and biological warfare agents. Pentagon sources acknowledge that tests are being conducted to determine whether certain substances can penetrate the current models of U.S. gas masks and chemical protective gear.

Under the terms of the 1972 Biological Weapons Convention, the U. S. government has declared the following facilities where maximum high-risk defensive biological research takes place:

1. **Center for Infectious Diseases at the Centers for Disease Control**
Atlanta, Ga.

2. **National Cancer Institute, Frederick Research Facility**
Frederick, Md.

3. **National Institutes of Public Health Service**
Bethesda, Md.

4. **Plum Island (N.Y.) Animal Disease Center**
Plum Island, N.Y.

5. **U.S. Army Medical Research Institute of Infectious Diseases**
(Fort Detrick), Frederick, Md.

6. **Government Services Division, the Salk Institute**
Swiftwater, Pa.

Additional biological defense research is conducted by:

Walter Reed Army Institute of Research

U.S. Army Chemical Research, Development and Engineering Center

U.S. Army Natick Research, Development and Engineering Center

U.S. Army Dugway Proving Ground

U.S. Atmospheric Sciences Library

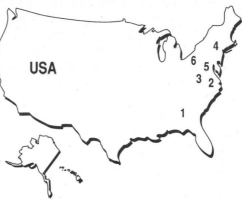

USA

U.S. Army Research Office

U.S. Army Human Engineering Laboratory

Los Alamos National Laboratory

Lawrence Livermore Laboratory

Department of the Interior

Naval Research Laboratory

Department of Energy

Uniformed Services University of Health Science

Department of Commerce

NASA, Veterans Administration

Centers for Disease Control

National Academy of Sciences

Figure 9-1 (continued)
High-Risk Biological Warfare Research

In December 1988, in response to a federal lawsuit filed by the Foundation for Economic Trends (a private watchdog organization), the Defense Department revealed that it was researching a veritable rogues' gallery of bacteria, viruses, and toxins. Among the substances are such bacteria as *Yersina pestis* (the Black Death of the fourteenth century); and tularemia (rabbit fever), which is known to cause blisters, high fevers, and, in some cases, death. Also on the list are viral diseases, including such well-known types as yellow fever and polio, and exotic ones such as Chikungunya and O'Nyong Nyong. The Pentagon acknowledged in the legal proceeding that it was conducting research on the military uses of cobra toxins, Mojave rattlesnake venom, and toxins from scorpions and shellfish.

These bacteria are lethal in their own right, but Pentagon strategists say there is a possibility that novel agents could, in effect, combine the worst aspects of the lot—with nightmarish battlefield results. General Howard Eggleston, head of the Army's Space and Special Weapons Directorate, sketched out one possible scenario (Thatcher, 1989, A6): one day, Army medics confront an outbreak of disease that seems to be a highly infectious fever. But when they begin treatment, the symptoms suddenly begin to resemble poisoning by snake venom. Worse, says Eggleston, it is conceivable that the treatment administered for the first symptoms—the fever—could actually trigger the onset of the second—the snakebite poisoning. Treatment would then become a macabre guessing game. Eggleston claims the Pentagon has even considered the possibility that computers, using artificial intelligence techniques, could be used to concoct formulas for such deadly potions. The Pentagon, he says, must try to anticipate such threats and ensure that American soldiers are protected. This is probably the same line of argument one hears in the Kremlin.

Nuclear Weapons

While the use of chemical and biological weapons by terrorists is more feasible technologically, nuclear terrorism—detonation of a nuclear device, use of fissionable material as a radioactive poison, and seizure and sabotage of nuclear facilities—has received far greater attention from both the media and the experts. Examples of some of the more obvious possibilities that are technically feasible and politically plausible include the threat or use of a nuclear option by political or environmental extremists seeking to carry out acts of symbolic violence against nuclear facilities; by a revolutionary group acting against its own government or against a foreign country to increase pressure on the home government to meet the revolutionaries' demands; by a national liberation movement working against the imperialist government in the mother country; by a terrorist group engaged in a proxy war initiated by an outside state or even a nuclear power; and by a suicidally inclined group of people with disturbed personalities who are willing to use nihilistic violence for its own sake (Alexander, 1983, 232).

Such developments are extremely serious because they could result either in a broad-scale nuclear war or in deepening the risk of a nuclear war. The likelihood increases in situations where nuclear terrorism can be used as a form of war by proxy or as a tactical weapon by desperate terrorist groups. It is conceivable, for example, that if Israel were the target of a surrogate nuclear attack by the PLO, the U.S. and the USSR might reach a point of confrontation that greatly increases the dangers of a nuclear war between them.

Military stockpiles around the world contain tens of thousands of strategic and tactical nuclear weapons. Although the "nuclear club" is limited in membership, it is expected that some forty to fifty nations will have access to peaceful nuclear materials and technology by the end of the century. Expansion in the nuclear arsenal is indeed alarming, not only because of the total number of weapons stockpiled, but also because many nuclear weapons will not be protected from theft by the electronic safety locks and other security devices that more sophisticated nuclear powers use.

The increasing availability of fissionable material provides an alternative for terrorists to the theft of a nuclear weapon from a military stockpile. As early as the 1960s (Alexander, 1983, 234–235), various reports indicated that persons using only unclassified information along with literature available to the public could design and build a crude nuclear device. In 1975, an undergraduate at the Massachusetts Institute of Technology designed a workable bomb of low yield; in 1976, a Princeton undergraduate designed a bomb that could be built for about $2000. If bright undergraduates have the technological know-how to design nuclear bombs, then obviously any proficient terrorist group that can obtain the fissionable material and emulate these students' feats has a reasonable chance of "going nuclear."

Another aspect of nuclear terrorism is the problem of radioactive weapons dispersal. A plausible alternative to the explosion or threatened explosion of a nuclear device is the utilization of plutonium or any other radioactive nuclides for the dispersal of radioactivity in any given area, or the contamination of natural resources. A dispersal threat would be more credible than a bomb threat, if only because it requires less material and a lower level of technological expertise. Thus, a determined terrorist group, could place only three and one-half ounces of plutonium in an acrosol canister to produce a radiological weapon with potentially devastating effects (Alexander, 1983, 235). Introduced into the air-conditioning system of a large office building, for example, several thousand people would die over a period of time, depending on the level of the dosage absorbed. Alexander quotes the British expert, Sir Brian Flowers, on this kind of risk: "Because of its toxic and fissile properties, plutonium offers a unique and powerful weapon to those who are sufficiently determined to impose their will. I do not believe it is a question of whether someone will deliberately acquire it for purposes of terrorism and blackmail, but only of when and how often."

Thinking the Unthinkable

Among those whose appointed—or, perhaps, self-appointed—task is to "think the unthinkable," various scenarios begin with an assumption about the use of weapons by terrorist individuals, organizations, or states. The scenarios may range from coldly realistic to warmly imaginative, but they share the common property that each has precedents and none is totally implausible, given the rate at which technological development occurs today.

In 1985, more than 150 specialists from thirteen countries met in Washington, D.C., for a conference on "International Terrorism: The Nuclear Dimension." Participants included members of the international business community and specialists in international terrorism, nuclear weapons design and deployment, civilian nuclear commerce and proliferation, international law, national and industrial security, crisis management, and civil defense. The national security implications of terrorism were heightened by the coincidence of the conference with the airline hostage crisis in Beirut and the Air India disasters over Ireland and in Japan.

The members of this working group noted that some 155 bombings or other attacks had taken place during the preceding two decades at the sites of nuclear reactors in Europe or America. None, however, had caused a serious accident. Most of the incidents had been the work of nuclear protesters rather than terrorists—the same pattern exhibited in a recent arrest of three suspects in an Arizona nuclear power plant sabotage case (Feldman & Meyer, 1989). The nuclear weapons sector was considered less vulnerable to attack because substantial resources had been allocated to protective measures such as the PAL systems (permissive action links) with features that rendered stolen weapons useless. Not all tactical nuclear weapons, however, have as yet been fitted with advanced self-protecting systems, including those aboard ships. More vulnerable to both theft and sabotage are civilian nuclear facilities, such as power reactors and research reactors. The conference experts believe that, although nuclear bomb making may not be as simple as previously believed, it is still feasible with a sufficient quantity of reactor-grade plutonium or highly enriched uranium.

Laqueur (1987, 316) makes the important point that nuclear terrorism could not only pose a major threat to individual nations, it could also lead to a major international crisis. These dangers prompted U.S. Senators Sam Nunn and John Warner in 1985 to suggest establishment of U.S.-USSR Nuclear Risk Reduction Centers, to coordinate the superpowers' responses to nuclear terrorist threats. Provision would be made for exchanging information through existing hot-line facilities and arranging possible common actions. American and Soviet representatives met in Geneva in 1986 to consider steps leading to establishment of such centers.

Toxic chemicals and lethal biological agents involve fewer technological problems than nuclear weapons, but their use is subject to a number of other constraints. For one thing, terrorists usually claim to act on behalf of the people: they aspire to popular support. As Brian Jenkins has stated, "They want a lot of people watching, not a lot of people dead." Weapons of mass destruction are not likely to add to their popularity, and their use entails the risk of intolerable losses of life. It seems unlikely that the IRA, for example, would use chemical or biological toxins in Northern Ireland, where such weapons might incur casualties as heavy among Catholics as among the "enemies" (i.e., Protestants and British soldiers). More likely would be the use of chemical, biological, or nuclear weapons by the PLO or Libyan terrorists against "enemy" populations in Israel. But even in Israel, where Arabs and Jews live in close proximity to one another in many places, the indiscriminate nature of weapons of mass destruction makes them equally deadly for both friends and foes. Such considerations lead to the cautious conclusion, therefore, that although use of these weapons can never be entirely ruled out, the probability of their use seems low.

New Vulnerabilities

Most of the speculation on future terrorist threats has focused on chemical, bacteriological, and nuclear weapons, with comparatively little attention given to possible attacks on the technological infrastructure of modern society. Modern industrial societies have vulnerabilities that terrorists or criminals could successfully exploit. In many instances, a small band of determined, knowledgeable individuals could carry out actions that, if successful, could have far-reaching consequences. Modern society's vulnerabilities include water supply systems, transportation systems, energy systems, communications systems, computerized management and information systems, and certain critical industries. The vulnerabilities may lie in the complexity and interdependence of the systems themselves, or in certain vulnerable portions of a given system.

Jenkins and Rubin (1978) have identified two kinds of operations that could be directed against the technological infrastructure: (1) those that could cause disruption of vital systems leading to widespread inconvenience, and possibly some degree of public alarm, but that do not directly threaten life; and (2) actions that represent a direct threat, or the appearance of a direct threat, to human life. Examples of the first kind are interruption of telecommunications or the destruction of computer-stored records to disrupt a country's financial system. Either act would certainly create serious problems but would not imperil human life. Examples of the second type are sabotage of liquefied natural gas facilities or of tank cars carrying lethal chemicals; both could present a grave danger to public safety.

Modern communication systems are vulnerable to physical disruption and passive tampering, for example, the introduction of a "virus," a parasite program that can defeat carefully designed security barriers and wipe out major data banks and control systems. In 1985, Japanese terrorist groups simultaneously attacked twenty-three nodes on the Tokyo metro system (Laqueur, 1987, 320).

Jenkins and Rubin (1978) note that terrorists have exploited the new vulnerabilities of advanced industrial societies in limited and specific ways. Although they have no compunctions about killing small numbers of people to gain attention and cause alarm, they are apparently unwilling to anger a large number of people by some act of sabotage that could cause widespread inconvenience. Terrorists seem to prefer to force the government to take security measures that inconvenience the public, such as surrounding a shopping area with a security fence and requiring shoppers to submit to a search. Terrorists have bombed transformers but have seldom tried to blow up power stations. They have not interfered with water supply systems. They have not forced evacuations by setting fires in chemical manufacturing plants or by blowing up tanks of hazardous chemicals, although publicity given to accidental chemical spills and fires may inspire terrorists to give serious thought to copycat actions.

The vulnerability that modern terrorists regularly exploit is civil aviation, primarily because aircraft are vulnerable and convenient containers of hostages or a guaranteed number of victims.

Despite the faint reassurance one may draw from the fact that terrorists have thus far not used exotic weapons of mass destruction or conventional weapons to cause mass casualties, and that they have not, with the exception of civil aviation, struck at the technological vulnerabilities of modern society, we cannot depend on the permanence of political or moral constraints on the activities of political extremists. These constraints will inevitably erode in the case of terrorists operating internationally if the terrorists can reach sanctuary and if governments are prevented from responding effectively by respect for the sovereignty of other states and by political considerations. If a group does not depend on a local constituency for supply and can rely on refuge elsewhere, it may be less concerned about alienating its target population.

One should not forget that antiterrorist technology and tactics are also bound to make progress in the coming years. Potential progress applies to defensive measures such as remote-sensing capacities that are able to distinguish terrorists from their victims; high-explosives detection techniques; high-speed discovery techniques that detect the presence of a single molecule of a toxin; and so forth. So far antiterrorist technology has always been reactive, lagging behind the terrorist threat. But if the terrorist threat should grow, higher priority will be given to funding not only deterrents to attack but also to means of paralyzing terrorist efforts altogether.

Summary

Chemical weapons became the focus of public attention recently when the Iraqi government used poison gas against its own dissident Kurdish population. Libya has also received a great deal of attention as a result of disclosures that West German materials and technical assistance have contributed to the creation of a Libyan chemical weapons capability.

Poison gas, used by both sides during World War I, was outlawed by the Geneva Protocol of 1925, but this did not prevent the Italians from conducting chemical warfare against the Ethiopians or the Japanese from using poison gas against the Chinese during the 1930s. Chemical weapons are simple to manufacture, inexpensive, and can be delivered against a target in various ways. As the recent Paris conference has shown, it is nearly impossible to set up a system for effectively monitoring a ban on such weapons.

Similar observations apply to biological weapons. Both the U.S. and the Soviet Union maintain research and manufacturing capabilities for producing a variety of biological toxins. The advantage of biological and chemical toxic agents to terrorists are low cost, relative accessibility, and ease of deployment. Their principal disadvantages are lack of precision and indiscriminate diffusion.

Despite the attention that potential terrorist use of nuclear weapons has received in the professional literature, the relatively few incidents that have occurred thus far have mostly involved protesters rather than terrorists. Other areas of vulnerability to terrorist attack in modern industrialized countries include transportation, energy, and communications systems.

Key Terms

binary explosive device	blistering agents
blood agents	choking agents
Geneva Protocol	mustard gas
nerve agents	"new vulnerabilities"
"novel agents"	Nuclear Risk Reduction Center
Paris conference	thiodiglycol (TDG)
toxins	unitary explosive device
Washington Treaty	

Questions for Discussion and Review

1. What efforts were made following World War I to outlaw use of chemical weapons? How successful were the efforts?
2. Distinguish between unitary and binary explosive devices for delivering a chemical agent to a target.
3. How did the Iraqi government acquire the capacity to make chemical weapons?
4. What goals were sought in the 1989 Paris conference on limiting chemical weapons? How does this conference compare with previous international conferences on chemical weaponry?
5. What are "novel agents" in biological weaponry?
6. Discuss the major constraints that currently limit the probability that nuclear weapons will be used by terrorist groups. What are the principal dangers we face in the future?
7. Identify some of the risks involved in modern life to terrorist threats against "new vulnerabilities."

References

Alexander, Y. "Terrorism and High Technology Weapons." In *Perspectives on Terrorism*, edited by L. Z. Freedman and Y. Alexander, 225–240. Scholarly Resources: Wilmington, DE, 1983.

Banks, T., and Karniol, R. "Special Report: Chemical Weapons." *Jane's Defence Weekly*, 14 (July 14, 1990): 51–58.

Bar, M. "Strategic Lessons of Chemical War: Historical Approach." *IDF Journal* 20 (Summer 1990): 48–55.

Corddry, C.W. "Poison Gas Use Alarms U.S., Israel." *The Oregonian* (December 28, 1988): A7.

Doerner, W.R. "On Second Thought." *Time* 44 (January 23, 1989): 30–31.

Engelberg, S. and Gordon, M.R. "West German Company Linked to Libyan Plant." *The Oregonian* (January 1, 1989): A23.

Feldman, P. and Meyer, R.E. "Police Surprise, Arrest Three Suspects in Nuclear Power Plant Sabotage Case." *The Oregonian* (June 1, 1989): A12.

Grier, P. "U.S. Moves to Modernize Toxic Arsenal." *The Oregonian* (January 2, 1989): A9.

Griffith, G.W. "Biological Warfare and the Urban Battleground." *Enforcement Journal* 14(1) (1975): 4–5.

Henry, D. "149 Nations Oppose Chemical Weapons." *The Oregonian* (January 12, 1989): A1, A14.

Jenkins, B.M. and Rubin, A.P. "New Vulnerabilities and the Acquisition of New Weapons by Nongovernment Groups." In *Legal Aspects of Terrorism*, edited by A.E. Evans and J.F. Murphy, 221–276. Lexington, MA: D.C. Heath, 1978.

Laqueur, W. *The Age of Terrorism*. Boston: Little, Brown, 1987.

Smolowe, J. "Return of the Silent Killer." *Time* 44 (August 22, 1988): 47–49.

Thatcher, G. "Size of Soviets' Chemical Threat." *The Oregonian* (January 2, 1989): A8.

Thatcher, G. "Science Opens 'Pandora's Box' of Toxins." *The Oregonian* (January 3, 1989): A6; A7.

Thatcher, G. and Aeppel, T. "How Iraq Got Way to Wage Chemical War." *The Oregonian* (January 1, 1989): A22.

Tuohy, W. "State-owned Company Tied to Libyan Plant." *The Oregonian* (January 25, 1989): A7.

Watson, R. and Barry, J. "Letting a Genie Out of a Bottle." *Newsweek* CXII (September 19, 1988): 30–31.

Watson, R., Barry, J., Walter, D., Warner, M.G., and Rogers, M. "The 'Winds of Death'." *Newsweek* CXIII (January 16, 1989): 22–25.

White, T. and White, K. "Biological Weapons—How Big a Threat?" *International Defense Review* 23 (August 1990): 843–846.

Part Three

Transnational Perspectives

10
Terrorism and Law

Terrorists and their actions can be viewed from the perspectives of both domestic and international law. Some terrorist acts may be perpetrated within national boundaries or in territory over which a nation has sovereignty by individuals who are citizens of that country. Other acts of terrorism may be committed by persons who are not citizens of the country—and whose victims may also be nationals of some other country.

In international law, a crime is whatever nations recognize to be a crime; for example, most nations agree that murder committed in another country is as serious as murder committed within their own national boundaries. Therefore, not only is murder recognized as a crime, but there is also reciprocity in the way nations choose to regard it.

Political crime, however, is a different matter. Whereas all nations may recognize a general category such as treason, specific acts of treason may have markedly different value from one country to another. A treasonous act against the U.S. may horrify and outrage the British, the French or Germans may feel indifferent; the Libyans may rejoice.

Schreiber poses the question democracies such as the U.S. face in dealing with political crimes that may include terrorism:

> How should a country, committed to granting asylum to those persecuted for political crimes in their native countries, and even to encouraging their activities against oppressive governments, treat those refugees whose "political crimes" were also terrorist acts? (1978, 150)

One answer might be: If the political crimes consisted of crimes against the person (murder, attempted murder, robbery, assault), the criminals should be extradited to stand trial in the country where the crimes occurred or to be prosecuted by the lawful authorities of the country within which the offenses were committed. This is the position prescribed in the legal phrase *aut dedere aut punire* ("either extradite or punish").

Matters can become more complicated when a crime takes place in international air space or international waters. The *Achille Lauro* incident illustrates how the international law against piracy fails to control politically motivated crimes that also happen to involve common law crimes. The hijackers murdered an American citizen, Leon Klinghoffer, and stole money and jewelry from the ship's passengers (a crime of robbery in common law) but their primary purpose in seizing the ship was political—that is, they were seeking to commit acts of violence in Israel, where the vessel was scheduled to dock.

After taking control of the *Achille Lauro*, they demanded that Israel release certain terrorists it had imprisoned. Is an enterprise of this kind "piracy"? Was their murder of Leon Klinghoffer a common crime or a political crime?

A political crime, of course, may result from nothing more than an exercise of the faculty of speech: divulging a secret, inciting a crowd, speaking to an enemy. Political crimes like these bear little or no resemblance to common crimes of a violent or fraudulent nature. Other states may be reluctant to condemn the individual who commits a political crime of this kind—one that is not against common humanity but only against a specific state or regime. Indeed, the perpetrator may be highly praised. Pursuing this line of thought, Bassiouni defines and tests what constitutes political crime:

> A purely political offense is one whereby the conduct of the actor manifests an exercise in freedom of thought, expression, and belief (by words, symbolic acts or writings not inciting to violence) [or] freedom of association and religious practice which are in violation of laws designed to prohibit such conduct. (1975, 408)

Schreiber (1978, 154) proposes to call common crimes with political overtones *complex crimes*. To the extent that they are common, most—but not all—nations will agree that the perpetrators should be prosecuted; to the extent that the crimes are political, most—but not all—nations will disagree and often try to avoid the issue.

Terrorism and Common Crime

As noted, the terrorist's actions in a domestic setting may not differ appreciably from those committed by conventional criminal offenders; that is, a single terrorist incident may include the offenses of kidnapping, aggravated assault, armed robbery, and homicide. In the criminal codes of most modern nations, these offenses are likely to be defined without reference to such considerations as ideological or political motivation. If apprehended, the perpetrators may be tried and convicted on the basis of administration of justice standards that are recognized and upheld in nearly all jurisdictions. The judge of a Palestine court that tried Youssef Said Abu Dourrah in 1941 for a "political" murder committed in England observed: "We know nothing in the criminal law of this country or of England that creates a specific offense called political murder" (Bassiouni, 1975, 409).

It is also worth noting that many terrorist organizations have engaged, and may continue to engage, in purely criminal activities such as bank robberies, kidnappings for ransom, and extortion as a means to obtain funds to support their continued existence.

Murder has always been a crime that admitted various degrees of severity, depending on the intentions of the murderer. Was the murder premeditated? Was it impulsive? Was it committed while the perpetrator was temporarily insane? Was it done in reaction to a perceived threat to life or limb? Depending on one's point of view, a political motive for murder might be extenuating or complicating. The jurist, however, is not concerned with such issues.

> The element of intent required for all serious crimes bears upon the state of mind of the actor at the time the *actus reus* [the act] was committed. As such the *mens rea* [mind] does not contemplate the reason why, the ultimate purpose, or the motivating factors which brought about this state of mind. Certainly motive is relevant in proving intent, but it is not an element of the crime and, therefore, has no bearing on whether or not the actor's overall conduct, the accompanying mental state and its resulting harm, will be characterized a crime. It will, however, be relevant in the determination of the sentence. (Bassiouni, 1975, 409)

By this reasoning, Schreiber (1978) points out, when a man is charged with murder, the fact that the victim was an ambassador and the intent was to disrupt the ambassador's state should have no bearing on his eligibility for asylum or, once he is brought to trial, on the prosecution of the case. On the other hand, those facts may result in a light sentence, if he is tried in a country sympathetic to his purpose—or in execution, if he is tried by the ambassador's government. Recognizing this likelihood, prosecutors in the state in which the murderer seeks refuge can hardly be indifferent to his pleas for asylum on the ground that his is a political crime, even though the political motive was ruled out as a basis for deciding on extradition!

Crimes and International Law

When the focus shifts to the international scene, there is no international criminal code, no international police force to enforce the laws, and no international criminal court with jurisdiction over the prosecution and disposition of those charged with committing international crimes. Legal scholar John Murphy points out that there is no internationally agreed-upon definition of terrorism and, therefore, no international crime of terrorism.

> Rather, there are treaty provisions for suppression of aircraft hijacking, unlawful acts against the safety of civil aviation, unlawful acts against internationally protected persons, including diplomatic agents, the taking of hostages and the theft of nuclear materials. Although these treaty provisons are often loosely described as "anti-terrorist," the acts they cover are criminalized regardless of whether they, in any particular case, could be classified as "terrorism." (Lynch, 1987, 68)

In a lecture delivered at Columbia University on April 5, 1986, Abraham D. Sofaer, legal adviser to the U.S. Department of State and former U.S. District Court Judge in New York, asked: "What good is the law in fighting international terrorism?" (1986, 901). His answer to this rhetorical question is a rather bleak one: Not only have terrorist acts been excluded from the reach of legal sanctions, but strenuous efforts have been made—quite successfully—to legitimize terrorism by conferring on it a status that obscures or denies its fundamentally criminal character. Much, but not all, of this dismal tale has unfolded within the United Nations.

International Terrorism and the United Nations

The United Nations, in Wilkinson's view, has proven "a broken reed on the whole subject of terrorism" (1986, 284). To our way of thinking, this seems a remarkably mild judgment. In fact, attempts by the U.S. and other democratic nations to secure effective multilateral action against terrorism have been consistently stymied in the councils of the United Nations. The United Nations is deeply divided among its member-states on a basic working definition of terrorism. This division is nowhere more clearly revealed than in what happened to the U.S. proposal in 1972 for a Draft Convention for the Punishment of Certain Acts of International Terrorism.

In the aftermath of the Munich Olympics massacre, the convention had the praiseworthy aim of trying to limit the *spread* of international terrorism. As Wilkinson notes, it left the business of prosecution and punishment for *internal* acts of terrorism to the domestic jurisdiction of individual states.

> Yet even this relatively cautious and practical step was opposed and ultimately defeated by the clamorous objections of the so-called "non-aligned group" of U.N. member-states. The General Assembly refused to take any action on the U.S. Draft Convention other than to refer it to a 35-member *ad hoc* Committee on Terrorism to study the subject. As a result of the pressure of the fourteen non-aligned members of this committee, "terrorism" was completely redefined as "Acts of violence and other repressive acts by colonial, racist, and alien regimes against peoples struggling for their liberation." (Wilkinson, 1986, 285)

The representative from Cuba rejected any proposal of rules "for the purpose of assigning legal limits" to revolutionary armed struggle. The representative from Madagascar condemned terrorist acts committed for personal gain, but suggested that acts of political terrorism, committed in the service of "hallowed rights" recognized by the United Nations, were to be commended. Almost as an afterthought, the gentleman from Madagascar noted with regret that sometimes actions that fit the latter category "affected innocent persons" (Sofaer, 1986, 904).

Two years later, the General Assembly adopted by consensus a Convention on the Prevention and Punishment of Crimes against Internationally Protected Persons, including Diplomatic Agents. On the face of it, this convention appears to provide for making such offenses crimes by international law. As Green comments, however, the resolution to which the convention is annexed expressly requires that its provisions are "related" to the convention and "shall always be published together with it" (1979, 186). Paragraph 4 of the resolution makes it abundantly clear why this proviso was attached:

> The provisions of the annexed Convention could not in any way prejudice the exercise of the legitimate right to self-determination and independence, in

accordance with the purposes and principles of the United Nations and the Declaration on Principles of International Law concerning Friendly Relations and Cooperation among States in accordance with the Charter of the United Nations, by peoples struggling against colonialism, alien domination, foreign occupation, racial discrimination, and apartheid.

Thus, an act of terrorism is sanctified and no longer considered a crime if it is committed in what Green calls "the sacred name of twentieth-century holy writ: self-determination."

In 1979, a U.N. resolution for the first time condemned terrorist acts, but it referred to the 1977 Protocols to the Geneva Convention, which seek to extend to groups engaged in wars of national liberation the protection of the laws of war. It was not until December 1985 that the General Assembly adopted a resolution that "unequivocally condemns, as criminal, all acts, methods, and practices of terrorism." But the debates that preceded and followed adoption of this resolution left no doubt whatever that many United Nations member-states continue to maintain that terrorist acts are justified and excused by characterizing them as part of a "war of national liberation." The U.S. and other countries seeking effective action against international terrorism are thus obliged to pursue multilateral arrangements outside the scope of the United Nations.

Extradition and the Political Offense Exception

Most countries have treaties that obligate them to extradite to other states persons accused of committing, in those states, crimes associated with terrorism, such as murder, hijacking, bombing, armed assault, and robbery. Yet extradition requests are often refused because the offenses are characterized as "political" conduct, which the law exempts from extradition.

In 1972, five individuals hijacked a plane in the United States, extorted $1 million, and flew to Algeria, where they were received as political militants. In 1976, they made their way to France, which refused to extradite the five, although they had presented no evidence of political motivation beyond the claim that they were escaping racial segregation in the U.S. and were associated with the "black liberation movement."

More recently, the U.S. failed to obtain extradition of Abu Abbas, thought to have masterminded the *Achille Lauro* piracy, from two countries through which he passed following the incident (Italy and Yugoslavia). Despite U.S. assertions of their treaty obligation to hold Abbas, these states released him. Yugoslavia claimed that he was entitled to diplomatic immunity because he carried an Iraqi diplomatic passport.

Some decisons by U.S. courts are equally dubious; for example, they have refused to extradite Irish Republican Army gunmen on the ground that an uprising is taking place in Northern Ireland that makes crimes in furtherance of the revolt "political."

Historical Background

Sofaer observes that the "political offense" claim as a defense against extradition has "noble roots" (1986, 907). It developed during the period of the French and American revolutions and reflected the values the new democracies placed on political freedom. Thomas Jefferson commented, for instance, that "unsuccessful strugglers against tyranny have been the chief martyrs of treason laws in all countries." At that time, political offenses were associated with acts against the security of a state, such as treason, espionage, and sedition.

The concept was soon expanded, however, to so-called "relative" political offenses—ordinary crimes committed in a political context or with political motivation. In an important early case on this point (*In re Castioni*, 1891), English courts denied extradition for a killing that occurred in the midst of a demonstration against the government of a Swiss canton that refused to submit its new constitution to a popular vote. The shooting served no purpose, but the court found it "political" because it was incidental to, and part of, a political disturbance. Even if an act is "cruel and against all reason," the court held, its perpetrator is protected if he acted "for the purpose of furthering and in furtherance of a political rising." *Castioni* was quickly qualified in England when, in 1894, one of the many anarchists of the period, Theophile Meunier, was extradited to France for placing bombs in a Parisian cafe and an army barracks. But the decision took hold in the U.S. and elsewhere.

In the same year the Meunier case was decided, a U.S. court (*In re Ezeta*, 1894) refused to extradite high officials of El Salvador accused of murders in their unsuccessful effort to retain power. Relying on *Castioni*, the court held that all acts associated with an uprising were political offenses. The court accepted without discussion the premise that protection should be given equally to democrats and dictators. It also explicitly rejected the notion that the offender's conduct in killing noncombatants could disqualify him from the court's protection. During hostilities, said the court, "crimes may have been committed by the contending forces of the most atrocious and inhuman character, and still the perpetrators of such crimes escape punishment as fugitives beyond the reach of extradition."

The ruling in *Ezeta* had some support in U.S. and foreign practice during the nineteenth century. Granting asylum to revolutionaries and victims of revolutions was considered enlightened—this was the period during which republican governments first became a widespread reality. But the political offense doctrine has another side. Several incidents, diplomatic decisions, and rulings during the nineteenth and twentieth centuries indicate that the U.S. and other countries have taken their particular interests and political ideals into account in formulating the contours of the political offense exception doctrine. This self-interest has led to certain limitations of the concept of a political offense.

A particularly dramatic instance followed the assassination of Abraham Lincoln. Despite the crime's political nature, the U.S. sought and received assurances from Great Britain and Italy, respectively, for the apprehension abroad of John Wilkes Booth and John H. Surratt, one of Booth's suspected conspirators. Surratt was actually captured in Egypt and sent back to the U.S. on an American Navy vessel. The need to protect heads of state was recognized by other nations as well. Schreiber quotes King Edward VII of England in 1905 as he recalled the 1903 assassination of King Alexander of Serbia:

> My particular business is that of being king. King Alexander was also by his trade a king. As you see, we belonged to the same guild, as laborers or professional men. I cannot be indifferent to the assassination of a member of my guild. We should be obliged to shut up our businesses if we, the kings, were to consider the assassination of kings as no consequence at all. (1978, 152)

The protection of heads of state is now a widely recognized qualification to the political-offense doctrine.

Recent Applications and Issues

The more recent problem of skyjacking demonstrates how the political offense exception doctrine can still be applied in accordance with U.S. national interests. During the 1950s, despite America's strong opposition to aircraft hijackings, the U.S. and its Western allies refused requests from Czechoslovakia, the USSR, Poland, Yugoslavia, and other Communist regimes for the return of persons who hijacked planes, trains, or ships to escape Communist rule. But when skyjacking reached epidemic proportions in the late 1960s and early 1970s, the U.S. determined that hijacking of aircraft carrying passengers was too serious a problem and too great a threat to the safety of innocent people to be tolerated. The U.S. reexamined its policy and concluded that "the hijacker of a commercial aircraft carrying passengers for hire should be returned regardless of any claim that he was fleeing political persecution."

Thus, during consideration of the Hague Convention on Hijacking, the U.S. suggested in 1969 that the political offense exception should be eliminated for that crime. The suggestion was rejected, and the political-offense exception was retained in both the Hague hijacking convention and the Montreal sabotage convention. Nations therefore remain authorized (though not required) to refuse, on political grounds, to extradite suspects in such universally recognized crimes as hijacking and sabotage.

For several years, the U.S. has been prepared to revise its treaties with democratic allies to narrow the political offense exception and make it inapplicable to crimes of violence and breaches of antiterrorist conventions. In 1983, for example, the U.S. signed a revised treaty with Italy that narrowed the political-offense exception to exclude, in certain circumstances, offenses covered by a multilateral agreement, such as the hostage-taking or aircraft hijacking conventions. The rationale for the treaty revision is that the U.S. and its people are opposed to rebellions, revolutions, and political assassinations in democratic countries, because their political systems provide a peaceful means to seek change (Sofaer, 1986). Thus, revolutionaries should not be encouraged in a democracy by the treatment of their violent acts as acceptable political conduct. A doctrine born to reflect the belief in freedom should not be permitted to serve the interests of those seeking to impose undemocratic views through force.

The problem with this position, as Pyle points out in his critique of the revised treaty signed in 1986 by the Reagan and Thatcher governments (called the Supplementary Treaty Concerning the Extradition Treaty Between the Government of the United States and the Government of the United Kingdom of Great Britain and Northern Ireland), is that "almost every country on earth now calls itself a democracy" (1986, 66). In addition, says Pyle, even the most democratic countries—including the United States and Great Britain—have conquered and ruled other lands by nondemocratic means. Pyle believes that attacks on the political offense exception doctrine and opposition to judicial inquiries into the capacity of foreign regimes to do justice will not end when the last arguable democracy has been signed up:

> They will continue until the law of extradition has been restored to its medieval form and princes can again surrender fugitives for reasons of state. The extradition bureaucrats will not be content until they have the power to meet their counterparts at America's borders and say, "We'll give you three of your terrorists if you give us Robert Vesco." (1986, 78)

Terrorism and the Laws of War

Terrorist groups have repeatedly sought to secure a legal status that exempts their actions from criminal sanctions. One means they have pursued involves recognition of terrorists as combatants entitled to treatment under the Geneva conventions of 1949. The line of demarcation between actions that are criminal and those committed as part of combat is often difficult to draw precisely, as we have learned again and again in a succession of armed conflicts. But few authorities would hesitate to condemn as criminal homicide the massacre of civilians, including women and children, at Oradour-sur-Glane by troops of the 12th SS Hitler Jugend Panzer Division in 1944, despite the fact that these men were in uniform and belonged to a combat unit during World War II.

The laws of war were designed to protect persons serving as members of a military force in wartime from harsh and summary punishment when taken prisoner by the enemy. The Geneva conventions attempted to set humanitarian limits to the treatment of prisoners of war.

Radical groups responsible for terrorist acts have long sought legitimacy by securing recognition as combatants under the laws of war. They registered a significant success in the Geneva Diplomatic Conference on the Reaffirmation of International Law Applicable in Armed Conflict, which met between 1974 and 1977. This conference, under the auspices of the International Committee for the Red Cross (ICRC), was called to improve the laws of war set forth in the Geneva conventions of 1949. It produced two additional protocols to the Geneva conventions: Protocol I, dealing with international armed conflict, and Protocol II, dealing with noninternational armed conflict. The U.S. participated in the conference and signed the protocols, but neither protocol has been ratified by the Senate.

From the beginning of the conference, an effort was made to extend the law of international armed conflict to cover activities of the PLO and other radical groups, many of whom were accorded observer status at the conference. In its first session, the conference adopted what is now Article 1(4) of Protocol I, which would make the laws of international armed conflict applicable to "armed conflicts in which peoples are fighting against colonial domination and alien occupation and against racist regimes in the exercise of the right of self- determination." Never before, Sofaer remarks, has the applicability of the rules of war been made to turn on the purported aims of a conflict (1986, 913). This provision obliterates the traditional distinction between international and noninternational conflict. Any group within a national boundary that claims to be fighting against colonial domination, alien occupation, or a racist regime can now claim that it is protected by the laws of war and that its members are entitled to prisoner-of-war status for their otherwise criminal acts.

The Geneva conference went even further in accommodating the aims of radical groups at the expense of the civilian population that humanitarian law is supposed to protect. A fundamental premise of the Geneva conventions is that soldiers must earn the right to protection as military fighters by wearing uniforms and carrying their weapons openly. According to the 1949 conventions, fighters who attempt to take advantage of civilians by hiding among them in civilian dress, with their weapons concealed, forfeit their claim to be treated as soldiers.

The terrorist groups that attended the conference had no intention of modifying their conduct to satisfy the traditional rules of engagement. Terrorists are not soldiers; they do not wear uniforms. They hide among civilians and, after striking, they try to escape once again into civilian groups. Instead of modifying their conduct, the terrorist groups succeeded in modifying the law.

> Article 44(3) of Protocol I recognizes that "to promote protection of the civilian population from the effects of hostility, combatants are obliged to distinguish themselves from the civilian population when they are engaged in an attack or in a military operation preparatory to an attack." But the provision goes on to state "that there are situations in armed conflicts where, owing to the nature of the hostilities, an armed combatant cannot so distinguish himself." In such situations, "he shall retain his status as a combatant, provided. . . he carries his arms openly: (a) during each military engagement, and (b) during such time as he is visible to the adversary while he is engaging in a military deployment preceding the launching of an attack in which he is to participate." (Sofaer, 1986, 914–915)

These changes in the traditional rules undermine the notion that the protocol has secured an advantage for humanitarian law by granting revolutionary groups protection as combatants. Under the Geneva conventions, a terrorist could not hide among civilians until just before an attack; under

Protocol I, he may do so—he need only carry his arms openly while visibly engaged in a deployment or an actual engagement.

The radical groups represented at the conference lobbied hard for these changes and succeeded. After the vote on Protocol I, the PLO's representative "expressed his deep satisfaction at the result of the vote." He then specifically cited Article 1(4) as authority for the PLO's terrorist actions in Israel.

Aut Dedire Aut Punire

In 1972, the Third International Symposium sponsored by the International Institute for Advanced Criminal Sciences produced a document enunciating the following principles:

1. An alleged terrorist offender in custody should be effectively prosecuted and punished or else extradited to a state which requested him and intends to prosecute him.

2. Extradition to a requesting state should be granted if the state with custody chooses not to prosecute, unless an international court is created with jurisdiction over such matters, in which case the accused should be surrendered to the court's jurisdiction.

3. All states should be vested with universal jurisdiction with respect to crimes of terrorism.

4. Whenever a state other than the state in which the act of terrorism was committed seeks to prosecute a terrorist, a reasonable number of observers should be allowed to see the evidence and attend all proceedings.

5. Whenever extradition is contemplated, the ideological motives of the accused should not be the sole basis for the granting of asylum or for denying the extradition request.

6. If the act at issue involves grave crimes, extradition should be granted regardless of the ideological motives of the actor.

7. In all other cases, when a grave common crime has not been committed and the defendant alleges he is being charged with a political crime and thus should be immune to extradition, the court making the decision must weigh the harm committed against the values the defendant was seeking to preserve and the means he employed in relation to the goal he sought.

8. In the event of multiple extradition requests for the same offender, priority should be given to the state relying on territorial jurisdiction in its request (that is, that state in whose boundaries the crime was committed, followed by the state relying on the theory of prosecuting fundamental national interests.

9. The rights of the individual in extradition proceedings must always be upheld and he or she should not be precluded from raising any defenses available under extradition law and other relevant aspects of national and international law.

10. Extradition should not be granted when the individual sought is to be tried by an exceptional tribunal or under a procedure in patent violation of fundamental human rights. In such cases, however, the state with custody must prosecute the accused.

11. To prevent circumstances from arising in which states seeking an alleged terrorist will resort to extralegal measures to secure him, extradition procedures

should be expedited but without sacrificing the protections afforded to the individuals, and states that do not choose to extradite should prosecute their prisoners without delay.

12. Finally, judges, public officials, lawyers, and others who may become involved with terrorists in the course of their duties should become familiar with international criminal law, in particular those provisions relating to the extradition of those charged with terrorism. (Schreiber, 1978, 162–163)

Schreiber views such draft conventions as "an important step toward provisions in international law governing the treatment of suspected terrorists" (1978, 164). This laudable objective, unfortunately, is apt to founder on the issue we have already identified as the fundamental weakness in international law: the fact that not every nation wants to prosecute terrorists, because not every nation is willing to acknowledge that actions associated with them are reprehensible. In particular, Third World nations object strenuously to attempts by United Nations committees to codify the sentiments of powerful nations and impose them on the rest of the world.

Schreiber concludes that the primary effect of international conventions covering prosecution and extradition for terrorism is to assert once again the rule of law in the face of systematic, politically motivated lawlessness. Such conventions thus make a statement of principle, however helpless they are in deterring the dedicated terrorist.

Judicial Processing and Disposition

As mentioned earlier, a terrorist incident may involve crimes such as kidnapping, murder, robbery, assault, and extortion, which, although they may differ in the motivations of the perpetrators, do not differ in the way the offenses are defined in terms of criminal law. It is tempting, therefore, to conclude that apprehension, prosecution, adjudication, and sentencing of terrorist/offenders present no special problems with which the criminal justice system at the local, state, or federal level cannot deal. When we focus on the judicial processing of terrorists charged with common crimes, however, we immediately encounter a number of problems. How does one go about preparing a criminal case against a political terrorist? The simple answer to this question is: with great difficulty.

Prosecuting of conventional crimes relies on the investigative work of police and the testimony of witnesses. But in cases involving terrorism, it is difficult for the ordinary citizen to accept the heavy burden of responsibility inherent in testifying. The clearest danger for witnesses is the visibility they acquire in the atmosphere of intimidation that usually surrounds such cases.

We can distinguish three types of witnesses: victims, collaborators, and observers. Victims, because of their experience, are likely to be frightened and wish to forget the whole business as quickly as possible. Asking them to prolong the ordeal in a sometimes lengthy and sensational trial may be too much; hence, this traditional source of evidence is one on which the court can seldom rely in terrorism cases.

The same situation may apply to collaborators, though for different reasons. These potential witnesses may refuse to testify out of loyalty to the terrorist cause or out of fear of retaliation if they turn state's evidence.

Observers are the last recourse. The ordinary citizen who saw something that could be used by the prosecution may be subject to the same fears as those of the victim, whether or not the fears are justified. In such cases, the reality of the threat is not what is important, but rather the belief that it exists. The result is that the only reliable source of witnesses consists of observers who were on the scene by virtue of official duties—that is, police officers. They may be the only witnesses who both know the facts and are willing to report them.

Given this primary dependence on the police for eyewitness testimony and their monopoly on criminal investigation, we see that the police play a particularly significant role in cases involving political terrorism. In view of the special challenge the political terrorist poses, the law enforcement community can easily feel pressured to make successful cases. Public sentiment, particularly as reflected in melodramatic media coverage, can exacerbate this attitude and lead to the belief that there is no room for failure without risking confidence in the criminal justice system and its officials.

Emotionally charged situations of this kind tend to raise issues of national security and to produce high expectations for effective action and immediate results.

> Some of the possible dangers that can arise in the process of investigation and preparation of a case include the use of illegal methods for acquiring evidence, the infringement on civil rights, and the tampering with any evidence that is available. Once a case is brought to court, further possible pitfalls include the relaxing of the rules of evidence, the admission of biased testimony, collusion between prosecution and defense, or prejudicial interventions by the presiding judge. (Crelinsten, Laberge-Altmejd, & Szabo, 1978, 32)

History is replete with cases in which questions of national security and the accompanying public outcry led to hasty judicial decisions that were later proven questionable or even wrong. The conspiracy trial of the Chicago Seven in 1969–1970 tarnished the image of the judicial process because the presiding judge allowed himself to be provoked by the defendants' inflammatory rhetoric and actions.

Sentencing and Disposition

The final and most important step in the judicial process is sentencing. A sentence represents the penalty or sanction for a given crime as established by the legislature, imposed by the court, and carried out by the correctional system. Generally, five different kinds of sentences are available to the court to impose on a convicted offender: (1) a fine; (2) probation; (3) a suspended sentence; (4) imprisonment; and (5) capital punishment.

A fine is usually exacted in the case of a minor offense and is unlikely to be imposed in the case of terrorists, who are almost invariably prosecuted for major, rather than minor, violations of the law.

The most common sentence in the American judicial system is probation, under which the offender is permitted to live in the community subject to compliance with legally imposed conditions. Often, where leniency is appropriate, a suspended sentence is imposed in lieu of a sentence of imprisonment; it, too, allows the offender to remain in the community.

The atmosphere surrounding cases of political terrorism tends to demand harsh sentences, and probation is less likely. One possible result of pressures to act quickly and severely is that long sentences may be handed down in the heat of controversy, only to be followed later by such practices as pardons, amnesties, or early releases on parole after the sense of urgency is gone. These practices minimize the impact of the sentence and illustrate the need to consider adapting judicial procedures to the special problems raised by the prosecution of terrorists *before* being compelled to do so by public hue and cry.

If fines or probation are excluded as probable options in sentencing terrorist/offenders, we are left with imprisonment and execution. Of the two choices, imprisonment is the far more probable disposition. It is generally recognized that the goals of imprisonment are threefold: (1) punishment; (2) incapacitation; and (3) rehabilitation. These goals are not mutually exclusive and can be emphasized in varying degrees in different penal policies.

How do the three goals of imprisonment and their possible interactions apply to the political terrorist? In theory, at least, punishment is directed at the act rather than the actor. We judge a person insofar as he has committed a prohibited act, not as a person per se; we sentence the perpetrator, not the person. Even so, the motive behind the act is not forgotten altogether. Traditionally, motives serve as mitigating factors; for instance, in extradition and sentencing. Of course, motives can be used the other way: the motive behind terrorist acts may be cited in a demand for harsher sentences and to ensure that the perpetrators are properly punished.

Depending on the point of view, a convicted terrorist can be considered either a political prisoner or a criminal offender. The use of punishment as retribution works as well for political terrorists as for any other kind of offender. But punishment is supposed to be more than mere revenge: it is conceived as a means of deterrence. Even though the deterrent effects of imprisonment are nearly impossible to substantiate in the case of criminal offenses, they appear to be totally inappropriate in the case of terrorist offenses. Possible imprisonment, let alone death, is one of the risks a terrorist assumes in the name of a particular cause.

In view of the committed terrorist's imperviousness to punishment and deterrence, the goal of incapacitation appears to be more appropriate. The rationale for incapacitation is quite simple: imprisonment is justified on the grounds that as long as the offender is held in confinement, he is not free to commit further crimes. Extreme forms of punishment, such as execution or life imprisonment, constitute total incapacitation. Both supporters and critics of the punitive approach seem to regard this rationale as the most plausible of the utilitarian arguments on the side of punishment.

Implicit in incapacitation is the belief that the best basis for predicting future behavior is past behavior. In the case of criminal behavior, the presumption is that the one who has committed a particular type of crime is likely to commit more of those crimes or crimes of some other type.

> This latter justification does not seem to figure largely in the justification for incapacitation as a mode of prevention. To the extent that we lock up burglars because we fear that they will commit further offenses, our prediction is not that they will if left unchecked violate the antitrust laws, or cheat on their income taxes, but rather that they will commit further burglaries, or other crimes associated with burglary, such as homicide or bodily injury. The premise is that the person may have a tendency to commit further crimes like the one for which he is now being punished and that punishing him will restrain him from doing so (Packer, 1968, 50).

In every case, Packer reminds us, it is an empirical question whether or not the prediction is valid.

In the case of terrorists, there seems little doubt that the terrorist will return to his previous associates and activities as soon as he is released. But the terrorist presents an additional problem during his confinement. Political prisoners, which includes terrorists, represent a potentially disruptive element in the prison population. In fact, in Italy, the prisons constitute one of the primary recruiting grounds for extremist groups. As a result, officials tend to opt for segregation of those prisoners whom they feel are engaging in recruitment. Although segregation avoids this problem, others ensue that are detrimental.

Segregated groups of prisoners who share ideological views or a political cause tend to organize along military lines, and to maintain a high degree of internal cohesiveness. The result is an esprit de corps that makes communication between prisoners and staff extremely difficult, if not impossible. Prison authorities have little control over the activities of individual group members and, at the same time, individuals who wish to dissociate themselves from the group are essentially locked in.

The Death Penalty

By the end of 1988, the death row population in the U.S. had topped 2,000—the highest number since recordkeeping began in 1953. Southern states held three-quarters of the condemned, including women; Florida, Georgia, and Texas accounted for more than half of those on death row.

In 1972, when the total death row population stood at 631, the highest total reached to that point, the U.S. Supreme Court ruled in *Furman v. Georgia* that "the imposition and carrying out of the death penalty in the instant cases constitutes cruel and unusual punishment in violation of the Eighth and Fourteenth Amendment" (239–240). As a result of the *Furman* decision, the death sentences of the 631 death row inmates were vacated. Had the Supreme Court struck a mortal blow to the advocates of capital punishment?

There was no consensus by the Court in *Furman*. The decision was 5:4, and each of the nine justices wrote an opinion on the constitutionality of the death penalty. Four of the justices stated that imposition of the death penalty, even then, did not run afoul of the Constitution. Only two justices (Brennan and Marshall) stated their belief that capital punishment was per se unconstitutional under all circumstances. And three justices agreed that historically the death penalty had been arbitrarily and capriciously imposed—especially against blacks, the poor, and men. They found it unnecessary to decide in *Furman*, however, whether the death penalty could ever be imposed given new legislative guidelines.

The legislative response around the country to *Furman* was swift. Thirty-six jurisdictions (including the U. S. Congress) passed new death penalty legislation designed to remove the discriminatory effects that had permeated the American system for many years. But the legislative packages were anything but uniform. Some states made the death penalty mandatory following a conviction for first-degree murder. Other states left the sentencing decision exclusively to the convicting jury; others permitted a sentencing recommendation from the jury, but rested the ultimate decision with the trial judge. Most states provided legislative guidelines to juries and judges as to their sentencing authority in capital cases. All present occupants of death row in the U.S. were convicted under these post-*Furman* statutes; however, opponents of the death penalty, including the American Civil Liberties Union and Amnesty International, contend that sentencing under the new laws exhibits the same pattern of arbitrariness and racial discrimination that originally led the Supreme Court to the *Furman* decision. One study, based on statistics from Texas, Ohio, Florida, and Georgia for the years 1972 through 1977, concluded that blacks convicted of murdering whites had been sentenced to death eighteen times as frequently as whites convicted of murdering whites. It also shows that 170 of the 1,015 blacks convicted of murdering whites had been sentenced to death, whereas only three of the 341 whites convicted of murdering blacks received the death penalty.

Discussions between opponents and supporters of capital punishment tend to be dominated by emotional rather than intellectual considerations. Issues raised by the death penalty tap some extremely deep levels of primitive belief. Our answers to questions about the taking of human life in socially sanctioned circumstances are therefore likely to express our primitive beliefs; the intellectual arguments we subsequently use to justify our choice fall into the catetory of rationalizations. One principal rationalization involves the deterrence argument. The rationale underlying this theory is that people will refrain from committing criminal acts because they fear the consequences of punishment. Supporters of the death penalty might argue, therefore, that since fear of death is likely to be the most powerful kind of motivation in human behavior, capital punishment provides a powerful defense against any crime that incurs the death penalty. Opponents of the death penalty point out that this position is based on a simplistic notion of human conduct, requiring that human beings be rational creatures who can weigh the potential consequences of their actions and make informed choices among possible alternatives. This position, of course, comes close to the free will doctrine on which criminal law is based.

Once it is cast within this mold, the issue of capital punishment is fought out on the question of whether the evidence supports or refutes the contention that the death penalty is a deterrent to the commission of specific crimes. Supporters of capital punishment take refuge from accusations that they are barbaric and bloodthirsty by claiming that the death penalty works to reduce the incidence of heinous murders. Abolitionists say "Just show us satisfactory scientific evidence that the death penalty is an effective deterrent against such crimes and we shall renounce our opposition to capital punishment."

Scores of studies by criminologists, psychologists, and economists have thus far failed to produce the kind of scientific evidence that would satisfy the abolitionists, and there are some who claim that such evidence is beyond the reach of scientific verification, now or ever.

Sometimes the discussion of capital punishment brings in irrelevant or misleading arguments; for example, Ellison and Buckhout claim that "Murder is seldom a cold-blooded crime but is nearly always committed in the heat of violent passion, when the murderer is obviously incapable of rationally considering the consequences of his or her act" (1981, 267). This description fits the kind of homicide that typically involves people who are closely, even intimately, connected with or related to one another: husband, wife, and lover, or friends, neighbors, or close acquaintances—these are the ingredients of a "crime of passion." But these crimes usually result in indictments for second-degree murder, not murder in the first degree. It is not people convicted of second-degree murder who end up on death row; it is the person who, in the overwhelming majority of instances, was convicted of first-degree murder under the felony murder doctrine—that is, one who committed murder while carrying out rape, robbery, kidnapping, burglary, or some other type of felonious offense. It is appropriate to examine the issue of deterrence in relation to second-degree murder, but different considerations are involved in the potential effects of deterrence on a person who is capable of committing felony murder.

Each time an execution is carried out, there is a flood of speculation in the press that we may be on the brink of a large-scale resumption of capital punishment that will boost the figures for executions to the levels they reached back in the 1930s. These speculations are buttressed by the results of public opinion polls, which appear to indicate a major shift during the 1980s from two decades ago, when a minority of the public favored the death penalty, to majority support for capital punishment at present. Much of the editorial comment accompanying these reports seeks to convey the impression that most people are fed up with interminable delays imposed by appellate procedures in death penalty cases and are impatient to push on with the distasteful but necessary task of executing condemned murderers.

Given these background considerations with regard to capital punishment, it is difficult to visualize any situations in which the death penalty is likely to be invoked for terrorists who have been convicted of first-degree murder. One thing is absolutely certain: the accused will not be a terrorist who was apprehended in West Germany. The case of Mohammed Ali Samadhi, who was tried in the Federal Republic for killing Robert Stethem, an American sailor on a hijacked TWA flight in 1985, demonstrated the refusal of the Bonn government to extradite a terrorist to the U.S., where he faced the possibility of a death sentence. Other countries that have abolished the death penalty are also unwilling to cooperate in extraditing terrorists. In fact, Canada refused to extradite one of the three young men involved in the robbery and mass murder of thirteen people—Seattle's infamous Wah Mee massacre—until Washington's attorney general agreed to waive the death penalty if the accused individual were convicted.

Thus, we are left by default with imprisonment as the likeliest sentence a U.S. court will impose on persons convicted of terrorist crimes—and imprisonment for anything less than life certainly means that the individual will eventually be released.

Summary

When terrorists commit such crimes as murder, robbery, assault, and kidnapping, they are not given special consideration because their offenses are politically motivated. Offenders may either be extradited or prosecuted in the country where the offense occurred. Political crimes that do not involve common law violations, however, raise a number of rather complicated legal issues.

International law lacks a criminal code, law enforcement agencies, and courts to deal with "international crimes." Most importantly, there is no agreed-upon definition of terrorism that assigns it the status of a crime. Thus, terrorism becomes a problem for multilateral arrangements among nations.

Efforts by the Western democracies within the United Nations to establish a common international ground for fighting terrorism have been stymied by representatives of the so-called nonaligned nations. Equally frustrating have been U.S. attempts to strip international terrorism from the protective cover provided by the "political offense exception" to extradition. The result has been that extradition of individuals charged with terrorist acts, including crimes of violence, is increasingly difficult to obtain.

States identified with sponsorship of terrorism have also supported the initiatives of terrorist groups and organizations to secure prisoner of war status for apprehended terrorists. The U.S. and a number of other countries have refused to extend the POW provisions of the Geneva Convention to terrorists, but their example has not been followed by many nations.

Imprisonment, which is the criminal sanction most likely to be imposed on convicted terrorists, creates nearly as many problems for the captors as it does for the captives. Capital punishment is surrounded with so many controversies that we are unlikely to see it used as a disposition for individuals convicted of terrorism in the near future.

Key Terms

aut dedire aut punire	common crimes
complex crimes	death penalty
deterrence	Geneva Convention
Furman v. Georgia	Hague Convention
incapacitation	Leon Klinghoffer
Achille Lauro incident	political offense exception
punishment	Mohammed Ali Samadhi

Questions for Discussion and Review

1. Can a democratic country offer asylum to a person whose political crime includes an act of terrorism?
2. Are crimes such as assassination (murder) justified by political motivation?
3. Has the United Nations taken the lead in seeking to reduce or eliminate international terrorism?
4. Briefly sketch the historical background to the "political offense exception" to extradition. Did the countries that were signatories to the Hague Convention on Hijacking adopt the U.S. suggestion to eliminate the political offense exception for this crime?
5. What are the basic objections to accepting revisions of the Geneva Conventions that extend prisoner of war treatment to terrorists?
6. Summarize the problems in successfully prosecuting terrorists as criminal offenders. If terrorists are convicted, what dispositions are available to the courts?
7. Are we likely to see the death penalty imposed in the foreseeable future for murder convictions in cases involving terrorism?

References

Bassiouni, M.C. "Criminological policy." In *Legal Aspects of International Terrorism,* edited by A.E. Evans and J.F. Murphy, pp. 523–534. Lexington, MA: D.C. Heath, 1978.

Bassiouni, M.C. "The Political Offense Exception in Extradition Law and Practice." In *International Terrorism and Political Crimes,* edited by M.C. Bassiouni, pp. 398–447. Springfield, IL: Charles C. Thomas, 1975.

Crelinsten, R.D., Laberge-Altmejd, D., and Szabo, D. *Terrorism and Criminal Justice.* Lexington, MA: D.C. Heath, 1978.

Ellison, K.W. and Buckhout, R. *Psychology and Criminal Justice.* New York: Harper & Row, 1981.

Green, L.C. "The Legislation of Terrorism." In *Terrorism in Theory and Practice,* edited by Y. Alexander, D. Carlton, and P. Wilkinson, pp. 173–197. Boulder, CO: Westview Press, 1979.

Lewis, P.W., Mannle, H.W., Allen, H.E., and Vetter, H.J. "A Post-*Furman* Profile of Florida's Condemned—A Question of Discrimination in Terms of the Race of the Victim and a Comment on *Spinkellink* v. *Wainwright.*" *Stetson Law Review* 9 (1979): 1–45.

Murphy, J.F. As cited by Lynch, E.A. "International Terrorism: The Search for a Policy." *Terrorism: An International Journal* 9 (1987): 1–85.

Packer, H., *The Limits of the Criminal Sanction.* Palo Alto, CA: Stanford University Press, 1968.

Pyle, C.H. "Defining Terrorism." *Foreign Policy* 64 (1986): 63–78.

Schreiber, J. *The Ultimate Weapon: Terrorists and World Order.* New York: William Morrow, 1978.

Sofaer, A. "Terrorism and the Law." *Foreign Affairs* 64 (1986): 901–922.

Wilkinson, P. *Terrorism and the Liberal State.* New York: New York University Press, 1986.

11

A Question of Policy

Policy: a definite course or method of action selected (as by a government, institution, group or individual) from among alternatives and in the light of given conditions to guide and usually determine present and future decisions (5a).

Webster's Third International Dictionary, p. 1754

The Monroe Doctrine and the Truman Doctrine are national policies that long outlived the administrations under which they were promulgated. The policies represented unity of purpose and consistency of action in the service of national interests. They identified, for friend and foe alike, a coherent pattern of official action and reaction to situations affecting American security and stability that transcended political parties.

Does the U.S. have a national policy toward terrorism in the sense conveyed by the dictionary definition of policy? A national policy toward terrorism would imply broad agreement between the executive and legislative branches of government regarding appropriate measures and countermeasures for dealing with terrorism and terrorist actions, and rational, coherent guidelines for responding to terrorist incidents that can be recognized by the country's friends and adversaries.

In May 1985, the Senate Judiciary Committee held three days of joint hearings on international terrorism, insurgency, and drug trafficking. Commenting on the committee proceedings, Lynch states that:

> The most striking conclusion drawn from the Joint Judiciary Committee and Foreign Relations Committee hearings was the fact that the United States has neither a comprehensive nor a realistic policy on terrorism. Current policy is fragmented and not fully developed. (1987, 2)

Apart from agreeing that the U.S. would not engage in any formal or official negotiation with terrorists, there was little else on which witnesses from the Departments of State and Defense seemed able to reach a consensus.

Perhaps the best answer to the question of whether the U.S. does or does not have a national policy on terrorism can be found by examining how a succession of administrations has dealt with terrorism and by reviewing some of the more important legislative initiatives toward terrorism.

The Nixon Administration

In 1972, terrorist incidents occurred at Lod Airport in Tel Aviv and at the Olympic Games in Munich. Although neither incident directly involved American citizens or diplomatic installations, President Richard M. Nixon took the threat of international terrorism seriously enough to establish the Cabinet Committee to Combat Terrorism (CCCT). The committee, chaired by Secretary of State William Rogers, was made up of the Secretaries of the Treasury, Defense, and Transportation, the U.S. Attorney General, the Director of the Central Intelligence Agency, the U.S. Ambassador to the United Nations, the Acting Director of the FBI, the Assistant to the President for National Security Affairs, the Assistant to the President for Domestic Affairs, and any other officials the chairman deemed necessary.

In addition to the CCCT, a supplementary Working Group was established in October 1972 under the chairmanship of Ambassador Armin H. Meyer, the Special Assistant to the Secretary and Coordinator for Combatting Terrorism. The Working Group consisted of senior delegates selected by CCCT members. The composition of the CCCT and the Working Group is summarized in Table 11–1.

Table 11-1
Organization for Antiterrorism Planning, Coordination, and Policy Formulation

Nixon Administration	
Cabinet Committee to Combat Terrorism	
Secretary of State	U.S. Ambassador to U.N.
Secretary of State	Director of Central Intelligence
Secretary of Defense	Assistant to the President for
Secretary of Transportation	National Security Affairs
Attorney General	Assistant to the President for
	Domestic Affairs
	Acting Director of the FBI
Working Group	
Department of State (Chairman)	Central Intelligence Agency
Department of the Treasury	Federal Bureau of Investigation
Department of Defense	National Security Council Staff
Department of Justice	U.S. Mission to the U.N.
Department of Transportation	Domestic Affairts Council Staff

SOURCE: Farrell, W.R. The U.S. Government Response to Terrorism: In Search of an Effective Strategy. Boulder, CO: Westview Press, Inc. 1982.

The operational tasks of the CCCT included assignment of the responsibility for interagency coordination of efforts to prevent terrorism—specifically, the global collection of intelligence and security of foreign and domestic personnel and installations; evaluation of the programs and activities and recommendations for their improvement; design of response procedures for acts of terrorism; suggestions to the Director of the Office of Management and the Budget for funding; and submission of progress reports to the President (*Public Papers of the President of the United States Richard Nixon*, 1974, 912).

During the next five years, the CCCT held only a single meeting. Its inactivity, plus the desire of President Jimmy Carter to create a stronger policy toward terrorism, resulted in dismissal of the CCCT on September 16, 1977.

The Carter Administration

Under President Carter, the antiterrorism response program was reorganized into three levels. The first level was designated *national command and policy* and was represented by the Special Coordination Committee of the National Security Council. The second level was designated *coordination and control* and its membership consisted of executive agencies. The third level, *operations*, encompassed the four components of the federal antiterrorism response program: (1) prevention; (2) deterrence; (3) prediction; and (4) reaction. Membership at this level consisted of agencies serving on the Interagency Working Group to Combat Terrorism (Motley, 1983, 33). The organizational structure established by the Carter administration is presented in Table 11–2.

Table 11-2
Organization for Antiterrorism Planning, Coordination, and Policy Formulation

Carter Administration	
National Security Council/Special Coordination Committee	
NSC Adviser	Chairman, Joint Chiefs of Staff
Vice President	Director of Central Intelligence
Secretary of State	other concerned agencies
Secretary of Defense	
Executive Committee on Terrorism	
State	Transportation
Justice/FBI	Central Intelligence Agency
Defense/JCS	Energy
Treasury	NSC Staff

(continued)

Table 11-2 (continued)

Interagency Working Group to Combat Terrorism

State	Immigration & Naturalization
Justice	International Communications Admin.
Arms Control and Disarmament Agency	Law Enforcement Assistance Admin.
Agency for International Development	Metropolitan Police Dept.
Central Intelligence AGency	Naional Security Agency
Coast Guard	Nuclear Regulatory Commission
Commerce	Office of Management & Budget
Customs	Postal Service
Army	Transportation
Defense	Federal Aviation Admin.
Defense Intelligence Agency	Treasury
Energy	Alcohol, Tobacco, & Firearms
Federal Bureau of Investigation	Secret Service
Federal Preparedness Agency	U.S. Mission to the U.N.
Federal Protective Service	Health, Education, Welfare
	Joint Chiefs of Staff

Committees

Research & Development	Public Relations
Security Policy	International Initiatives
Contingency Planning & Crisis Management	

SOURCE: Farrell, W.R. The U.S. Government Response to Terrorism: In Search of an Effective Strategy. Boulder, CO: Westview Press, Inc. 1982.

This trilevel structure was designed after a study by the National Security Council (NSC) to evaluate the government's ability to respond to terrorist situations. Deputy Attorney General Benjamin R. Civiletti stated that the study "confirmed the need for an extremely flexible antiterrorism program at the federal level that would take into account the changeable nature of the contemporary terrorist threat and the wide range of resources that would have to be marshalled to meet all likely contingencies" (Motley, 1983, 32).

At the national command and policy level, the Special Coordination Committee of the NSC became the forum for discussion of special issues and incidents requiring decisions by the President and his most senior advisers. The purpose of the NSC is to aid the President in "analyzing, integrating, and facilitating foreign, defense, and intelligence decisions. International economic and other interdependence issues which are pertinent to national security are also considered by the NSC" (Farrell, 1982, 35).

In addition to President Carter's revision of the role of the NSC in managing terrorist incidents, he also changed the functions of the NSC itself. Two policy committees were created: the Policy Review Committee (PRC) and the Security Council Committee (SCC). Chairmanship of the PRC shifted, depending on the subject under consideration; the PRC was primarily involved in long-term projects. The SCC, which was always chaired by the

Assistant to the President for National Security Affairs, had the same membership as the NSC. Both the PRC and SCC had working groups. Depending on the nature of the project, the working groups were composed of delegates at the level of undersecretary or assistant security.

The Lead Agency Concept

The federal government's organizational strategy for the management of terrorist incidents is based on the concept of *lead agency*. This plan originated during the Nixon administration, but was described more recently by Ambassador Anthony C.E. Quainton, former Director of the State Department's Office for Combatting Terrorism:

> In practice, the SCC would probably directly exercise this responsibility only in the event of a major terrorist incident requiring the highest level decisions. In general, the U.S. government's response to terrorist incidents is based on the lead agency concept: The State Department has operational responsibility for international incidents and the FBI handles domestic incidents coming under Federal jurisdiction. They work closely with state and local law enforcement authorities where there is overlapping jurisdiction. Aircraft hijacking is a special case—the Congress has mandated by law that the Federal Aviation Administration shall have primary responsibility in this field. Each of these agencies can and does draw upon the support of other Federal agencies with relevant expertise. Where interagency policy issues arise during the course of an incident, senior officials of concerned agencies can meet, under NSC staff leadership, to resolve them. (Farrell, 1982, 35)

As Quainton's statement implies, the organization of federal response is delegated to the agency with the most direct operational role in dealing with a given terrorist incident. Acts of terrorism that occur outside the U.S. but are perpetrated against targets representing American interests are a matter of diplomacy; hence, the Department of State becomes the lead agency—specifically, the Office for Combatting Terrorism manages the incident. Depending on the nature of the incident, consultation and support may be enlisted from any of the geographic and functional bureaus within the Department of State that bear any relationship to the incident. In reponse to domestic acts of terrorism, the Department of Justice—operating through the FBI—is the lead agency. Each FBI field office has its own special weapons and tactics (SWAT) team and each has developed contingency plans for diplomatic and consular offices within its area. FBI contingency planning provides for an on-scene mobile command center, media relations, and the use of assault teams. In the event of a hijacking within U.S. air space, the lead agency is the FAA; once the aircraft has landed, the FBI replaces the FAA as the lead agency. (Presumably memoranda are exchanged between the two agencies to clarify which agency is to assume responsibility for managing the incident.)

At the control and coordination level of the federal antiterrorism program was the Executive Committee on Terrorism (ECT), consisting of officials from the Departments of State, Defense, Treasury, Justice, Transportation, and Energy, along with the CIA and the NSC staff, all of whom were directly accountable to the SCC. Delegates assigned to the ECT typically had extensive background in policy analysis and coordination and control of military or law enforcement operations. The ECT was chaired by a State Department official, with a Department of Justice official as deputy chairman.

The Interagency Working Group to Combat Terrorism

Shortly after Ambassador Quainton assumed the directorship of the Department of State's Office for Combatting Terrorism in July of 1978, he decided that the Working Group was too large and cumbersome to operate effectively. Accordingly, responsibilities were delegated to a series of committees: Research and Development; Contingency Planning and Crisis Management; Security Policy Committee; Public Information; and International Initiatives. With the reorganization of the Executive Committee into the present organizational structure, most of the earlier committees have become defunct; others still exist on official records but appear to serve no meaningful purpose.

The Reagan Administration

Shortly after President Reagan's inauguration, the new administration established the Interdepartmental Group on Terrorism, which was intended to function at the coordination and control level of the federal government's antiterrorism program. The IG/T, as it is known in Washington bureaucratic circles, replaced the Executive Committee on Terrorism that had been introduced during the Carter administration. Chaired by the Department of State with the Department of Justice as Deputy Chairman, the IG/T consists of delegates from various federal agencies that bear a direct responsibility for responding to terrorism. The agencies represented on the IG/T include the Office of the Vice President; National Security Council (Special Coordination Committee); Departments of State, Defense (Joint Chiefs of Staff), Justice, Treasury, Energy, and Transportation; and the Central Intelligence Agency. The IG/T convenes bimonthly for interagency coordination of antiterrorism programs.

With the abolition of the Interagency Working Group to Combat Terrorism, it became necessary to provide support to the IG/T from many other federal agencies with a jurisdictional interest in the suppression of terrorism. Presently thirty federal agencies comprise the Advisory Group on Terrorism, as listed in Table 11–3.

Table 11-3
Organization for Antiterrorism Planning, Coordination, and
Policy Formulation

Reagan Administration
National Security Council/Special Coordination Committee

Senior Interdepartmental Group
Deputy Secretary of State, Chmn

Interdepartmental Group on Terrorism

Vice President	Department of Defense
National Security Council	Department of Energy
Department of State (Chmn)	Department of Transportation
Department of Justice (Dep. Chmn)	Central Intelligence Agency
Department of the Treasury	

Advisory Group on Terrorism

Agency for International Development	Federal Protective Service
Arms Control and Disarmament Agency	Immigration and Naturalization Service
Bureau of Alcohol, Tobacco & Firearms	International Communications Agency
Center for Disease Control	Joint Chiefs of Staff
Central Intelligence Agency	Metropolitan Police Department
Defense Intelligence Agency	National Security Agency
Department of the Army	Nuclear Regulatory Commission
Department of Energy	Office of Justice Assistance, Research and Statistics
Department of Interior	
Department of Justice	Office of Management and Budget
Department of State	Office of the Undersecretary of Defense
Department of the Treasury	United States Coast Guard
Department of Transportation	United States Customs Service
Federal Aviation Administration	Unitred States Postal Service
Federal Bureau of Investigation	United States Secret Service
Federal Emergency Management Agency	

SOURCE: Farrell, W.R. The U.S. Government Response to Terrorism: In Search of an Effective Strategy. Boulder, CO: Westview Press, Inc. 1982.

The Central Intelligence Agency is the primary agency involved in collecting and interpreting information pertinent to terrorism. On January 24, 1978, President Jimmy Carter promulgated Executive Order 12036, which empowered the Director of the CIA to create the National Foreign Intelligence Program budget and to supervise the entire intelligence community's collection operations. Other members of the intelligence community with which the CIA coordinates are the National Security Agency, the Defense Intelligence Agency, military officials involved in reconnaisance and intelligence operations, the Department of State's Bureau of Intelligence and Research, the FBI, the Department of the Treasury, the Department of Energy, and the Drug Enforcement Administration.

The Department of Defense has two functions in the area of counterterrorism: it must provide security for its personnel and for installations abroad. Failure to ensure such protection for the U.S. Marine barracks at Beirut International Airport led to the massacre of more than 200 Americans on October 23, 1983. The Department of Defense is also responsible for providing military assistance to local law enforcement agencies when constitutionally justified under the Posse Comitatus Act. This legislation prohibits use of the Army or Air Force to enforce any laws except those authorized by the U.S. Constitution (e.g., providing for the common defense) or the Congress. Under certain conditions, the Department of Defense is authorized to provide assistance in the form of technical and advisory personnel and equipment to the FBI when responding to a domestic terrorism incident.

The Department of Defense recognizes a distinction between *antiterrorism* and *counterterrorism*. The former refers to preventive measures accomplished through diplomatic and strategic policy planning; the latter is generally applied to a military context emphasizing the tactical force option. (We will look at this distinction more closely in chapter 12 and consider its implications for dealing defensively with terrorism.)

Within the Department of Defense, the Defense Nuclear Agency (DNA) provides technical support to the Office of the Secretary of Defense and Joint Chiefs of Staff on various aspects of nuclear weapons operation. Two principal areas over which the DNA has jurisdiction are nuclear security and responding to nuclear accidents and incidents. The Nuclear Security Division of DNA conducts exploratory research in the areas of technology development, tactical concept development, and proof of feasibility under the auspices of the Department's Physical Security Research and Development Program.

Since 1972, the FBI has had standard operating procedures and contingency plans for dealing with terrorism in effect for all fifty-nine of its agencies. As mentioned, many of the field offices have trained hostage negotiators and SWAT forces at their disposal. In April 1977, the Terrorism Section of the Criminal Investigations Division was established at FBI headquarters in Washington, DC.

The tactical response to a domestic terrorist incident is made by the FBI Special Agent in Charge (SA/C) at the location. The SA/C is accountable to the director of the FBI, who bears the responsibility for resolution of the situation. It is the Attorney General, however, who is responsible for coordinating the government's response, which includes policy decisions and legal judgments pertaining to such incidents (Motley, 1983, 43). Communication between the on-site SA/C and the task force is carried out through the Operations Command Center of the Department of Justice.

Two units within the FBI have a significant role in dealing with terrorism: the Special Operations and Research Staff (SOAR) and the Terrorism Research and Bomb Data Unit (TRABDU). The SOARS unit consists of special agents with backgrounds in psychology and criminology and experience in criminal investigation. The purpose of the SOARS unit is to collect and analyze information concerning terrorist incidents and to convey this information to other law enforcement agencies with an interest in terrorism. The Terrorism and Bomb Data Unit studies the membership of terrorist organizations to develop more sophisticated investigative methods for dealing with such groups.

The Federal Emergency Management Agency (FEMA) was created in 1980 by the fusion of about a half-dozen agencies charged with managing the consequences of natural or man-made disasters. The most recent responsibility conferred upon FEMA by executive order is the organization of a response to a terrorist incident that would require mass evacuation and public transportation systems rerouting. Specific circumstances warranting FEMA involvement would include: (1) nuclear, chemical, or biological threats; (2) sabotage of nuclear facilities; (3) detonation of a nuclear device; and (4) sabotage of susceptible public utilities systems (e.g., petroleum and natural gas, electrical power, transportation systems, and telecommunications networks).

The executive order conferred upon FEMA the responsibility for managing the aftermath of certain types of incidents and empowers the agency to coordinate the government's response plan. The term *coordination* implies generating policy guidance and supervision of planning and implementation of consequence management. To fulfill its mission, FEMA must be reliably informed and able to participate in both the preparedness and crisis management phases of response. The agency's National Emergency Training Center in Emmitsburg, Maryland, consisting of the U.S. Fire Academy and the Emergency Management Institute, has worked at developing training programs for state and local law enforcement and fire officials to help prepare them for handling a variety of emergencies (Giuffrida, 1982, 120–121).

The Bush Administration

The administration that took office in January 1989 under George Bush, former Vice-President in the Reagan administration, has made no changes of any consequence in the organizational structure it inherited. This may indicate satisfaction with existing arrangements or, more probably, that President Bush has been concerned with other priorities. Bush has been criticized in Congress and the media for excessive caution in foreign policy initiatives. But no one in official Washington, including Bush's critics, predicted the nature, extent, and rapidity of developments in Eastern Europe that marked the end of the Cold War. Many of those same critics, however, have castigated Bush for recklessness in approving such actions as "Operation Just Cause," the military incursion into Panama to seize Manuel Noriega.

Bush also inherited the terror bombing of Pan Am Flight 103 that crashed in Lockerbie, Scotland, while en route from London to New York on December 21, 1988. In addition to the 259 passengers and crew members who perished in the explosion, falling debris and a fireball of aviation fuel cost the lives of eleven residents of the small Scottish town. Within a matter of days, investi-gators had gathered sufficient evidence to prove that the bombing had been carried out for an unknown sum of money at Iran's behest by the Popular Front for the Liberation of Palestine-General Command, a terrorist organiza-tion headed by Ahmed Jibril, in retaliation for the downing of an Iranian airbus in the Persian Gulf by the *U.S.S. Vincennes* on July 3, 1988 (Emerson & Duffy, 1990). Reportedly, two months before the disaster, West German officials had held the maker of the bomb, Marwan Khreeshat, and subsequently released him. Emerson and Duffy claim that German authorities covered up the resulting scandal.

A policy decision taken by the Bush administration that has implications for terrorism concerns the "war on drugs." One of Bush's more important political appointments was to make William Bennett, Secretary of Education in the previous administration, head of the Office of National Drug Control Policy. Promptly dubbed the "Drug Czar" by the media, Bennett spent months preparing a 235-page policy paper that is notable for its cautious outlook. It rejects the legalization of addictive drugs and rebuts the view that drug abuse can be fought only by attacking the social causes of crime and addiction in low-income neighborhoods. Bennett supports more aid for federal law en-forcement, expansion of state and federal prison capacities, increased funding for education and treatment, and tougher legal sanctions against casual drug users.

Despite the obvious evidence that interdiction, the Reagan administration's primary strategy against Latin American drug trafficking, has been a failure, Bennett has publicly rejected the idea of using U.S. military forces in the interdiction effort. He is also skeptical of the State Department's preferred tactic, which is to try to eradicate the coca-plant fields in Bolivia, Columbia, and Peru. Instead, he argues for substantial improvement in U.S. intelligence-gathering activities targeted at cocaine trafficking, coupled with increased U.S. law enforcement and economic aid to Latin America.

Antiterrorism Legislation

Official Washington has viewed, and continues to view, the problems of terrorism as principally the responsibility of the executive branch of govern-ment. That view is supported by the fact that most of the personnel, material, and administrative apparatus for dealing with terrorism is in the Departments of State, Defense, Justice, and other executive departments of the government, as we have seen. Nevertheless, the Congress has made efforts from time to time to enact legislation specifically aimed at terrorism. One of the first efforts, the Antihijacking Act of 1974 (PL 93–366), was actually the amendment of the Federal Aviation Act of 1958 to reinterpret the "special aircraft jurisdiction of the U.S." and to redefine the crime of air piracy to meet the criteria of the Hague Convention for the Suppression of the Unlawful Seizure of Aircraft

(1970), which requires contracting states to either extradite apprehended hijackers to their country of origin or to prosecute them under the judicial code of the recipient state. In addition to its criminal provisions, the Act empowers the President to suspend passenger air service to and from any country suspected of supporting terrorist enterprises.

Subsequent legislative initiatives have encountered considerable opposition. Two bills illustrate some of the difficulties generated by passage of antiterrorism laws in Congress.

During the 95th Congress, Senator Abraham Ribicoff (D-CT) introduced an antiterrorism bill designated the "Omnibus Antiterrorism Act of 1977" (S. 2236). At the time, Senator Ribicoff was Chairman of the Committee on Governmental Affairs. His bill was described as an attempt to integrate "diplomatic initiatives with a strong unilateral U.S. policy to combat terrorism" (Fields, 1981, 6). The original provisions of the 1977 bill were (1) reorganization of antiterrorist responsibilities within the executive branch; (2) criteria for reporting terrorist incidents; (3) creating a List of Countries Aiding Terrorist Enterprises (LOCATE), which also included a series of sanctions against such countries; (4) a List of Dangerous Airports; and (5) the institution of legislation from the Montreal Convention.

Following evaluation of the bill by the Governmental Affairs, Foreign Relations, and Select Intelligence Committees of the U.S. Senate, several changes were made. The provisions for reorganization in the executive branch were eliminated; the list of countries aiding international terrorism was modified and the LOCATE acronym was dropped; the series of sanctions applicable to the countries listed was reduced; and the list of dangerous airports was discarded. It seems anticlimactic to report that this emasculated bill was not acted upon before expiration of the 95th Congress.

In 1979, Senator Ribicoff's bill was resurrected and presented to the Congress as the "Omnibus Antiterrorism Act of 1979" (S.333). The revived bill also provided for reorganization of antiterrorism responsibility within the Office of the President. It was suggested in Title I, Section 101 that a new bureaucratic mechanism called the Council to Combat Terrorism would be a suitable alternative to existing arrangements; however, in testimony before Senator Ribicoff and the other Committee members, Ambassador Quainton expressed the dissenting opinion that the newly institutionalized NSC/SCC organizational structure was working as effectively as could be expected and that replacing it with another comparable structure would serve no useful purpose.

With respect to Section 106, which empowers the President to respond to the problem of "patron states" by imposing sanctions, further modifications of the bill were deemed necessary. Quainton objected to the concept of a set of predetermined sanctions that would be automatically imposed against any country that engaged in or supported terrorism. Stressing the need to consider all relevant factors and response options in dealing with terrorist groups, Quainton said, "We feel we can be most effective in combatting terrorism if we are able to make these crucial judgments on a case-by-case basis" (Omnibus Antiterrorism Act of 1979, 5). He made it clear that this stipulation was not intended to belittle the value of sanctions; rather, it was believed that the President should be given maximum flexibility in the selection of appropriate diplomatic measures, including sanctions, for individual countries.

One major provision of the 1979 bill that was well received was modification of the U.S. Code to accommodate the 1971 Montreal Convention on Aircraft Sabotage. Section 306 made additional criminal provisions for the prosecution of individuals charged with air piracy. It was believed that timely integration of this international convention into the U.S. Code would provide a powerful deterrent to persons who threaten the safety of civilian air transportation.

In mid-August 1983, Senator Gordon Humphrey (R-NH), member of the Senate Subcommittee on Security and Terrorism, introduced S.2255, which was enacted as the Antiterrorism and Foreign Mercenary Act. This act makes it a crime for U.S. citizens or corporate entities to provide logistical, mechanical, or technical assistance to other governments for the purpose of supporting terrorist organizations or regimes. According to Senator Jeremiah Denton (R-AL):

> Events in recent years have shown that some renegade former employees of U.S. intelligence agencies and some U.S. companies have undertaken to supply terrorist dictatorships and their agents with training and support to augment their military and intelligence services. The supplies have even extended to supplying the basic ingredients for murder. (American Bar Association, 1983, 6)

Senator Denton also made the point that there is no statutory constraint forbidding American citizens to engage in contracts to participate in missions for terrorist governments such as Libya. During the Libyan invasion of Chad, it was revealed that Libya enlisted American citizens to fly equipment and supplies to the Libyan military forces. This bill had the warm support of the Department of State, Department of Justice, and the Central Intelligence Agency.

The Intelligence Component

It is commonplace to assert that the ability of an open society such as ours to deal with terrorism depends on its intelligence capability (Cooper, 1978; Farrell, 1982, 32–48; Rivers, 1986, 201–223; Wilkinson, 1986, 136–142). Democratic societies, sometimes justified by events, however, often fear that those who have administrative control over intelligence organizations and their activities will overstep their bounds. Crozier has expressed the dilemma in the following terms: "The problem for the open society is how to have, build up and preserve this essential tool of defense—which, in the long run, is indispensable for the protection of ordinary people—and not so outrage the liberal conscience that the legitimate exercise of state power is frustrated" (1974, 154). Crozier believes that the greatest weakness of modern liberal nations in the area of internal defense is their reluctance or inability to see subversion as a problem until it is too late.

Evolution of U.S. Intelligence Capability

In World War II, President Franklin D. Roosevelt established the Office of Strategic Services (OSS) to carry out a variety of tasks involving the gathering of intelligence information and counterintelligence functions. The OSS grew in size and competence; its principal teacher was the British military intelligence service (MI5), the oldest and most effective organization of its kind in the Western world, and it learned from contacts and experience with other American allies, including France, China, and the USSR. But President Truman disbanded the OSS in 1945, and its functions were absorbed by the War and State Departments. In 1946, Truman signed a Presidential Directive that established the Central Intelligence Group (CIG), under the direction of the National Intelligence Authority (NIA). In 1947, Congress passed the National Security Act, which replaced the NIA and CIG and established the Central Intelligence Agency (CIA), the National Security Council (NSC), and other U.S. intelligence agencies.

What is commonly referred to in Washington as the "intelligence community" is composed of a number of organizations and agencies with various missions. We have already identified most of these agencies; the best known is the CIA, whose director is a member of the President's Cabinet. Other organizations include the National Security Agency / Central Security Service; the Defense Intelligence Agency, which is responsible for coordinating military intelligence; the Department of State's Bureau of Intelligence and Research; the Department of Justice's Internal Security Section, Office of Intelligence Policy and Review, and the Federal Bureau of Investigation; and the Department of Energy's Office of Defense Programs, which direct the nation's nuclear weapons research, development, testing, production, and surveillance efforts. In the Executive Office of the President are the National Security Council, the President's Foreign Intelligence Advisory Board, and the President's Intelligence Oversight Board.

The U.S. Constitution, in effect, gives both the President and the Congress certain roles and powers in the conduct of foreign affairs. The President directs foreign policy, and the Congress has the "power of the purse"; this separation of powers is one of the Constitutional checks and balances. Within the separation of powers dimension is the question of whether the Congressional role inhibits the President's ability to conduct foreign policy. In many instances, foreign policy involves the issue of administering intelligence activities, especially those of a covert or clandestine nature.

Intelligence Oversight

The U.S. has never been comfortable with clandestine operations. With the rise of Communism and the ascendancy of the U.S. as a world power, it became increasingly necessary to resort to tactics that most Americans find objectionable. When James Doolittle reviewed covert operations for President Eisenhower in 1954, he might have been speaking for William Casey or for Oliver North: "It is now clear that we are facing an implacable enemy whose avowed objective is world domination. . . . There are no rules in such a game. Hitherto acceptable norms of human conduct do not apply. We must learn to subvert, sabotage and destroy our enemies by more clever and more effective methods than those used against us" (Kramer, 1987, 15).

The success of covert operations depends on two factors: deception and secrecy. Deception is a more polite term than lying, but means much the same thing. The "good" lies told to deceive our enemies, unfortunately, became the "bad" lies used to deceive our own people. By the time the Vietnam war reached its climacteric, there was no longer any question of whether the American government was lying to the American people; the question became whether the government's actions were "plausibly deniable," that is, whether the government's lies were convincing.

As Kramer put it: "Something had to be done, and it was. A set of rules was promulgated, not to *outlaw* covert operations, but to insure that they be conducted legally" (1987, 15). The key piece of legislation for accomplishing this purpose was the Hughes-Ryan Amendment to the Foreign Assistance Act of 1961. The Amendment directed the President to report CIA covert operations to the Congress. The main requirement was that Congress be notified— Congress did not have to assent to the operations, it merely had to be told.

But secrecy, which is the other indispensable ingredient of covert operations, is a rare commodity in talkative democracies. What happened subsequently with "intelligence oversight" illustrates the problems open societies face in attempting to deal with external threats of an unconventional nature; that is, those that require unconventional responses such as the kind covered by the term *covert operations*. The American intelligence community came under continual and intense pressure from a variety of sources: from the executive branch, which tried to establish strict controls over intelligence gathering activities; from Congress, which imposed rules and oversight procedures intended to create broad legislative supervision over the intelligence community; from the American people, who were bombarded with media criticism of intelligence activities. According to Stafford T. Thomas,

> No country had ever subjected its secret organs of government to such open and extensive review. . . . The Congressional Committees conducted their business openly and publicly, adopted an adversarial, accusatory, an investigative approach, and, perhaps, inevitably and irresistibly, dramatized its proceedings. . . . It rarely acknowledged any legitimate reasons for clandestine operations and operated under the assumptions that most clandestine or secret operations were indefensible. (1983, 42)

The result was that the effectiveness of the Central Intelligence Agency (CIA) and other intelligence agencies was reduced to a level from which it has not yet fully recovered. Morale and prestige reached an all-time low and led to the resignations of many able people. In addition, a series of legal and political constraints were put into place, many of which remain today. Sarkesian claims that many intelligence personnel "became more concerned with operating according to a strict interpretation of the law, than with developing innovative and imaginative concepts and procedures" (1986, 214–215). Miller concludes:

> Foreign intelligence agents operate in our midst, and we are faced with a hostile adversary. Defensive measures remain inadequate in the face of criticism by those who view them as endangering civil liberties. Counterintelligence is thus hamstrung, ill-defined and misunderstood, organizationally fragmented and unequal to the task of protecting our institutions. (1983, 45)

At least part of the blame, Sarkesian maintains, can be placed on the intelligence community itself. Intelligence agencies are caught up in bureaucratic "turf" struggles, are reluctant to cooperate and share information, and exhibit an unfortunate tendency to resort to a rigid "need-to-know" policy in dealing with other intelligence agencies.

Wilkinson (1986, 139) believes that democratic societies can maintain a constitutional government and still have effective intelligence agencies. The task is not easy, but it can be done, and there are cases where it has been successful. The Western European countries, through the European Economic Community (EEC), have set up an organization designed for discussion and sharing of intelligence information. TREVI (terrorism, radicalism, and violence international) brings together the police administrators from the EEC countries. The heads of the intelligence services meet regularly in Switzerland. The Republic of Ireland is not represented at these meetings and Israel and Switzerland, non-EEC members, are represented (Dobson & Payne, 1982, 10). The North Atlantic Treaty Organization (NATO) has developed a network for exchanging information on terrorists, their organization techniques, and the weapons at their disposal. This network permits the U.S. and Canada to share information with their European allies.

The Germans have successfully combined intelligence gathering with technology. Under the control of the Federal Criminal Investigation Department, the computer at Wiesbaden plays a key role in Germany's counterterrorism efforts. Every bit of information about terrorists, including information about every object found at the scene of a terrorist attack, no matter how seemingly trivial, is stored in the computer. The computer has proved successful in the capture of several wanted terrorists. The police of the western democracies are linking their information systems with the computer at Wiesbaden, cooperating in the intelligence gathering process.

Developing Policy

Several administrations have subscribed to the rhetoric, if not to the reality, that the U.S. government has had, and continues to maintain, a consistent policy toward terrorism, which declares that no concessions are to be made to terrorist blackmail of any type and that all terrorist acts are to be condemned as criminal. This "no concessions" policy dates back to the Nixon administration and is based on the assumption that once terrorists' demands have been granted, especially in incidents of prolonged duration (such as hijacking and hostage-holding), the U.S. will be perceived as willing to submit to extortion.

Despite the official position of not yielding to terrorist demands, diplomatic channels are held open for initiatives leading to negotiation. In situations where captives are being held, attempts have been made to initiate and maintain a dialogue with the terrorists so as to learn as much as possible about their origins, backgrounds, and objectives in the interests of designing alternate strategies for securing the release of the hostages, while maintaining, at the same time, the position that the U.S. government will not succumb to blackmail.

As noted, Lynch contends that "the United States has neither a comprehensive nor a realistic policy on terrorism" (1987, 2). Our brief examination of executive and legislative initiatives toward terrorism discloses nothing to contradict that bleak observation. It seems almost superfluous to add that, in the absence of a consistent policy on terrorism, no coherent strategy either to retaliate against terrorist attacks or to prevent them has been apparent since terrorism first became an issue for the Nixon administration.

There is a pervasive lack of coordination among the various agencies of the executive branch. Senator Jeremiah Denton, Chairman of the Subcommittee on Security and Terrorism of the Judiciary Committee and Co-Chairman of the Joint Hearings, said in his opening statement,

> There appears to be a great need to coordinate the collection and analysis of the information we get. We have the FBI, Department of State, CIA, the Defense Intelligence Agency, NSA, DEA, and various Armed Forces intelligence groups collecting, analyzing, and disseminating information on terrorism. And although there is some measure of coordination and cooperation, it is not sufficient. We must ensure adequate and appropriate efforts among all our agencies in every step of the intelligence process. (Lynch, 1987, 2)

Any reader who has had to cope with a profusion of three-letter federal agencies can appreciate the cogency of Senator Denton's comments. Although the proliferation of agencies with counterterrorism responsibilities results, in part, from greater awareness of the terrorist threat, there is a danger that bureaucratic complexities will encourage less than complete cooperation among the agencies. Lines of authority are vague, responsibilities are uncertain, and accountability is virtually impossible. There is a pressing need for creation of a mechanism with the capacity to coordinate intelligence data and minimize bureaucratic competition; otherwise, those in a decision-making position will continue to respond to each new terrorism incident on an ad hoc basis, without ever devising effective strategies to deal with terrorism as a recurring problem. A mechanism of this kind would have the additional advantage of bringing to bear all available resources to deal with a particular terrorist event.

An especially disquieting consequence of the Committee hearings was the disclosure of widespread lack of expertise on terrorism among the members of the U.S. Congress. This is all the more disturbing, given the Congressional oversight role, particularly in authorizing and funding agency programs related to terrorism. Under Secretary of Defense Fred C. Ikle said in his opening remarks to the Committee that Congress, since the early 1970s, has chosen to involve itself in foreign policy matters and intelligence operations—actions for which primary responsibility lies with the executive branch of government—to a much greater extent and to play a far more pervasive role than in previous administrations (Lynch, 1987, 3). By doing so, Congress has assumed responsibility for nearly every foreign policy and intelligence operation, not only in terms of the budget and general oversight as envisaged by the Constitution, but in terms of the most detailed tactics and methods. The involvement of Congress in these areas, which accelerated in the wake of the Watergate scandal, is a serious responsibility, but it entails an even more serious accountability to acquire basic knowledge about terrorism if an informed legislative policy is ever to emerge.

It is a sad commentary on the state of U.S. policy toward terrorism, Lynch notes, that not only does no such realistic policy exist, but even before making recommendations, it is necessary to first explain what is meant by "policy." In the context of international terrorism, policy can be defined as a *set of guidelines determining that certain actions will be taken and a predetermination of what those actions will be and under what criteria they will be employed.*

The aspects of current policy revealed at the Joint Hearings do not meet this definition, as the following excerpt from the statement of a Reagan administration witness clearly demonstrates. Ambassador Robert B. Oakley, Director of the Office for Counter-Terrorism and Emergency Planning, submitted a 35-page statement that devoted only two paragraphs to answering the question: What is U.S. policy on terrorism?

> U.S. policy is direct. We will make no concessions to terrorists. We pay no ransoms nor permit releases of prisoners nor agree to other acts which might encourage additional terrorism. We make no changes in U.S. policy because of terrorists' threats or acts. If U.S. personnel are taken hostage or endangered, we are prepared to consider a broad range of actions appropriate to the threat. We encourage other governments to take similar strong stands against terrorism. Finally, we are determined to act in a strong manner without surrendering our basic freedoms or endangering our democratic principles. (Lynch, 1987, 74)

These assertions, as Lynch observes, are integral to the fight against terrorism and should not be altered, but they do not add up to a policy. They are a declaration of intentions. Missing are the guidelines for action. Also missing is any evidence that the U.S. has considered the sorts of questions that must inevitably arise in discussions of the use of force: What level of violence is the U.S. prepared to reach? How many civilian casualties are acceptable? And so on.

This is not to say that spokespersons for the present administration should openly announce exactly what the guidelines are, but there should be some indication that the questions have been asked, even if not yet fully answered. The degree to which loss of life is politically acceptable, what legal measures the U.S. is willing to pursue, when reprisal and retaliation are appropriate, and the risks of war we are willing to assume as the U.S. confronts nations that support terrorism must be worked out at the earliest possible moment.

Policies for dealing with terrorism can be divided into two general categories: *defensive* or passive strategies, designed to make the targets of terrorism more secure and eventually make specific terrorist acts less attractive; and *offensive* strategies, designed to disrupt terrorist operations and make terrorism as a policy less attractive.

The best defensive strategies and cooperative efforts in the world will not end the threat of terrorism. The U.S. must develop offensive strategies, both military and nonmilitary, to make terrorism as a policy—and not just specific terrorist actions—as unattractive as possible, especially to state sponsors.

It is vitally important to build a consensus behind the policy once it is developed. The struggle against terrorism will require the U.S. to commit substantial resources of material, time, effort, and, sometimes, lives. This means that policies to defeat terrorism, once developed, cannot be allowed to be thwarted, threatened, or even interrupted because of partisan squabbles within Congress or changes of administration. Once the elements of policy are in place, the key to their success will be steadfastness of purpose and dependability of resolve. These absolutely require bipartisan support in Congress.

Summary

The seriousness of the terrorism problem led President Nixon to establish a committee, and later a working group, of Cabinet-level officials to develop and implement plans for dealing with terrorism. Under the Carter administration, the antiterrorism program begun by President Nixon was reorganized in three levels: command and policy, coordination, and operations. Another innovation was the lead agency concept, which assigned operational priorities to various federal agencies for coping with terrorist incidents.

Still further reorganizations occurred during the Reagan administration. Thus far, the Bush administration has made no major changes in the existing organizational structure for managing terrorism and antiterrorist initiatives.

Congressional antiterrorism legislative initiatives that took place during this same period did not meet with success, possibly because Congress sees antiterrorism as primarily a responsibility of the executive branch.

There are problems raised by intelligence oversight for U.S. antiterrorist operations, especially those requiring covert or clandestine responses to unconventional conflicts. Not all the problems faced by the intelligence community can be blamed on oversight; some of the difficulties can be attributed to a lack of interagency cooperation.

Key Terms

antiterrorism
Central Intelligence Agency (CIA)
counterterrorism
intelligence community
Interagency Working Group
National Security Council (NSC)
offensive strategies

Cabinet Committee to Combat
 Terrorism (CCCT)
defensive strategies
intelligence oversight
lead agency
Office for Combatting Terrorism

Questions for Discussion and Review

1. What are the two basic components of a national policy on terrorism?
2. What major changes did President Jimmy Carter make in the antiterrorism program initiated by the Nixon administration?
3. Discuss the lead agency concept and indicate how it would operate in a given terrorist incident.
4. How does the Department of Defense distinguish between antiterrorism and counterterrorism?
5. What are the functions of the two units within the FBI that play a significant role in dealing with terrorism?
6. Discuss the issues involved in "intelligence oversight."
7. What needs to be done to provide the U.S. with a comprehensive, rational, and effective national policy toward terrorism?

References

American Bar Association. *Standing Committee on Law and National Security Intelligence Report*, vol. 5, no. 9. September 1983.

Committee on Government Affairs. U.S. Senate. Omnibus Antiterrorism Act of 1979. 96th Congress, 1st Session. Washington, DC: U.S. Government Printing Office, 1979.

Cooper, H.H.A. "Terrorism and the Intelligence Function." In *Contemporary Terrorism: Selected Readings*, edited by J.D. Elliott and L.K. Gibson, pp. 181–190. Gaithersburg, MD: International Association of Chiefs of Police, 1978.

Crozier, B. *A Theory of Conflict*. New York: Scribner's, 1974.

Emerson, S. and Duffy, B. "Probe of Pan Am 103 Runs Into Cover-Up by W. German Police." *The Oregonian* (March 18, 1990): A2–A3.

Farrell, W.R. *The U.S. Government Response to Terrorism: In Search of an Effective Strategy*. Boulder, CO: Westview Press, 1982.

Fields, L.G. Terrorism: Summary of Applicable United States and International Law. Department of State, February 1, 1981.

Giuffrida, L.O. "FEMA's Role in Consequence Management of Terroristic Incidents." *The Police Chief* XLIX (January, 1982): 120–122.

Kramer, M. "Covert Operations: Play by the Rules." *U.S. News & World Report* 103, (July, 20, 1987): 15.

Lynch, E.A. "International Terrorism: The Search for a Policy." *Terrorism: An International Journal* 9 (1987): 1–85.

Miller, N.S. "Counterintelligence at the Crossroads." In *Intelligence Requirements for the 1980's: Elements of Intelligence,* edited by R.C. Godson, pp. 36–48. Washington, DC: National Strategy Information Center, 1983.

Motley, J.B. "U.S. Strategy to Counter Domestic Political Terrorism." *National Security Affairs Monograph Series,* 1983 (Serial No. 83–2).

Public Papers of the Presidents of the United States: Richard M. Nixon, 1972. Washington, DC: U.S. Government Printing Office, 1974.

Rivers, G. *The War Against the Terrorists: How to Win It.* New York: Stein & Day, 1986.

Sarkesian, S.C. "Defensive Responses." In *Hydra of Carnage,* edited by U. Ra'anan, R.L. Pfaltzgraff, Jr., R.H. Schultz, E. Halperin, I. Lukes, pp. 201–220, Lexington, MA: Lexington Books, 1986.

Sterling, C. *The Terror Network: The Secret War of International Terrorism.* New York: Holt, Rinehart, & Winston, 1981.

Thomas, S.T. *The U.S. Intelligence Community.* Lanham, MD: University Press of America, 1983.

Wilkinson, P. *Political Terrorism.* London: Macmillan, 1974.

Wilkinson, P. *Terrorism and the Liberal State.* New York: New York University Press, 1986.

12
Counterterrorism
and the Spectrum of Conflict

As we have seen, terrorism can be viewed as a type of criminal behavior, a form of intense political competition and subversion, a manifestation of the changing nature of warfare, a new form of warfare—indeed, as *all* of these. Obviously, the official view of terrorism does much to determine how the U.S. government proposes to deal with the issue of counterterrorism. As long as agencies of the federal government see terrorism *exclusively* as a form of criminal behavior, counterterrorism will be considered a task for law enforcement. This viewpoint is entirely appropriate for incidents of domestic terrorism, many of which can and should be treated as criminal offenses. Unfortunately, international terrorism has assumed more and more the characteristics of what Sarkesian calls *unconventional conflicts*—a broad range of unorthodox conflicts, the most common and dangerous forms of which are terrorism and revolution (1986, 202). Obviously, dealing with international terrorism, especially the state-sponsored type, calls for radically different responses from those that law enforcement authorities use in handling criminal offenders.

Unconventional conflicts appear to have become a permanent feature of the international landscape, despite some recent developments that have lowered the tension level in a number of the world's chronic troublespots. The dangers that such conflicts pose to open societies may, in the long run, be as serious as those posed by nuclear warfare. Recent history has demonstrated that open societies such as ours are least prepared to respond effectively to terrorism and unconventional conflict.

One of our aims in this chapter is to discuss the issue of terrorism within the context of unconventional conflicts and attempt to identify appropriate defensive measures for dealing effectively with the challenges these conflicts present for an open society. Much of the following discussion is heavily indebted to the significant contributions Sarkesian (1986) and Sloan (1987) make to clarifying the conceptual basis for unconventional conflict and its associated terminology. Their goal was not to design operational directives, but rather to develop concepts and guidelines that may eventually provide a basis for policy and strategy.

In chapter 11, we distinguished between defensive and offensive strategies toward terrorism. The former focuses on what has often been called "target hardening"—operations aimed primarily at creating a protective barrier or security screen around critical targets and significant political personages to raise the stakes and increase the costs for those engaged in terrorism. Most authorities are quick to agree that such passive measures by themselves are not sufficient to succeed against determined adversaries, although defensive measures constitute a basis for developing comprehensive policies and strategies.

Offensive measures may include both nonmilitary and military options. Nonmilitary options may include economic sanctions, airport and travel boycotts, and diplomatic sanctions, such as closing the embassies of sponsoring states and restricting travel of diplomats accredited to the United Nations from those states. Appropriate actions can be taken for failure to sign treaties for the suppression of terrorism, such as the Hague Convention on Hijacking.

James Adams (1986) has published the only serious study of where terrorists get their financial resources and how they spend them. He refers to a report from the Israeli Defense Force, which claimed to have seized an enormous quantity of arms and military equipment from the PLO during *Operation Peace for Galilee*—the Israeli invasion of Lebanon. Itemized were: 4,670 tons of ammunition; more than 1,000 combat vehicles, including 80 tanks; nearly 30,000 small arms; 70 heavy artillery pieces; 158 antitank weapons; and a substantial number of mortars, recoilless rifles, rocket launchers, and field communications equipment. The general assumption, encouraged by Israeli propaganda, was that the arms were supplied by the USSR as a gesture of solidarity with the PLO. "In fact," says Adams, "the PLO has had to pay cash for every bullet, rocket, and tank received from the Soviets since the struggle for Palestine independence began" (1986, 47).

To many Western journalists and government officials, such an assertion must seem farfetched. It seems safe to say that the average American's conception of the PLO, which has been continually reinforced by coverage of the squalid conditions of refugee camps in Lebanon and the Gaza Strip, is that the PLO is largely composed of people living on the precarious edge of starvation. In fact, the PLO is a very affluent organization, with investments in banks, factories, real estate, a securities portfolio, and various other financial instrumentalities. Adams claims that the total worth of PLO assets is approximately $9 billion, which earns an annual return in excess of $1 billion.

The subtitle of the Adams book is: "Behind the PLO, IRA, Red Brigades, and M19 Stand the Paymasters." Each of the four groups listed has its own distinctive fund-raising base. The PLO relies heavily on donations from oil-rich Middle Eastern states. The Irish Republican Army allegedly has a dollar pipeline from an Irish-American group known as Noraid. The Red Brigades depend heavily on kidnap ransoms and robberies, while the M-19 (the Colombian revolutionary group) leans toward cocaine trafficking.

Adams notes that, over the years, there have been about two dozen conferences at which terrorist groups have attempted to map out some sort of information clearinghouse or other cooperative arrangement. These have never produced any lasting results, so the terrorists have never had a chance to teach one another about their specialized fund-raising skills, or consider setting up some sort of central bank to serve the common terrorist interest. Adams maintains that governments that are seriously committed to combatting terrorism must attack these various sources of financial support.

The use of military options against terrorism is a topic fraught with controversy. It is not merely that the U.S., as an open society committed to the rule of law both at home and abroad, faces special problems in employing military force in unconventional conflicts. Military experts themselves are sharply divided on the the nature of the distinction between unconventional and conventional conflicts—and, consequently, on appropriate tactics, strategies, policies, and organizations for dealing with a range of unorthodox conflicts, including revolution and terrorism.

We have approached this concluding chapter with many serious reservations. At a time when these matters are being vigorously debated in the highest national councils, it is easy to appear presumptuous in discussing them in a book whose major purpose is instruction, rather than analysis. Nevertheless, we feel strongly that failure to explore the implications and consequences of a multifaceted approach to counterterrorism would compromise our coverage of this crucial topic.

Unconventional Conflicts

The conflict spectrum shown in Figure 12–1 provides a general classification of conflicts. At one end of the spectrum are conflicts of the type that are least likely to develop into armed conflict, that is, acts of individual terrorists. At the opposite end of the spectrum is major nuclear warfare—the ultimate in conflict. The spectrum also identifies, from the U.S. perspective, two major dimensions of unconventional conflicts: *special operations* (terror and counterterror) and *low-intensity conflicts* (revolution and counterrevolution). Other types of conflicts are grouped into "conventional" and "nuclear." Figure 12–2 provides details of the unconventional conflict categories. We need to examine the distinctions between special operations and low-intensity conflicts to arrive at a clearer understanding of what they mean with respect to defensive measures undertaken by an open society.

Special Operations

Sarkesian identifies three patterns of terrorism: *terror qua terror, revolutionary terror,* and *state-supported terrorism* (1986, 204–205).

Terror qua terror is the term usually applied to incidents perpetrated by groups whose primary goal is the terrorist act itself. Their principal purpose is to conduct terror for the sake of terror. This designation appears to fit the pattern of the Baader-Meinhof Gang and the Japanese Red Army, whose activities we characterized in chapter 1 as nihilistic.

NONCOMBAT	UNCONVENTIONAL	LIMITED	MAJOR
•Shows of force	•Special operations	•Conventional	•Conventional
•Assistance	•Low-intensity conflicts	•Nuclear (?)	•Nuclear

Figure 12-1

The Contemporary Conflict Spectrum

SOURCE: From Sarkesian, S.C. "Defensive responses." Reprinted by permission of the publisher, from *Hydra of Carnage* by Uri Ra'anan, Robert L. Pfaltzgraff, Jr., Richard H. Schultz, Ernst Halperin, Igor Lukes (Lexington, Mass.: Lexington Books, D.C. Heath and Company), Copyright 1986, Uri Ra'anan, Robert L. Pfaltzgraff, Jr., Richard H. Shultz, Ernst Hallperin, and Igor Lukes.

*NON-COMBAT	**SPECIAL OPERATIONS	LOW-INTENSITY CONFLICTS	CON-VENTIONAL	NUCLEAR
		•Revolution / Counterrevolution	• Limited major	• Limited strategic

*** I II III IV

——————— Most likely contingencies ——————————|

*Shows of force; Economic assistance and military advisors
**Hit-run raids, counterterror, rescue, spearhead
***Phase I: Combined economic and other nonmilitary assistance; weapons training teams, military and advisory groups; beyond noncombat assistance
Phase II: Special force teams + Phase I
Phase III: Special forces B, C, and D teams, U.S. ground troop commitment-defensive role + Phases I and II
Phase IV: Vietnam-type involvement

Figure 12-2

Revised Conflict Spectrum

SOURCE: From Sarkesian, S.C. "Defensive responses." Reprinted by permission of the publisher, from *Hydra of Carnage* by Uri Ra'anan, Robert L. Pfaltzgraff, Jr., Richard H. Schultz, Ernst Halperin, Igor Lukes (Lexington, Mass.: Lexington Books, D.C. Heath and Company), Copyright 1986, Uri Ra'anan, Robert L. Pfaltzgraff, Jr., Richard H. Shultz, Ernst Hallperin, and Igor Lukes.

Revolutionary terror is a tactical concept employed by insurgents such as the PLO, the IRA, and the Viet Cong. Groups that perpetrate such incidents are generally under the direction of a revolutionary system whose political purpose and objectives are relatively clear. Within this context, the terrorist act is an extension of the revolution and is carried out to assist the revolutionary struggle.

State-supported terrorism is primarily a means for a state to achieve certain political goals. Thus, a state may support any terrorist group if its objectives or tactics serve the state. If terrorist groups are not readily available, the state may create groups for that specific purpose. Support can range from providing financial assistance, weapons, training, equipment, and transportation to actual operational direction. Objectives of state-supported terrorism vary; they include destabilization of a state or region, intimidation, and coercive diplomacy.

Although specifically designed for counterterrorism operations, special operations evolve primarily from conventional roots employing Ranger- and Commando-type units. (Later we will describe several units of this kind that have been developed by various European countries, Britain, and the U.S.) Special operations missions include hit-and-run raids, rescue of hostages, and spearhead operations such as Grenada. According to Sarkesian, special operations tend to be of a "quick strike and withdrawal" type and are directed against targets that are limited in scope and readily identifiable (1986, 206). Many special operations can be conducted as a joint civilian-military undertaking.

Low-Intensity Conflicts

Low-intensity conflicts include revolutionary and counterrevolutionary situations that are extended in time and differ considerably from conventional conflicts and special operations. Revolutions seek to overthrow the existing system and replace it with revolutionary leadership and ideology. The general revolutionary strategy combines unconventional warfare with political mobilization and psychological warfare. Revolution incorporates its own morality and ethics; that is, success of the revolution is the ultimate morality, and any means used to reach this goal is ipso facto held to be moral and ethical.

Counterrevolution is difficult to conceptualize except as strategy in reponse to revolution:

> Although evolving from the same patterns as revolution, counterrevolution differs in purpose, organization, targets, and political-strategic posture. The most effective counterrevolutionary strategy is effective government and all that this entails with respect to leadership, effectiveness of governing instruments, and responsiveness to popular grievances. (Sarkesian, 1986, 206)

Although it is hard to take exception to Sarkesian's contention that effective government is the best antidote to revolution, Latin America provides a series of dreary examples of the interminable revolutionary/counterrevolutionary cycle that is a likelier alternative than effective government in that part of the world (Andersen, 1988/89).

Nonterritorial Terrorism

Terrorism has become a major instrument in prolonged or extended political warfare within an environment of neither war nor peace. Terrorism on an

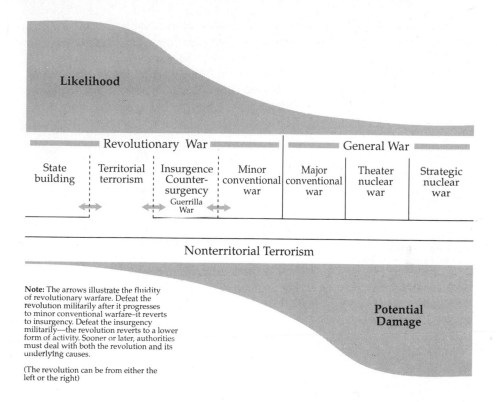

Figure 12-3

Spectrum of Conflict

SOURCE: *Beating International Terrorism: Counterterrorism Operations* is a government publication published by the Air University Press, a directorate within the Center for Aerospace Doctrine Research, and Education at Maxwell AFB, Alabama.

organizational or governmental level—as contrasted to the level of individual motivation—must be viewed within the context of intense political competition. It has been, and will continue to be, used as an instrument of political subversion. Terrorism is therefore one of the tactics and strategies associated with the concept of "indirect aggression," as developed by the Soviet Union and practiced by a number of states. It is the "systematic attempt to undermine a society with the ultimate goal of causing the collapse of law and order and the loss of confidence in the state" (Goren, 1984, 14).

Technological change ushered in a new form of terrorism in the 1950s and 1960s. The introduction of jet aircraft gave terrorists the capacity to strike at global targets of opportunity in a matter of hours. Terrorism was no longer a tactic associated with campaigns of political or armed subversion whose primary goal was the seizure of state power in a territorially based conflict. Thanks to technological enhancement, modern terrorists could now engage in operations thousands of miles from their base of operations or from a disputed strife zone. In effect, the past two decades have been marked by the development of *nonterritorial terrorism,* which has become strategic in nature, as indicated in Figure 12–3. It is a form of terrorism not confined to a specific geographical area. It is essential to differentiate between this form of terrorism and the terrorism associated with tactics of insurgency. Nonterritorial terrorism does not fit neatly within that part of the spectrum of conflict referred to as "low-intensity conflict." Klingaman states,

> Terrorism is an important aspect of low-intensity conflict. A proper definition should specify local internal terrorism to distinguish this form of violence from nonterritorial terrorism, a form that is not necessarily low-intensity in nature. Local internal terrorism is properly described as a tactic employed in the low-intensity phase of guerrilla warfare and insurrection. International terrorism has strategic implications in the field of armed diplomacy. (Sloan, 1987, 5)

Therefore, existing doctrine, strategy, and forces that have been developed to engage in low-intensity conflict may not be appropriate to counter modern nonterritorial terrorism.

In an even broader perspective, the strategic, as contrasted with the tactical, importance of international terrorism is largely the result of technology's having transformed the international system. Both superpowers and smaller states have employed terrorism as a significant weapon in the changing international environment.

At the level of superpower confrontation, the massive destructive power of both nuclear and conventional weapons limits the behavior of the U.S. and the Soviet Union based on their mutual recognition that unless alternatives to direct military confrontation can be found, the ultimate result could be global holocaust—a condition termed the "balance of nuclear terror." The confrontation experience of the Cuban missile crisis may partly explain why the U.S. resorted to only limited action in attempting to free the hostages in Iran. To avoid direct confrontation, the superpowers have sought to limit their use of military force at a lower level. The Soviet Union in particular has supported client states (East Germany, Bulgaria, Cuba) who, in turn, have trained and equipped various groups to use terrorism as a form of "indirect aggression" that can challenge Washington's global strategic position. This is not to suggest that Moscow is behind a unified "terror network" (Sterling, 1981), but it serves to emphasize how the Soviets have used terrorism as a strategic weapon through the use of "active measures [which] constitute a dynamic and integrated array of overt and covert techniques for influencing events and behavior in, and actions of, foreign countries" (Shultz & Godson, 1984, 16).

To the USSR, terrorism is not narrowly defined as simply a form of violence; it is placed within a broad spectrum of political warfare and armed conflict that ranges from overt and covert propaganda to paramilitary operations, composed of a wide variety of Soviet activities in support of terrorist groups and insurgent movements. Terrorism is therefore an offensive weapon in what is ultimately a systematic campaign of intensive political conflict. It is just one element in an approach that integrates the tactics and strategies of political and armed conflict. In combatting terrorism, the U.S. will have to address the issue of whether it can develop its own variant of "active measures," Soviet style, as one means of taking the offensive against terrorist groups and their state sponsors.

If the Soviet Union has employed terrorism as a way of avoiding the technological nightmare of nuclear war, other states have used it to compensate for the preponderance of military power held by Washington and Moscow. The seizure of the hostages in Iran points to another ominous characteristic of modern terrorism: states are not only sponsoring terrorist groups, but are emulating their tactics as an instrument of foreign policy. It is not important in the Iranian case that the seizure of hostages may have been initiated by nongovernmental groups; what is significant is that holding the hostages in Iran became a state-sanctioned and state-sponsored terrorist act employed as a means of pressuring a more powerful state to overreact or acquiesce to a series of demands. In this enterprise, the Iranians were highly successful. The title of ABC's long-running coverage of the incident, "America Held Hostage," effectively conveyed the similarity between an act committed by an international terrorist group and by a government employing the tactics of international terrorism.

The Iranian seizure of the U.S. embassy was not the traditional "state terrorism" or "enforcement terrorism" of the past, aimed at controlling or intimidating the local population. It was directed at a foreign adversary and audience whose official diplomatic representatives were held captive. What we are now witnessing is a variation on the gunboat diplomacy practiced by the imperial powers during the last century. Now smaller states can threaten major powers with relative impunity. When and if these rogue states and the terrorist groups they support achieve nuclear capability, they will be able to engage in a form of intimidation unknown or even imagined in the past.

Counterterrorist Units

Our Western European and British allies, who have had to deal with a substantial amount of terrorism in their countries, have developed and utilized special units trained to engage in counterterrorist actions.

West Germany

Post-war Germany had been organized to prevent the reemergence of Nazi-style military groups. There was a decentralization of government powers into semiautonomous states on a federal principle. Events at the Munich Olympic Games in 1972, when the Black September terrorists killed the Israeli athletes, however, showed Germany that it was unprepared for the organization of modern terrorist groups. The Munich tragedy resulted in the decision that led to formation of Grenzschutzgruppe 9 (GSG9).[1] GSG9 was made part of the Federal Border Guard, a police organization under the control of the central government. According to Ulrich Wegener, GSG9's First Commander, "the tactical concept of the group is based on tight control, flexible leadership, high mobility, surprise, the careful utilization of weapons of all kinds, self-discipline of each member of the unit, and resourcefulness and cunning. The hallmark of Group 9 is the coordination of airborne and motorized forces in accomplishing a joint mission" (Dobson & Payne, 1982, 97). It is a civilian police force that stresses knowledge of the law, especially as it applies to antiterrorist operations. Recruits undergo mental and physical tests in which half are eliminated in the initial two-day selection course. Besides the use of weapons, they are trained in the ideology and tactics of various terrorist groups and continually practice freeing hostages from aircraft and other situations.

The first major test of GSG9 came in 1977, when a Lufthansa plane was hijacked to Mogadishu, Somalia. The German government received permission from the Somalian authorities, and sent GSG9. Using listening devices and special magnesium-based grenades, they attacked and successfully rescued the hostages.

Besides the federal unit, the Germans have also developed other counterterrorist units. The individual states have special groups that combine weapons training with the use of undercover activities. Another unit, formed by the Federal Investigation Department, studies in great detail the life and activities of a particular terrorist. The unit, with the cooperation of foreign governments, tracks down terrorists, arrests them, and returns them to Germany for trial. The unit has had cooperation and success in Bulgaria, France, and other countries.

Great Britain

Great Britain has also had its share of experience with terrorism and how to combat it. Probably the best-known British counterterrorist unit is also the most secretive; known as the Special Air Service (SAS), it gained prominence on May 5, 1980, during "Operation Nimrod" when an SAS team assaulted the Iranian Embassy in London, rescuing nineteen hostages unharmed and killing five terrorists. Unlike GSG9, SAS is a military unit that first came into being in World War II. Selection and training of SAS members is grueling. They are put through strenuous mental and physical tests and are trained in medicine, languages, and close-quarter marksmanship. Technology is also important to the SAS. Their own research developed the "stun-grenade" utilized by GSG9 at Mogadishu, and with their advice, the British government has developed electronic devices that tell, with sight and sound, what is happening in an aircraft or building where hostages are being held.

Because the SAS is a military unit, it is not used without a great deal of thought and preparation. British law clearly points out under what circumstances the military can provide assistance to civil authorities, and military units are used only when it is felt that the police are inadequately equipped to deal with a crisis. This was the case in London when Iranians opposed to the regime of the Ayatollah Khomeini took over the Iranian embassy. The government crisis committee, composed of the Home Secretary, the Secretary of the Cabinet Office, and others representing the Police Force, Ministry of Defense, and the Foreign Office, is empowered to decide whether a situation warrants military intervention. After six days of negotiation, the terrorists killed a hostage and threatened to kill others. The committee decided to use the military, and the official in charge of the police handed over command to the military. At the conclusion of the operation, the SAS returned control to the police and immediately left the scene. Besides participation in the 1980 Iranian Embassy siege, the SAS has operated in Northern Ireland against the Provisional IRA.

The British also use other military units as part of their counterterrorist program. The Royal Marines have a role in protecting the North Sea oil installations, and the Special Boat Squadron (SBS) has counterterrorist duties involving ships and certain shore installations. The SBS also works closely with Scandinavian units that have similar duties in the North Sea.

Britain also has several civilian units that are part of their counterterrorist capabilities. The Royal Ulster Constabulary are continually involved in the struggle against terrorists. They are well trained and equipped, but still require military assistance. The London Metropolitan Police have an Anti-Terrorist squad that has expertise in explosives and in hostage negotiations, where they have had great success. The police also have an equivalent of the SAS they can use before calling on the army; called D11, the unit is trained primarily for containment and as snipers.[2]

United States

The U.S. has developed hostage negotiation techniques, and local police departments have Special Weapons and Tactics units (SWAT) used to handle criminals in siege situations. It was not until 1977, however, that we developed a military force capable of critical operations such as GSG9 performed at Mogadishu. In November 1977, Colonel Charles Beckwith was given command of SFOD-Delta. The project was designed to recruit and train a force capable of operating as a counterterrorist unit on a par with SAS or GSG9. Most of the recruits came from the Special Forces and the Rangers, and training was based on the SAS training course.

The unit was sent on its first mission in April 1980. Colonel Beckwith led ninety of his group in an attempt to rescue the fifty-three American hostages held in the U.S. Embassy in Teheran. The mission failed, but there was no criticism of Delta itself; criticisms had to do with the helicopters, pilots, and excessive secrecy (Dobson & Payne, 1982, 73; Thompson, 1986, 107).

After the failure of the mission, the Joint Chiefs of Staff organized a panel to oversee training and operational plans intended to improve Delta's proficiency (Farrell, 1982, 65). Delta was sent to Cyprus in 1985 when a TWA flight was hijacked, but was not utilized. Its effectiveness is still not known.

If a terrorist attack occurred in the U.S., primary responsibility for action would rest with local police. Delta's responsibility, normally, is to deal only with acts of terrorism outside the U.S. The Posse Comitatus act provides that the military should not be used to execute civil and criminal law except under extreme circumstances. Local police departments' ability to respond to terrorism is uneven. As recently as May 1986, the President of the Police Executive Research Forum expressed concern that medium and small departments were not prepared to respond to terrorism. Large police departments like New York and Los Angeles have a high degree of efficiency, but this is often not the case for the smaller cities.[3] A recent survey revealed that even though police departments were well equipped with hardware such as grenades, night vision devices, and automatic weapons, they lacked sufficient training in hostage negotiation and crisis management, and did not take part often enough in training exercises (Dobson & Payne, 1982, 66). The assault on the Move house by the Philadelphia police department in 1985, where over 10,000 rounds of ammunition were fired and police used military explosives that destroyed 61 houses, clearly shows why local counterterrorist units need better training (Rivers, 1986, 36–57).

The federal law enforcement agencies also have counterterrorist units. The FBI has a hostage response team that has had extensive training and utilizes tactics similar to those of the SAS. Unfortunately, the unit is not a full-time counterterrorist unit, and some authorities are concerned that this may hurt its effectiveness (Thompson, 1986, 110).

The U.S. may have effective counterterrorist units, but they appear to lack the potential for quick activation. Also, there appear to be jurisdictional disputes that need to be worked out, as shown by the squabbling over whether the FBI or the Los Angeles police would handle a terrorist incident at the 1984 Olympic Games (Thompson, 1986, 111).

Counterterrorism: Doctrinal Issues

Organizations such as GSG9, SAS, and Delta are extremely valuable resources when it comes to dealing with ad hoc rescue attempts in response to terrorist incidents. This is the precise mission for which forces of this type are recruited and trained. But as we have observed, terrorism is not a single, simple, unitary phenomenon, but rather a variety of complex, interrelated phenomena. Taken as a working proposition, this observation means that counterterrorism of necessity becomes not one but a number of operations of different kinds with varying goals, methods, and approaches.

A Department of Defense Directive (1982, 1) purports to update "established uniform DOD policies and responsibilities" and provide guidance on dealing with assassinations, bombings, and other terrorist threats. Two types of procedures are specified to deal with the threat:

Antiterrorism. Defensive measures used by the Department of Defense to reduce vulnerability of DOD personnel, their dependents, facilities, and equipment to terrorist acts.

Counterterrorism. Offensive measures taken to respond to terrorist acts, including the gathering of information and threat analysis in support of those measures.

Although the definition of antiterrorism is clear enough, the definition of counterterrorism contains a basic contradiction. The "offensive measures" defined as counterterrorism are taken to "respond to terrorist acts." Sloan is charitable in characterizing this as a "quasi-offensive posture" (1987, 11–12). In our judgment, it establishes a purely reactive policy position; that is, before a terrorist act can be responded to, it must first have been committed. There is nothing in this specification that truly allows for an offensive (preemptive) approach to terrorism. As Sloan points out, current counterterrorism measures are passive ones taken primarily to prevent terrorism: they are neither offensive nor responsive to a particular act.

Terrorism Preemption

It is a truism among critics of the military establishment that military professionals are continually engaged in preparing to wage the last war. There is just enough truth in this jibe to cause military establishments in the U.S. and elsewhere to maintain institutes and agencies whose function is to provide a congenial intellectual environment in which experts of all kinds can congregate and "think the unthinkable." What follows is an agenda of the kind that might be discussed and developed within such an institute or agency.

If the U.S. is to achieve a genuine doctrine and national policy of counterterrorism that goes beyond a merely passive or reactive posture, it may prove necessary to recognize a new category of measures that Sloan places under the heading of *terrorism preemption* (1987, 14). This term is defined as "those offensive military and associated reactions by the services and other appropriate agencies that are initiated against terrorists, their organizations, supporters, and sponsor states to prevent or deter acts or campaigns of terrorism directed against U.S. citizens and interests."

Specific measures that might be employed in missions and campaigns of terrorism preemption are of primary concern to those who are professionally qualified to carry them out. We can assume that the capability of engaging in terrorism preemption is available to the U.S. if and when such professionals are called upon to carry it out. Sloan points out that the answer to the question of whether or not such a call will be made is a matter of national policy, as discussed in chapter 11. Nevertheless, says Sloan, a basic guideline for target and force selection can be stated: *The more ambiguous the terrorist target, the more likely the requirement for a preemptive target of a covert nature* (1987, 26).

If terrorist preemption becomes an officially approved strategy, it will be necessary to identify the selection of targets and forces in specific operations.

Sloan proposes an analytical framework for accomplishing this purpose that includes these factors: (1) the type of target; (2) the type of force; (3) the constraints on the use of force; and (4) the degree of operational disclosure. Although each situation differs, Figure 12–4 shows how various patterns can be used as a means of engaging in proper force selection and application.

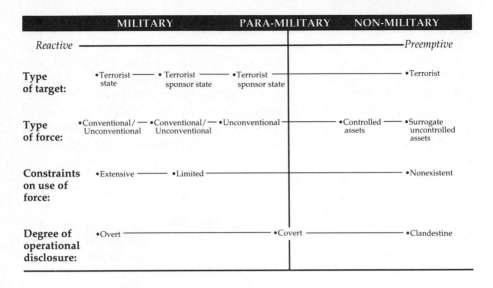

Figure 12-4

Analytical Framework for Counterterrorism Operations

SOURCE: *Beating International Terrorism: Counterterrorism Operations* is a government publication published by the Air University Press, a directorate within the Center for Aerospace Doctrine Research, and Education at Maxwell AFB, Alabama.

Terrorist State

In this scenario, a country is overtly using the tactics of nonterritorial international terrorism against U.S. citizens and interests overseas. Seizure of hostages, an assault on an embassy or other American installation, holding a skyjacked aircraft, and similar incidents would fall under this heading. Although this is not a form of state-sponsored terrorism, it is, in effect, a terrorist state practicing the most violent form of "armed diplomacy." Such an act is close enough to actual warfare to justify the initiation of counterterrorist operations as quickly as possible, because the action probably does not lend itself to extensive negotiation. Although negotiation is not employed to seek the release of hostages, it can be used to buy time to launch operations.

The type of target selected for a retaliatory strike could be a government installation, particularly a military base. Conventional or special forces could be used, either individually or jointly. Extensive constraints would be necessary on the use of force in "surgical strikes" to lessen the possibility of civilian casualties and retaliation against U.S. citizens, since public disclosure would be widespread once the operation was launched. This type of overt action would signal to the American public the government's resolution and capability to respond effectively to an incident. It would also signal to the terrorist state that such actions could not be carried out with impunity. The same selection of forces and targets could be applied preemptively when there is overwhelming evidence that the terrorist state is about to initiate an attack against American citizens or interests.

State-Sponsored Terrorism

In this scenario, it is more difficult to ascertain whether the state is directly involved in preparing for or engaging in an act of terrorism. (It may be doing so while lying about that support to the rest of the world.) The state may actually be supporting nonterritorial international terrorist groups as a form of "indirect aggression" against the target state—for our purposes, the U.S. Nevertheless, if there is a clear indication of the state's culpability, direct action can be taken against the sponsoring state and the terrorist organization, just as in the case against the terrorist state. Since the relationship between the state and the terrorist group is less clear, a requirement for covert operations may have to be considered with the provision to engage in "plausible denial," if necessary.

Both conventional and special operations forces could be employed overtly, so there continues to be a requirement for constraints on the use of force. The choice of targets, however, is no longer limited to regular military forces and installations, but may include specific terrorist groups and their home installations, requiring covert actions.

Terrorist Groups Without State Sponsorship

In this scenario, one moves further into the ambiguous area of neither war nor peace. It is difficult to initiate action against a government that is either unwilling or unable to deal with its own terrorists. Furthermore, the terrorist groups can essentially be viewed as "nonstate actors," and it is therefore difficult to consider the use of regular military forces against them.

Because there may not be a "smoking gun" to prove state culpability or involvement, there are serious questions concerning the use of any military forces in either counterterrorism or terrorism preemption operations. If we recognize, however, that such terrorists are engaging in a form of warfare, we can consider covert military operations, particularly by special forces personnel. *It may prove advisable for the U.S. to develop a new force to fight this kind of war in the shadows.* We might take a page from the Soviet book in this field: active measures—*dezinformatsia*—run the gamut of overt and covert techniques, diplomacy, public information, propaganda, economic and military assistance, and the use of *spetsnaz* (specially trained) units (Adams, 1987).

In operations against groups without state sponsorship, the targets may be irregular forces and terrorist organizations. Because the operations would be covert, there would be fewer constraints on the use of force. The operation would signal to the terrorist groups that they will pay the price for their actions. Inasmuch as the operations would be covert, the signal would not be meant for broad public awareness.

Preemptive measures can be considered before such groups gain the capacity to initiate assaults against U.S. citizens and interests.

Terrorists

This is perhaps the most difficult type of scenario to consider. Whereas the terrorists may consider themselves to be engaging in their own form of nonterritorial, nonstate warfare, they nevertheless are civilians, and it is therefore difficult to justify using military forces against them. Moreover, since the targets are human and small in number, counterterrorism and terrorism preemption missions might best be carried out by the clandestine services of the intelligence community.

Even if the operation is complex, experience shows that once small terrorist cells go tactical, they are difficult to stop, especially when they select softer targets of opportunity. It is therefore vital to consider terrorism preemption before such individuals begin movement toward the potential target. As noted, it may be necessary to develop a new force, perhaps in emulation of the Soviet *spetsnaz* units, to carry out such missions. Terrorism is a form of warfare in a gray area, and a preemption force would have to have the ability to engage in black operations. Given the highly clandestine nature of such missions, constraints on the use of force would be virtually nonexistent, since no operational disclosure would be anticipated. It may be difficult in such operations not only to target the organizational structure of large terrorist groups, but even more challenging to target the individual cells of small, free-floating terrorist groups.

Finally, the use of surrogates for counterterrorism and terrorism preemption missions must be considered, keeping in mind that, while such operations might enhance plausible denial, once surrogates are employed it becomes increasingly difficult to exercise effective command and control over them. A good case in point is the alleged CIA involvement in training a counterterrorist unit implicated in a car bombing in Lebanon that killed more than 80 people and injured 200.

Conclusions

The operations we have outlined are only a few of the alternatives that must be considered in moving across the conflict spectrum from a reactive, overt posture to a preemptive, clandestine posture against terrorist warfare. Livingstone (1986) adds reprisals and retribution to the list of available proactive responses to terrorism that can be regarded as coercive measures short of actual war. All three of these measures are legally justified under Article 51 of the United Nations Charter, which reserves to nations the inherent right of self-defense.

Resistance to the proposal of an aggressive counterterrorist strategy, Tovar claims, will come from familiar quarters and will draw upon familiar arguments (1987, 235). Intervention in the internal affairs of sovereign states is naturally denounced, even by those who practice it most vigorously. Indeed, all states intervene to one degree or another when and if they can.

There is, of course, an alternative: continue to do nothing and wait for events to show that the experts erred. This seems to be the preferred stance of those who believe that we will become like the terrorists if we adopt realistic policies in our own defense. As Livingstone says, "The United States may yet perish as a nation of the delusion that it is necessary to be more moral than anyone else" (1986, 128). One is reminded of the poet William Blake whose friend, he said, "has observed the Golden Rule till he's become the Golden Fool." To the world inhabited by terrorists, this is an unflattering but remarkably accurate portrait of the United States of America.

Summary

International terrorism has become part of the conflict spectrum designated as unconventional conflicts. The danger to the U.S. and other democracies may equal or exceed the threat of conventional or even nuclear warfare. We can no longer afford to trivialize international terrorism by treating it as a problem for law enforcement and the criminal courts. Developing an effective defense begins with recognizing that terrorism is a novel kind of warfare.

Nonterritorial terrorism has been suggested as a more accurate description for international terrorism. This form of terrorism has strategic implications in the field of armed diplomacy. It provides rogue states, such as Iran and Libya, with the capacity to threaten major powers, including the U.S. and the Soviet Union, with relative impunity.

West German and British experience with terrorism has led to the formation, training, and deployment of specialized units to deal with terrorist incidents. The U.S. has followed their example with the creation of the Delta Force. The only instance in which Delta Force was used in an actual counterterrorism operation did not provide an adequate test of its capability. Units of this kind, however, must be regarded as ad hoc rescuers; their utilization is part of a reactive (i.e., passive) defense. If the U.S. is to move beyond a reactive posture and develop a preemptive (i.e., active) defense, it is necessary to formulate doctrines that provide for covert and clandestine operations. The Soviet Union has already developed both the doctrines and organizational structures to carry out "active measures" in its national interests. Failure to profit from that example leaves the open societies of the world in a position of growing risk.

Key Terms

"active measures"   antiterrorism
Colonel Charles Beckwith   conflict spectrum
counterrevolution   counterterrorism
Delta   *dezinformatsia*
GSG9   local internal terrorism
low-intensity conflicts   nonterritorial terrorism
revolutionary terror   Special Air Service (SAS)
special operations   *spetsnaz*
"target hardening"   terror qua terror
terrorism preemption   unconventional conflicts

Questions for Discussion and Review

1. What are some of the nonmilitary offensive options available to the U.S. in combatting terrorism?
2. Describe the conflict spectrum and identify its major points.
3. Distinguish among the three major patterns of terrorism Sarkesian defines and describes.
4. Discuss nonterritorial terrorism and its relationship to low-intensity conflicts.
5. What kinds of missions are assigned to counterterrorism units such as GSG9, SAS, and Delta? How are these units trained and equipped to accomplish their missions?
6. Does the Department of Defense make a clear distinction between antiterrorism and counterterrorism?
7. Discuss the underlying rationale for U.S. development of a terrorism preemption capability. What are the advantages and the risks involved in this kind of development?

Notes

1. M. Schreiber, Personal communication, February, 1984.
2. For a more detailed presentation of the GSG9 and the SAS, see Geraghty, 1983; Thompson, 1986; Tophoven, 1984; Warner, 1972.
3. Behan, C.J., *Testimony on Terrorism from the Local Police Perspective Before House Subcommittee on Civil and Constitutional Rights*, May 15, 1986.

References

Adams, J. *The Financing of Terror: Behind the PLO, IRA, Red Brigades and M19 Stand the Paymasters*. New York: Simon and Schuster, 1986.

Adams, J. *Secret Armies: The Full Story of S.A.S., Delta Force, and Spetsnaz*. New York: Atlantic Monthly Press, 1987.

Andersen, M.E. "The Military Obstacle to Latin Democracy." *Foreign Policy 73* (1988/89): 94–113.

Best, G. "Restraints on War by Land before 1945." In M. Howard, *Restraints on War*, pp. 17–37. Oxford: Oxford University Press, 1979.

Clausewitz, C.V. *On War*. Princeton, NJ: Princeton University Press, 1984.

Cooper, H.H.A. "Terrorism and the Intelligence Function." In *Contemporary Terrorism: Selected Readings*, edited by J.D. Elliott and L.K. Gibson, pp. 181–190. Gaithersburg, MD: International Association of Chiefs of Police, 1978.

Crozier, B. *A Theory of Conflict*. New York: Scribner's, 1974.

Department of Defense Directive 2000.12. *Protection of Department of Defense Personnel and Resources Against Terrorist Acts* (February 12, 1982).

Dobson, C. and Payne, R. *Counterattack: The West's Battle Against the Terrorists*. New York: Facts on File, 1982.

Farrell, W.R. *The U.S. Government Response to Terrorism: In Search of an Effective Strategy*. Boulder, CO: Westview Press, 1982.

Geraghty, T. *Who Dares Wins*. London: Arms and Armour Press, 1983.

Goren, R.D. *The Soviet Union and Terrorism*. London: George Allen and Unwin, 1984.

Horchem, H.J. "Political Terrorism—The German Perspective." In *On Terrorism and Combatting Terrorism*, edited by A. Merari, pp. 63–68. Frederick, MD: University Publications of America, 1985.

Karsten, P. *Law, Soldiers, and Combat*. Westport, CT: Greenwood Press, 1978.

Khadduri, M. *War and Peace in the Law of Islam*. Baltimore, MD: Johns Hopkins Press, 1955.

Livingstone, N.C. "Proactive Responses to Terrorism." In *Fighting Back: Winning the War Against Terrorism*, edited by N.C. Livingstone and T.E. Arnold, pp. 109–131. Lexington, MA: Lexington Books, 1986.

Perlstein, G.R. "The Changing Face of Terrorism: From Regicide to Homicide." *International Journal of Offender Therapy and Comparative Criminology* 30(3) (1986): 187–193.

Rivers, G. *The War Against the Terrorists: How to Win It*. New York: Stein & Day, 1986.

Sarkesian, S.C. "Defensive Responses." In *Hydra of Change*, edited by U. Ra'anan, R.L. Pfaltzgraff, Jr., R.H. Schultz, E. Halperin, I. Lukes, pp. 201–220. Lexington, MA: Lexington Books, 1986.

Shultz, R.H., and Godson, R. DEZINFORMATSIA: *Active Measures in Soviet Strategy*. Washington, DC: Pergamon-Brassey's, 1984.

Sloan, S. *Beating International Terrorism: An Action Strategy for Preemption and Punishment*. Maxwell Air Force Base, AL: Air University Press, 1987.

Sterling, C. *The Terror Network: The Secret War of International Terrorism*. New York: Holt, Rinehart, & Winston, 1981.

Thompson, L. *The Rescuers: The World's Top Anti-Terrorist Units*. Boulder, CO: Paladin Press, 1986.

Tophoven, R. *German Response to Terrorism*. Koblenz: Bernard and Graefe Verlag, 1984.

Tovar, B.H. "Active Responses." In *Hydra of Carnage*, edited by U. Ra'anan, R.L. Pfaltzgraff, Jr., R.H. Schultz, E. Halperin, and I. Lukes, pp. 231–249. Boston: Lexington Books, 1986.

Warner, P. *The Special Air Service*. London: William Kimber, 1972.

Wilkinson, P. *Political Terrorism*. London: Macmillan, 1974.

Wilkinson, P. *Terrorism and the Liberal State*. New York: New York University Press, 1986.

Glossary

Achille Lauro incident
In October 1985, the *Achille Lauro* cruise liner was hijacked by four members of the Palestine Liberation Front; an elderly American passenger, Leon Klinghoffer, was murdered. The hijackers surrendered to Egyptian authorities who were flying them to Tunisia when American planes forced them to land in Sicily.

active measures
A dynamic and integrated array of overt and covert techniques for influencing events and behavior in, and actions of, foreign countries.

advocacy v. portrayal
The controversy over whether media representatives can confine coverage of terrorist incidents to straightforward reporting without running the risk of legitimizing the terrorists and their views.

anarchists
Individuals who follow the political doctrine (anarchy) that all government authority is undesirable. Anarchists favor abolition of governments by any possible means, including violence.

Animal Liberation Front
A group of animal rights activists who have perpetrated bombings in the U.S. and Great Britain. In several European countries, they have also committed acts of product contamination.

antiterrorism
Preventive measures accomplished through diplomatic and strategic policy planning.

Armenian Nationalists
Members of groups such as the Justice Commandos of Armenian Genocide who have assassinated Turkish diplomats worldwide, including in the U.S. Their terrorist actions have been repudiated in Armenian communities.

Aryan Nations
The Church of Jesus Christ Christian was founded in Idaho in the 1970s as a religious organization. It preaches a type of fundamentalism that holds that

white Americans are the true descendants of the Lost Tribes of Israel, and that blacks and Jews are the subhuman offspring of Satan.

Assassins
Led by the "Old Man of the Mountains," this group gained notoriety for the murders of religious and political leaders in the Middle East during the eleventh century.

aut dedire aut punire
Latin for "Either extradite or punish." By international law, countries are obligated either to extradite individuals accused of certain terrorist acts to the nation in which they were committed or to punish the offenders themselves.

Balfour Declaration
A controversial policy enunciated in a letter by the British Foreign Secretary, Arthur Balfour, and approved by Lloyd George's cabinet in 1917, advocating establishment of a national home for the Jewish people.

Bernadine Dohrn
A member of the Weather Underground who was considered one of America's most sought-after terrorist.

binary explosive device
A bomb that includes two ingredients that are relatively harmless when separate but become lethal when combined.

Black Panthers
Founded in Oakland, California, in 1966, the Black Panther party advocated armed self-defense and revolutionary change. Black Panthers were involved in several shoot-outs and confrontations with police.

blistering agents
General tissue irritants with an additional systemic action; for example, mustard gas, which was employed on a massive scale during World War I.

blood agents
A designation denoting lethal chemical warfare agents that interfere with cell respiration. Hydrogen cyanide and cyanogen chloride are members of this class.

Cabinet Committee to Combat Terrorism
President Nixon established this Committee in 1972.

censorship
Official controls on media coverage of terrorist events.

Central Intelligence Agency (CIA)
The principal foreign intelligence-gathering organization of the U.S., formed under the National Security Act of 1947.

choking agents
A category of chemical weapon employed in gaseous form that cause victims to drown in their own body fluids.

common crimes
Activities that most nations agree are punishable crimes.

conflict spectrum
A general classification of conflicts with, at one end, conflicts that are least likely to develop into armed conflict, and, at the opposite end, major nuclear warfare.

counterrevolution
A strategy in response to revolution, the most effective of which is likely to be equitable and competent government.

counterterrorism
Measures emphasizing the tactical force option, for prevention, preemption, or retaliation against terrorist acts.

crazies
Part of Frederick Hacker's typology, *crazies* refers to individuals who are mentally and emotionally disturbed. The target of this type of terrorist usually has some relationship to the disturbed individual's psychopathology.

criminals
A component of Hacker's terrorist typology, of which bank robbers who take hostages to secure their getaway are an example.

Croatian Nationalists
Members of groups such as the Croatian Revolutionary Brotherhood and HRB (Hrvatsko Revolucionarno Bratstvo) who demand Croatia's independence from Yugoslavia. The arrest of Croatian skyjackers in 1976 appears to have ended their activities in the U.S.

crusaders
Part of Hacker's terrorist typology, crusaders are individuals who seek prestige and power in the service of a higher cause and who act to attain a collective goal.

death imagery
A phenomenon found in some survivors of life-threatening experiences in which, long after the incident, people have the feeling they are going to die.

defensive strategies
Designed to make targets of terrorism more secure and eventually make specific terrorist acts less attractive.

death penalty
A criminal sanction that, because of its controversial nature, will probably not be used for individuals convicted of terrorism.

Delta
First Special Forces Operational Detachment-Delta (SFOD-D), the antiterrorist unit of the U.S. Army. Activated in 1981, Delta is closely modelled on the British Special Air Service (SAS).

deterrence
Preventing either the first occurrence of a crime or further repetition of criminal acts by an offender.

dezinformatsia
A political strategy of Soviet origin wherein communications contain intentionally false and misleading material, often combined selectively with true information. The objective of the strategy is to induce the adversary to believe the truth of the material presented and to consequently act in the interests of the nation conducting the strategy.

Dozier kidnapping
In December 1981, U.S. Army Brigadier General James Dozier, an officer serving with NATO in Italy, was kidnapped by the Red Brigades. Italian police were able to rescue Dozier, and the information they gathered is said to have helped eliminate the Red Brigades as a fighting force.

Drug Enforcement Administration (DEA)
The federal agency that replaced the Bureau of Narcotics and Dangerous Drugs as the agency responsible for enforcing federal drug laws.

Easter Rising
In 1916, a small group of Irish nationalists seized control of several buildings, including the Dublin General Post Office, and proclaimed establishment of the Irish Republic. They were defeated, but the British execution of the leaders for treason created support among the Irish people for war against Britain.

El Rukns
A black street gang in Chicago, involved in drug trafficking, that has reportedly met with agents of the Libyan government in an effort to secure a contract with them to commit a terrorist act.

ERP (Ejercito Revolucionario Del Pueblo)
Established in 1970, the ERP was Argentina's most active left-wing terrorist group; it carried out assassinations and kidnappings until suppressed by the military regime that came to power in 1976.

FARC (Revolutionary Armed Forces of Colombia)
The largest insurgent group in Colombia. Once heavily into kidnapping to obtain funds, the FARC is now involved in the drug trade.

field training exercises (FTXS)
A technique for improving coping skills and evaluating individual vulnerabilities through simulations.

"flexible response" policy
A position that questions the practicality and wisdom of adhering to a single, standard policy of "no ransom."

FLN (National Liberation Front)
Algerian revolutionary group that fought French colonial rule from 1954 to 1962. After independence, the members became the dominant political party in Algeria until the overthrow of Ahmed Ben Bella.

Fran Stephanie Trutt
An animal rights activist arrested in 1988 while attempting to place a bomb, focusing national attention on the animal rights movement.

FUQRA
A black Islamic sect implicated in attacks on rival religious sects.

Furman v. Georgia
A 1972 Supreme Court decision that ruled capital punishment as then applied constituted cruel and unusual punishment and overturned existing death penalty statutes.

Geneva Convention
A conference held in Geneva between 1974 and 1977 under sponsorship of the International Red Cross whose purpose was to improve the laws of war contained in the 1949 Geneva Convention on the treatment of prisoners of war.

Geneva Protocol
Twenty-eight countries, including the USSR, agreed not to use poison gas in war.

George Jackson
"Black power" advocate who became famous for his book *Soledad Brothers*; killed in 1971 during a gun battle at San Quentin prison.

"Golden Triangle"
An area in Southeast Asia known as the principal source of opium growing and export.

GSG9 (Grenzchutzgruppe 9)
Established by the West German government as a counterterrorist unit after the death of eleven Israeli athletes in Munich. Part of the Federal Border Police, they received international acclaim for their rescue in 1977 of hostages in Mogadishu, Somalia.

Hague Convention
A meeting held under the auspices of the International Civil Aviation Organization that issued a policy statement against acts of air piracy.

Hanafi Muslim siege
On March 9, 1977, members of the Hanafi sect, under the leadership of Hamaas Abdul Khaalis, seized three buildings in Washington, DC, and held 134 people hostage for 39 hours.

"hard cop/soft cop" routine
A law enforcement interrogation technique in which the suspect is put off balance by officers playing the roles of the hard cop, who threatens to throw the book at him, versus the soft cop, who is sympathetic and wants to make things easier for him.

hijacking
The taking over of public-service vehicles usually, but not always, for political reasons. Some hijackings are calculated to draw world attention to a political cause, others to hold passengers hostage in exchange for achieving a political objective. Hijacking of aircraft reached a peak in the late 1960s and early 1970s.

hostage-taker typologies
Attempts to classify hostage-takers so as to prepare and formulate possible negotiating responses.

ideologues
Individuals belonging to groups whose purpose is to bring about change in the social, economic, or political status quo.

ideology continuum
A classification that "rates" assumptions about the way things are supposed to be, particularly with regard to the moral order and political arrangements.

illegitimate violence
Government violence for the purpose of denying rights to an "enemy of the people."

incapacitation
Punishment that involves imprisonment is justified on the grounds that as long as an offender is being held in confinement, he or she is not free to commit more crimes.

intelligence oversight
Rules established by Congress to create broad legislative supervision over the federal agencies involved in intelligence activities.

interagency working group
Part of the reorganization of the antiterrorism response program under President Carter. In 1978, it was decided that the working group was too cumbersome, and its responsibilities were delegated to committees.

Irish Republican Army (IRA)
The IRA was named by James Connolly during the Easter Rising in 1916. It fought against the British until the independence of Ireland. In the 1930s, the army resumed the fight to drive the British out of Northern Ireland, which continues into modern times. In the 1970s, they fragmented into the Marxist-oriented "Official" IRA and the traditionalist "Provisional" IRA.

Jewish Defense League (JDL)
U.S. militant Jewish group formed by Rabbi Meir Kehane in 1968 whose members have committed terrorist attacks against perceived enemies of Jews.

Jihad (Holy War)
A religious duty imposed on Muslims to spread Islam by war.

KINTEX
Bulgarian official import/export agency. There is evidence that, through KINTEX, guns have been sold to the Middle East in return for heroin, which is then imported into Europe and the U.S.

Ku Klux Klan
An organization begun in the defeated Confederacy during the late 1860s that conducted campaigns of violence and intimidation against freed slaves and their white supporters. Klan violence persists today.

lead agency
The concept of assigning authority and responsibility for dealing with terrorism to the federal agency with the most direct operational role in dealing with a given incident.

"left wing" and "right wing"
Distinctions referring to the extremities of the ideological continuum; "left wing" refers to individuals or groups opposed to the government and seeking change, and "right wing" refers to those who want to maintain the status quo.

legitimate violence
The government's legally permissible use of coercion or violence to maintain order.

Leila Khaled
A leader in the Popular Front for the Liberation of Palestine (PFLP) who helped arrange the initial training of the Japanese Red Army and West Germans in Lebanon and who also took part in several aircraft hijackings.

Lindbergh Law
The law, passed in 1933, that made kidnapping a federal offense; named after the kidnapping and murder of Colonel Charles Lindbergh's child in 1932.

local internal terrorism
A tactic employed in the low-intensity phase of guerrilla warfare and insurrection.

low-intensity conflicts
Limited political-military struggles to achieve political, social, economic, or psychological objectives. They are generally confined to a particular geographic area and are often characterized by constraints on weaponry, tactics, and level of violence.

M-19 Group (April 19 Movement)
A Colombian insurgent group that has engaged in several dramatic and spectacular incidents such as the 1980 seizure of the Dominican Embassy in Bogota and the 1985 taking of the Palace of Justice. Today, the group is involved in the drug trade to raise money.

"Mad Bomber"
A psychotic named George Metesky, an example of the crazy type of terrorist who, over a period of 17 years, placed more than 30 bombs in public places in New York City.

Margherita Cagol
Occupied a major position in the Italian Red Brigades (Brigatte Rossi) and may have led the commando raid that freed her husband from jail in 1975.

"masked crime"
Otto Pollak believed that the criminal behavior of women is easily hidden or "masked" by the traditional roles assigned to them.

Matt Liebowitz
A member of the Jewish Defense League who served more than two years in an Israeli prison for participation in the machine-gunning of a busload of Arab civilians.

Medellin Cartel
A group of wealthy drug dealers in Colombia who have assassinated government officials and police officers.

media access
The controversy over the media's right to seek information for the news versus the imposition of restrictions on news gathering for reasons of safety and security.

media-induced contagion
It is claimed that a media presentation of aggressive or violent behavior may produce similar behavior in others by action of emotional contagion.

Michael Bakunin
An anarchist who believed that the state will always be an instrument of the capitalist ruling class; advocated a revolution of both urban industrial workers and rural peasants.

Montoneros
Argentinian terrorist organization drawn mainly from the left wing of the Peronist movement. Its campaign of bombing, kidnapping, and extortion did much to provoke the military coup of 1976 and the "dirty war" of terrorist suppression that followed.

Mujaheddin (The Soldiers of God)
Orthodox Islamic guerrillas of Afghanistan who fought the Soviet Army until its withdrawal in 1989 and are still fighting to oust the USSR-supported Najib government in Kabul.

mustard gas
A blistering agent used during WWI that was the most extensively stockpiled chemical agent of WWII.

National Security Council (NSC)
The purpose of the NSC is to aid the President in analyzing, integrating, and facilitating foreign defense and intelligence decisions.

nerve agents
A designation of compounds that cause disruption of nerve impulse transmission. Of the several kinds that can be used for military operations, Sarin appears to be the most important.

new vulnerabilities
Basic features of modern industrialized society that are open to exploitation by terrorists or criminals, including water supply systems, transportation systems, energy systems, communication systems, computerized management and information systems, and certain critical industries.

"no ransom" policy dilemma
Although in the long run, "no ransom" is likely to be an effective policy against hostage seizures, in the short run, implementing the policy and establishing its credibility may be extremely costly.

nonterritorial terrorism
A form of terrorism not confined to a specific geographical area.

novel agents
Things that are unable to reproduce themselves in nature but can be reproduced in the laboratory.

Nuclear Risk Reduction Center
U.S. Senators Sam Nunn and John Warner suggested in 1985 establishing Nuclear Risk Reduction Centers. In 1986, American and Soviet representatives agreed to study the creation of centers to reduce nuclear risk. Its primary purpose would be identifying and monitoring critical situations that could lead to nuclear war.

NWLF (New World Liberation Front)
A leftist group, active in the 1970s, that published Marighella's *Minimanual of the Urban Guerrilla* and was responsible for many bombings in the San Francisco area; considered an umbrella for other terrorist groups in California.

oderint dum metuant
"Let them hate us as long as they fear us"—a military strategy in which the invading army inflicts atrocities upon captive civilian populations to maintain military control.

offensive strategies
Designed to disrupt terrorist operations and make terrorism less attractive.

Office for Combatting Terrorism
Special unit of the U.S. State Department set up in 1972 to coordinate the government's work against internal and external terrorism.

Operation Nimrod
The most famous operational deployment of the British SAS. In April 1980, Iranians opposed to the Ayatollah Khomeini took over the Iranian embassy in London and held twenty-six hostages. On the 5th of May, the terrorists killed a hostage, and the SAS assaulted the embassy. One hostage and five of the six terrorists were killed, and the other hostages were rescued. The operation lasted eleven minutes.

Order, The
A clandestine offshoot of the Aryan Nations that engages in violent acts such as murder, assault, and armed robbery. Members were accused of the murder of disk jockey Alan Berg, but were acquitted for lack of evidence.

Paris Conference
A 1989 meeting of 149 countries who called for the countries of the world to rededicate themselves to the principles of the Geneva Protocol.

Patty Hearst
The daughter of Randolph Hearst, Jr., was kidnapped by the Symbionese Liberation Army in 1974. She participated in at least one bank robbery and was arrested in 1975.

Peter Kropotkin
A nineteenth-century anarchist who believed that terrorist violence called attention to a problem more effectively than did distributing pamphlets or handbills.

political offense exception
Refusal of extradition requests because the offenses are characterized as "political conduct."

primary prevention
Withdrawing the rewards of terrorism and promptly punishing the perpetrators.

principled deviance
Engaging in acts of civil disobedience to underscore the alleged immorality of the law that is being violated.

Puerto Rican nationalists
Members of such groups as the FALN (Fuerzas Armada de Liberacion Nacional) who are seeking independence for Puerto Rico. They have been responsible for over one-hundred terrorist attacks in the U.S.

Samira (Fusako Shigenobu)
Leader of the Japanese Red Army (JRA), she helped plan the massacre at the Lod Airport in Israel.

secondary prevention
Efforts to reduce the harm a terrorist incident has caused, including resolving the situation and assisting the victims.

Sendero Luminoso ("Shining Path")
Peruvian terrorist organization that is a Maoist split from the Peruvian Communist Party. Members also think of themselves as heirs to the pre-Colombian Inca empire. A hallmark of the organization is assassinations in which the victim is ritually mutilated.

Shan United Army (SUA)
In the 1960s and 1970s, the SUA was an insurgent group in Burma; it used profits from the heroin trade to finance its insurgency. Now it is primarily engaged in the drug trade for profit.

Sicarii
A Jewish sect active in the Zealot struggle against Rome that used terrorist tactics against the Romans and Jewish moderates.

siege
A specific type of hostage-taking scenario in which hostages are held in a barricade situation, usually played out under media coverage.

skyjacking
A specific type of hijacking in which an airplane is commandeered.

"snatch racket"
A media term referring to the kidnapping epidemic of the 1930s.

special operations
Military operations conducted by specially trained, equipped, and organized forces against strategic or tactical targets in pursuit of national military, political, economic, or psychological objectives.

Special Air Service (SAS)
A unit of the British Army, formed in 1950, that is the modern equivalent of the various deep-penetration units organized during World War II. Today SAS is best known for its counterinsurgency role in Northern Ireland and rescue of the hostages in the Iranian Embassy in London.

spetsnaz
The special operations troops of the Soviet Army whose mission is to conduct "special reconnaissance," defined as operations carried out to subvert the political, economic, and military potential and morale of a potential or actual enemy.

state-sponsored terrorism
A cost-effective method of carrying on a kind of low-intensity warfare by supporting independent terrorist groups against a nation that cannot be defeated by conventional methods.

Stockholm Syndrome
In a prolonged siege, hijack victims or hostages may identify with and even support their captors. This phenomenon is named after a hostage-taking incident at the Stockholm Kreditbank in 1973.

Students for a Democratic Society (SDS)
Founded in 1959 to form an alliance of students, blacks, and peace groups that could influence the policies of the Democratic Party.

Sykes-Picot agreement
A secret agreement between the British and French governments in 1916 that awarded the French—without the knowledge or consent of the Arabs—a "sphere of influence" in much of the Arab-inhabited area in which Britain had promised to support an independent Arab state.

Symbionese Liberation Army (SLA)
A group composed of white radicals and black ex-convicts that, in 1973, murdered Marcus Foster, the Oakland Superintendent of Schools, and, in 1974, kidnapped Patty Hearst.

target hardening
Operations aimed primarily at creating a protective barrier around critical targets and significant political personages.

Tatiana Leontiev
Early Russian terrorist arrested for attempting to kill the Czar who later killed an innocent man in the mistaken belief that he was the Russian Minister of the Interior.

terror qua terror
A term applied to incidents perpetrated by groups whose primary goal is the terrorist act itself—the conduct of terror for the sake of terror.

terrorism from above
Acts of terror perpetrated by governments using their own military or police forces upon their citizens.

terrorism from below
Acts of terror perpetrated by individuals or groups seeking to usurp and replace the authority of the government.

terrorism preemption
Military offensive and associated reactions by the armed forces and other appropriate agencies undertaken against terrorists, their organizations, supporters, and sponsor states to prevent or deter acts or campaigns of terrorism directed against U.S. citizens and interests.

tertiary prevention
Efforts to help victims deal with the late effects and residual disability of a terrorist incident.

Theodore Herzl
A Jewish correspondent for a Vienna newspaper, Herzl was in the crowd that witnessed the public degradation of Captain Alfred Dreyfus, a French officer of Jewish extraction who was wrongfully accused of being a German spy. Concluding that the Jews must concentrate on seeking a state of their own, Herzl became the leader of the Zionist movement.

thiodiglycol (TDG)
A chemical used in textile printing, photo developing, and ballpoint pen ink that is only a step away from mustard gas.

Thugs
A Hindu sect in India that committed ritual murder by strangling and buried its victims in graves dug in advance.

toxins
Poisonous by-products of the metabolic processes of a living organism.

traumatic stress
Extreme stress caused by crisis conditions, such as being held hostage, that produces both immediate and long-range adverse reactions, including sleeplessness, anxiety, nightmares, flashbacks, depression, and feelings of insecurity.

triad
A secret society in China. One of the triads, the Boxers, contributed to the nationalist movement headed by Sun Yat-Sen.

TWA flight 847
This TWA flight from Cairo to Rome was skyjacked by the Islamic Jihad in 1985. The passengers and crew were released after seventeen days of negotiations, but an American Navy diver was murdered. The international media were severely criticized for their coverage of the incident.

typologies of terrorism
Classification of terrorists according to organizational structure, aims, motives, or ideologies in an attempt to understand the dynamics and consequences of terrorist acts.

Ulrike Meinhof
Female West German terrorist leader who was a journalist. She was involved in several bomb attacks on U.S. Army installations in West Germany. Her most spectacular raid occurred in 1970, when she freed fellow terrorist Andreas Baader. Her group became known in the media as the Baader-Meinhof Gang, but she called it The Red Army Faction. She committed suicide in her jail cell in 1976.

unconventional conflicts
A broad spectrum of military and paramilitary activities conducted in enemy or politically sensitive territory. It usually includes guerrilla warfare, subversion, sabotage, and other operations of low visibility or a clandestine nature.

unitary explosive device
The lethal agent contained in bombs that is released as an aerosol or in tiny droplets.

vigilantism
A distinctively American tradition of violence and intimidation designed to establish or reestablish the social order when formal authority is absent or powerless.

Washington Treaty
A treaty where the nations of the world tried to outlaw poison gas in war. France refused to sign, and the treaty lapsed.

Weather Underground
A faction of the Students for a Democratic Society organized in 1969. Members tried to establish a revolutionary movement in the U.S. and were involved in bombings of several buildings in New York and Washington, DC.

Zealots
A Jewish movement that revolted against Roman rule during the first century of the Roman Empire.

Zionism
A movement begun in Europe seeking to promote Jewish settlement in the Holy Land. It had its first clear expression in the writings of Leon Pinsker, but its major impetus came in the 1890s under the leadership of Theodore Herzl.

Index